Mono
A Developer's Notebook™

Mono
A Developer's Notebook™

Edd Dumbill and Niel M. Bornstein

O'REILLY®

Beijing · Cambridge · Farnham · Köln · Paris · Sebastopol · Taipei · Tokyo

Mono: A Developer's Notebook™
by Edd Dumbill and Niel M. Bornstein

Published by O'Reilly Media, Inc., 1005 Gravenstein Highway North, Sebastopol, CA 95472.

O'Reilly books may be purchased for educational, business, or sales promotional use. Online editions are also available for most titles (*safari.oreilly.com*). For more information, contact our corporate/institutional sales department: (800) 998-9938 or *corporate@oreilly.com*.

Editor:	Brian Jepson
Production Editor:	Sarah Sherman
Cover Designer:	Hanna Dyer
Interior Designer:	David Futato

Printing History:

July 2004:	First Edition.

 This book uses RepKover™, a durable and flexible lay-flat binding.

ISBN: 0-596-00792-2

[M]

Contents

Foreword

I am thrilled to see Edd's and Niel's finished book. They have written a fantastic guide on the Mono development platform.

We developed Mono to make desktop application development fun, and we wanted to make it easier to create powerful applications, and to create a common framework for application developers to build their software on. Mono started out of our own needs: we wanted to build more software in less time and be more productive, and spend more time creating interesting applications.

We believe we have achieved this.

Mono is an open source implementation of the .NET platform and it includes the tools, libraries, and compiler required to build software on a variety of platforms: Linux, MacOS X, Solaris, BSD, Windows spanning a vast range of computer architectures from the popular x86 based systems to the high-end s390 computers.

Mono is not a complete implementation of .NET: some elements are missing, such as Windows.Forms and Visual Basic. We hope to provide these elements in a future release. But in exchange, Mono ships with various new libraries that directly address the needs of developers targeting Unix; we developed the Gtk# toolkit to rapidly produce GUI applications while taking advantage of everything C# could offer. We provided bindings to the Mozilla browser, the synchronization platform and filesystem platform Simias/iFolder, LDAP support, and access to low-level Unix facilities, as well as support for most database servers; they are all part of Mono.

Mono works on Windows as well. You might wonder why we support Windows if developers could just use Microsoft's implementation. There are several reasons: for one, we provide the source code and all the rights for you to use, modify, and redistribute the code and its changes, but most importantly because the Mono development community is an heterogeneous one that includes Windows-based developers.

Although the book covers most of Mono from the C# perspective, you are not limited to this language. You can use third-party languages like Java, the functional language Nemerle, Object Pascal, or Python to write your code: Mono is an equal opportunity language execution system.

Mono is unique in many ways; it helps Windows developers to use their existing knowledge in other platforms. *Mono: A Developer's Notebook* introduces you to how things are different from Windows, and how you can author, port, and deploy applications to Linux.

Existing Linux developers that have been using other languages or frameworks will find that Mono's C# compiler is a friendly tool to develop software, and that Mono also integrates well with third-party languages; this integration is one of the core principles of the ECMA CLI virtual machine.

I hope that you have as much fun writing software with Mono as we did in creating it. Mono is in no way finished; as you read this, our team is already working on the 2.0 features that will include the latest additions to the C# language, support for more popular languages, and an improved application stack that takes advantage of more services offered by your native platform.

—Miguel de Icaza
May 2004

The Developer's Notebook Series

So, you've managed to pick this book up. Cool. Really, I'm excited about that! Of course, you may be wondering why these books have the odd-looking, college notebook sort of cover. I mean, this is O'Reilly, right? Where are the animals? And, really, do you *need* another series? Couldn't this just be a cookbook? How about a nutshell, or one of those cool hacks books that seems to be everywhere? The short answer is that a developer's notebook is none of those things—in fact, it's such an important idea that we came up with an entirely new look and feel, complete with cover, fonts, and even some notes in the margin. This is all a result of trying to get something into your hands you can actually use.

It's my strong belief that while the nineties were characterized by everyone wanting to learn everything (Why not? We all had six-figure incomes from dot-com companies), the new millennium is about information pain. People don't have time (or the income) to read through 600 page books, often learning 200 things, of which only about 4 apply to their current job. It would be much nicer to just sit near one of the uber-coders and look over his shoulder, wouldn't it? To ask the guys that are neck-deep in this stuff why they chose a particular method, how they performed this one tricky task, or how they avoided that threading issue when working with piped streams. The thinking has always been that books can't serve that particular need—they can inform, and let you decide, but ultimately a coder's mind was something that couldn't really be captured on a piece of paper.

This series says that assumption is patently wrong—and we aim to prove it.

A Developer's Notebook is just what it claims to be: the often-frantic scribbling and notes that a true-blue alpha geek mentally makes when working with a new language, API, or project. It's the no-nonsense code that solves problems, stripped of page-filling commentary that often serves more as a paperweight than an epiphany. It's hackery, focused not on what is nifty or might be fun to do when you've got some free time (when's the last time that happened?), but on what you need to simply "make it work." This isn't a lecture, folks—it's a lab. If you want a lot of concept, architecture, and UML diagrams, I'll happily and proudly point you to our animal and nutshell books. If you want every answer to every problem under the sun, our omnibus cookbooks are killer. And if you are into arcane and often quirky uses of technology, hacks books simply rock. But if you're a coder, down to your core, and you just want to get on with it, then you want a Developer's Notebook. Coffee stains and all, this is from the mind of a developer to yours, barely even cleaned up enough for print. I hope you enjoy it...we sure had a good time writing them.

Notebooks Are...

Example-driven guides

As you'll see in the "Organization" section, developer's notebooks are built entirely around example code. You'll see code on nearly every page, and it's code that *does something*—not trivial "Hello World!" programs that aren't worth more than the paper they're printed on.

Aimed at developers

Ever read a book that seems to be aimed at pointy-haired bosses, filled with buzzwords, and feels more like a marketing manifesto than a programming text? We have too—and these books are the antithesis of that. In fact, a good notebook is incomprehensible to someone who can't program (don't say we didn't warn you!), and that's just the way it's supposed to be. But for developers...it's as good as it gets.

Actually enjoyable to work through

Do you really have time to sit around reading something that isn't any fun? If you do, then maybe you're into thousand-page language references—but if you're like the rest of us, notebooks are a much better fit. Practical code samples, terse dialogue centered around practical examples, and even some humor here and there—these are the ingredients of a good developer's notebook.

About doing, not talking about doing

If you want to read a book late at night without a computer nearby, these books might not be that useful. The intent is that you're coding as you go along, knee deep in bytecode. For that reason, notebooks talk code, code, code. Fire up your editor before digging in.

Notebooks Aren't...

Lectures

We don't let just anyone write a developer's notebook—you've got to be a bona fide programmer, and preferably one who stays up a little too late coding. While full-time writers, academics, and theorists are great in some areas, these books are about programming in the trenches, and are filled with instruction, not lecture.

Filled with conceptual drawings and class hierarchies

This isn't a nutshell (there, we said it). You won't find 100-page indices with every method listed, and you won't see full-page UML diagrams with methods, inheritance trees, and flow charts. What you will find is page after page of source code. Are you starting to sense a recurring theme?

Long on explanation, light on application

It seems that many programming books these days have three, four, or more chapters before you even see any working code. I'm not sure who has authors convinced that it's good to keep a reader waiting this long, but it's not anybody working on *this* series. We believe that if you're not coding within ten pages, something's wrong. These books are also chock-full of practical application, taking you from an example in a book to putting things to work on your job, as quickly as possible.

Organization

Developer's Notebooks try to communicate different information than most books, and as a result, are organized differently. They do indeed have chapters, but that's about as far as the similarity between a notebook and a traditional programming book goes. First, you'll find that all the headings in each chapter are organized around a specific task. You'll note that we said *task*, not *concept*. That's one of the important things to get about these books—they are first and foremost about doing something. Each of these headings represents a single *lab*. A lab is just what it sounds like—steps to accomplish a specific goal. In fact, that's the first heading you'll see under each lab: "How do I do that?" This is the central question of each lab, and you'll find lots of down-and-dirty code and detail in these sections. Many labs offer alternatives and address common questions about different approaches to similar problems. These are the "What about..." sections, which will help give each task some context within the programming big picture.

And one last thing—on many pages, you'll find notes scrawled in the margins of the page. These aren't for decoration; they contain tips, tricks, insights from the developers of a product, and sometimes even a little humor, just to keep you going. These notes represent part of the overall communication flow—getting you as close to reading the mind of the developer-author as we can. Hopefully they'll get you that much closer to feeling like you are indeed learning from a master.

And most of all, remember—these books are...

All Lab, No Lecture

—Brett McLaughlin, Series Creator

Preface

Mono is an open source, cross-platform, implementation of the .NET development framework. It's based on the Common Language Infrastructure (CLI), standardized by the ECMA standards group and ratified as standards by ISO. Similar to Java, the Mono environment consists of a compiler, virtual machine, and API classes. Although .NET supports many languages, Mono's main compiler focus is on the C# language.

This book is for developers who want to get up to speed quickly with Mono. Light on theory and strong on no-nonsense code examples, this book will lead you through what you can do *now* with Mono and provides plenty of jumping-off points for finding out more. By working through a series of labs, each centered on a particular API, task, or feature, you will quickly obtain running code that can be used as a basis for further learning or evaluation.

What This Book Covers

As well as shipping with the basic ECMA standardized APIs, Mono comes with two sets of class libraries (known as assemblies in the .NET world): Microsoft compatibility APIs and Mono's own API set. The compatibility assemblies include ADO.NET for databases, ASP.NET for web applications, and Windows.Forms for desktop applications. The Mono assemblies include among other things the Gtk# user interface toolkit, interfaces to databases such as MySQL and PostgreSQL, and an interface to the Mozilla web browser.

This book is mainly about the standard ECMA libraries and those unique to Mono. It will lead you through discovering the following aspects of Mono:

Installation and configuration

Chapter 1 discusses setting up the Mono development platform on Linux, Mac OS X, and Windows, and creating a functional development environment with your tools of choice.

Mono programming basics

Chapter 2 provides a rapid tour of the major features of the C# programming language, and Chapter 3 introduces the basics of the system class libraries, including file IO, string handling, regular expressions, threads, and unit tests.

User interfaces

The preferred user interface toolkit for Mono is Gtk#. Chapters 4 and 5 cover programming with Gtk#, and include some more advanced widgets targeting the GNOME desktop environment.

Processing XML

XML is a major feature of modern software development, and Mono's System.Xml classes provide a rich variety of APIs for XML-related programming. These are discussed in Chapter 6.

Networking

Mono comes with a rich set of features for creating networking applications. The ASP.NET libraries are a framework for web applications and web services. Chapter 7 discusses ASP.NET, along with more conventional TCP/IP and HTTP applications, encryption, remote procedure calls and database access.

Advanced and experimental topics

Chapter 8 discusses packaging and distributing Mono applications using GNU automake and autoconf, running Java and Basic programs in Mono, writing cross-platform code, and using generics in C#.

The aspects of Mono not covered in this book include the Microsoft compatibility assemblies. In particular, the Windows.Forms user interface libraries are not covered. O'Reilly publishes various books that cover these topics well. For more information on these titles, visit *http:// dotnet.oreilly.com/*.

Why Mono?

Mono brings together many modern programming language features. While many of its technologies can be found in various alternative languages, it's the conjunction of them in a single platform that makes Mono attractive and exciting to develop with.

Provides a controlled environment

One of the main benefits of Mono is that programs are compiled into a bytecode known as the *Common Intermediate Language* (CIL) and run in a controlled environment; such code is known as *managed code*. This managed environment provides many advantages, some of which will be familiar already to users of Java or scripting languages.

No crash and burn

In traditional compiled environments, buggy code generates nasty errors and unexpected program termination, often complicated by misbehaving code scribbling over parts of the memory. Mono's exception handling and virtual machine environment means that errors can be isolated easily, and need not be fatal to a program.

Garbage collection

Memory management is the biggest headache for non–garbage-collected languages like C and C++. The freedom and perceived speed of compiled C is often outweighed by the headache of tracking down memory leaks. The Mono runtime takes the trash out so you don't have to. In an ideal world, memory management done by hand is faster than automatic memory management. In reality, automated garbage collection is as fast as manual.

Runtime checking

The managed environment won't let a program write beyond the end of an array, access a null pointer, or many of the other common causes of errors in nonmanaged programs. Instead, exceptions are used to allow the programmer to handle errors gracefully.

Security benefits

A comprehensive security model means that the access rights of programs to system and remote resources can be strictly controlled. Additionally, the runtime error checking minimizes the chances of a misbehaving program presenting opportunities for exploitation.

The escape hatch

For legacy integration reasons, developers usually need access to "unsafe" code and unmanaged structures. The runtime enables developers to incorporate such code, while still using a sandbox or disabling execution for untrusted code paths in certain environments.

Reuses existing code investments

Mono makes it easy to reuse existing investments in code libraries. The Platform Invocation Services, or P/Invoke, method allows access to almost any function in an existing binary library with just one or two extra lines of code. Java has a similar mechanism, but Mono makes it much simpler.

For access to Java libraries, the IKVM compiler ensures a smooth transition. IKVM enables Java bytecode to run in the Mono runtime, allowing access from Mono code to Java classes, and vice versa. Even highly complex Java applications such as Eclipse can be run on Mono using IKVM.

Fast to write, fast to run

In a world where computers are cheap but developers expensive, reducing development time is often much more important than reducing execution time. Developing with Mono and C# can bring significant productivity increases. C# can be quickly understood by programmers coming from either a Java or C++ programming background, and presents enough of the advantages of both of those environments to feel immediately comfortable. At the same time, C# adds some new language features that reduce the verbosity of programs, including:

Events and delegates
> Events are first-class constructs in C#. Together with delegates (similar to function pointers) they make event-based code such as a user interface easy to write.

Properties
> No more getFoo( ) and setFoo( ) methods. C# has syntactic sugar to allow properties to be accessed like variables, and also allows complex code behind the accessors.

For programmers moving from a C or scripting background into Mono, the benefits of a strongly and statically typed language can have a big impact on the development cycle. In a statically typed language, many errors are caught at compile time before they ever make it into a program. These advantages also translate well into team development settings, where formal interfaces between code modules are even more important.

Contrary to some expectations, CIL bytecode running in a virtual machine is not slow. The Mono runtime utilizes a just-in-time compiler (JIT) to translate bytecode into native machine code, maximizing application performance. Due to improvements made in the CIL design over Java bytecode, the Mono JIT is expected to match or exceed the speed of Java JITs.

Presents cross-platform code and migration paths

Unlike Microsoft's .NET implementation, Mono is cross-platform, supporting Windows, Linux, and Mac OS X, and hardware including x86, PowerPC, and SPARC processors. The JIT means that not only will Mono run on these platforms but that it will perform well. In addition, the Mono platform libraries, such as the Gtk# user interface toolkit, are also available on all these systems, enabling single codebase deployment across multiple platforms.

Mono presents a smooth migration path for developers working on .NET in Windows. The implementation of ADO.NET, ASP.NET, and Windows.Forms means applications can be brought over to Linux as is. Running applications on Mono makes it easier than ever to deploy Linux with minimal risk or up-front investment. Due to platform-specific assumptions made by developers, it's likely that some small porting effort will be needed, but occasionally the move will be as simple as copying over the compiled assemblies!

Provides a choice of languages

The common runtime is not restricted to C# alone. Java, JavaScript, Basic, C, and even Cobol have compilers available. Not all of these languages are statically typed like C#. The flexibility and expressiveness of scripting languages are also available. Importantly for many developers, a version of Python is being developed. Most likely, in the future, no major programming language will be without a compiler targeting the common runtime.

Works with familiar tools

Moving to Mono doesn't mean that you must throw away the existing environments and toolchains that you are used to. For instance there are several build systems available, each from different cultures:

NAnt
> A .NET port of Java's famous Ant build system

Autotools
> GNU *autoconf* and *automake* can be used easily with Mono, along with *pkg-config*

MonoDevelop
> Projects can be built with this IDE, compatible with the popular Windows-based SharpDevelop IDE

Additionally, C# editing modes are available for all popular text editors. Mono doesn't even impose any particular directory structure on the way source code is organized.

Provides a large community resources

As the basis for new Windows development, .NET has a substantial resource library available from MSDN and third-party publications. Given the wide array of complementary efforts in both the Microsoft .NET and Mono communities, developers won't often find themselves without help.

In addition to developer education, open source development tools, such as testing frameworks, are readily available, and more are ported or written every day. Developers can expect to plug into a large community of peers, and the associated body of support and emerging best practice. Employers can take advantage of a large pool of available skills.

Conventions Used in This Book

This book uses the following typographic conventions:

Constant width
> Used for program listings, classes, methods, variables, parameters, directives, keywords, and the output of command-line utilities.

Constant width italic
> Used to show items that need to be replaced in commands.

Italic
> Used for emphasis, for first use of a technical term, packages, channels, and URLs.

...
> Indicates text that has been omitted for clarity.

Using Code Examples

This book is here to help you get your job done. In general, you may use the code in this book in your programs and documentation. You do not need to contact us for permission unless you're reproducing a significant portion of the code. For example, writing a program that uses several chunks of code from this book does not require permission. Selling or distributing a CD-ROM of examples from O'Reilly books does require permission. Answering a question by citing this book and quoting example code does not require permission. Incorporating a significant amount of example code from this book into your product's documentation does require permission.

We appreciate, but do not require, attribution. An attribution usually includes the title, author, publisher, and ISBN. For example: "*Mono: A Developer's Notebook* by Edd Dumbill and Niel M. Bornstein. Copyright 2004 O'Reilly Media, Inc., 0-596-00792-2."

If you feel your use of code examples falls outside fair use or the permission given above, feel free to contact us at *permissions@oreilly.com*.

Comments and Questions

Please address any comments or questions concerning this book to the publisher:

> O'Reilly Media
> 1005 Gravenstein Highway North
> Sebastopol, CA 95472
> (800) 998-9938 (in the U.S. or Canada)
> (707) 829-0515 (international or local)
> (707) 829-0104 (fax)

To ask technical questions or comment on the book, send email to:

> *bookquestions@oreilly.com*

O'Reilly has a web site for this book where examples, errata, and any plans for future editions are listed. You can access this site at:

> *http://www.oreilly.com/catalog/monoadn*

For more information about this book and others, see the O'Reilly web site:

> *http://www.oreilly.com/*

Acknowledgments

Edd Dumbill

Without Miguel de Icaza and the Mono team, neither Mono nor this book would exist. I owe them a great deal of thanks for all their work and enthusiastic help in solving the problems I came across while writing this book. In particular, my thanks are due to Miguel, Todd Berman, Gonzalo Paniagua, Mike Kestner, Erik Dasque, and Jackson Harper.

I'd like to thank Niel Bornstein for being such an excellent co-author and an inspiring companion through the rapid development of this book. Dave Beckett's careful reviewing and comments have been invaluable, as has the input, encouragement, and cheerful optimism of our editor, Brian Jepson. I am indebted to Phil McCarthy for drawing the excellent monkey that adorns Chapters 4 and 5.

Finally, my thanks as ever to my wife Rachael, whose understanding, patience, and support has made this book possible.

Niel Bornstein

When Edd Dumbill approached me to cowrite this book with him, I jumped at the chance to write about the Mono project. Edd's constant encouragement and support have made this an incomparable writing experience. Thanks also to our editor, Brian Jepson, who made the short deadlines easier to meet by providing excellent editorial support. Special thanks go to Dave Beckett for his invaluable commentary on the text.

Thanks also to Miguel de Icaza and his team, who have accomplished an amazing task in producing a great set of tools. In particular, thanks to Todd Berman, Erik Dasque, Atsushi Eno, and Gonzalo Paniagua for answering my questions about Mono's inner workings.

Last, but by no means least, many thanks to my wife and son, Dawn and Nicholas, who have likely suffered more than anyone during this project. Thanks for your patience and encouragement, and I promise I'll be in bed at a reasonable hour for a few months now.

CHAPTER 1

Getting Mono Running

The labs in this chapter will guide you through obtaining, installing, and setting up Mono for Linux, Windows, and Mac OS X. The Mono system is comprised of the compiler, runtime, assemblies (code libraries), and documentation. In addition to these components, you will need a development environment and a build system. This chapter will cater to those needs too, whether using a graphical IDE or integrating Mono to fit snugly into your favorite and long-established editing environment.

Some of the labs in this chapter will only make complete sense after you've worked through Chapters 2 and 3, so feel free to come back and look around before you move on toChapter 4.

In this chapter:
- *"Install Mono"*
- *"Explore Mono"*
- *"Run the MonoDevelop IDE"*
- *"Fit Mono into Your World"*
- *"Join the Mono Community"*

Install Mono

Mono is distributed in three logical components: the Mono runtime and tools, the Mono API assemblies, and the Microsoft .NET compatibility API assemblies. Most of this book is about the Mono runtime, tools, and APIs, as described in the Preface. The exception is the coverage of ASP.NET, which allows you to develop web applications and web services.

Starting at the beginning, how do you set your hands on Mono?

This lab describes how to obtain and install Mono, and the major accompanying assemblies. The majority of the labs in this book can be completed using the packages installed as part of this lab. Where additional downloads are required, they will be noted in each lab concerned.

How to do it

The best way to install Mono is to use the official packages. The Mono project has released precompiled packages for Linux (Red Hat, SuSE, and Fedora Core), Windows, and Mac OS X platforms. In addition, Linux

We don't control Mono's web site, so you may find things change slightly. Keep an eye on the online errata for this book for any corrections.

distributions with their own download channels such as Debian or Gentoo have incorporated Mono into their usual repositories.

Linux

Packages for Linux systems with an x86 family CPU are available from the Mono download page, which you can access by clicking the "Download" link on the Mono home page, *http://www.go-mono.com/*. Users of RPM-based systems (Red Hat, SuSE, and Fedora Core) should download the RPMs suitable for their Linux distribution.

To make life easier, Fedora Core users can set up a *yum* channel. To do this, add the following code to */etc/yum.conf*, adjusting the URL to that given for Fedora from the Mono download page, and run yum check-update to verify everything's working.

```
[mono]
name=Mono 1.0
baseurl=http://www.mono2.ximian.com/archive/1.0/fedora-1-i386/
```

The download page explains the interdependencies of the packages. To obtain a functional Mono development environment, install the following packages: *mono-core, mono-core-devel, mono-posix, mono-xml-relaxng, mono-data-postgresql, mono-data-sqlite, gtk-sharp, monodoc, mono-web-services, mono-remoting,* and *bytefx-data-mysql*. Fedora Core users can use yum install to download and install these packages. Alternatively, you can download the RPMs and install them manually using rpm -i.

The *Ximian Red Carpet* package manager can also be used to simplify installation on Fedora Core, SuSE, and Red Hat platforms. Red Carpet can be downloaded from *http://www.ximian.com/products/redcarpet/*. Once installed, you can obtain the Mono packages from the *Mono* channel.

Users of Debian Unstable (on x86 or PowerPC) can install Mono using the following command, run as root:

```
# apt-get install mono monodoc gtk-sharp
```

Users of Gentoo Linux (on x86 or PowerPC) should compile and install Mono like this:

```
# export ACCEPT_KEYWORDS="~x86"
# USE="gtkhtml gnome" emerge mono monodoc gtk-sharp
```

Windows

Like Microsoft .NET, Mono requires Windows 2000 or later to run. To install Mono on Windows, download and run the installer from the download page at *http://www.go-mono.com/*. Gtk# is included in the installer.

The installer will deposit all the necessary files in *C:\Program Files\Mono-1.0*, but you can override that by entering a different folder.

Batch files that wrap each of the Mono executables will be installed in *C:\Program Files\Mono-1.0\bin*, so must add that to your PATH environment variable. The dialog box in Figure 1-1 will pop up after the installation to remind you to do this.

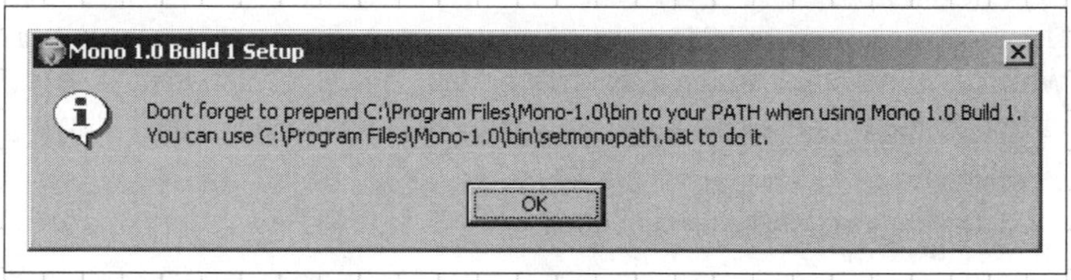

Figure 1-1. Mono Windows installer PATH reminder

You can use the batch file *setmonopath.bat* to add the directory to your path:

```
C:\>"C:\Program Files\Mono-1.0\bin\setmonopath.bat"
```

Mac OS X

Mono requires Mac OS X 10.3 or later to run. For Gtk#, X11 is also required. To install X11 for Mac OS X, either download it from *http://www.apple.com/macosx/features/x11/* or install it from the CD that came with Mac OS X 10.3. The X11 installer package will deposit everything needed to run X11 on your system.

Having installed X11, you must download and install Mono and Gtk#. Get the installer packages from the Mono download page at *http://www.go-mono.com/*. Be sure to read the documentation accompanying the packages.

You should also find Mono available through the fink and DarwinPorts software installers.

Installing from source

Mono is supported on more platforms than there are binary packages. In particular, Mono works on Solaris, HP/UX, and PowerPC Linux. For these platforms, you must compile Mono from source.

You can obtain source packages from the Mono web site's download page. Instructions for building from source can be found in the release notes. Mono itself is relatively straightforward to compile on Linux and Mac OS X, and is covered in this section. For Windows, you should check the release notes for special instructions.

You might find third-party precompiled Mono packages for lesser-used platforms, but don't count on it.

The minimum prerequisites for compiling Mono, aside from a functioning C compiler, are the development files for GLib. These will probably be available as *libglib2.0-dev*, *glib2.0-dev*, or *glib2-dev* packages on your Linux or Mac OS X system. They can also be compiled using the source code packages from *ftp://ftp.gnome.org/pub/gnome/sources/glib/*. Additional prerequisites for certain features are mentioned in the release notes but are not required for the labs in this book.

Decide where to install Mono to on your system, preferably not in */usr*, which is normally managed by the system package manager. A good choice is */opt/mono*. Configure and compile Mono using the following commands:

```
$ tar xfz mono-1.0.tar.gz
$ cd mono-1.0
$ ./configure --prefix=/opt/mono
$ make
$ su
# make install
```

Now that Mono is installed, you must configure some environmental variables before you can use Mono. Use the following commands, substituting your own paths if necessary:

```
$ export PATH=/opt/mono/bin:$PATH
$ export LD_LIBRARY_PATH=/opt/mono/lib:$LD_LIBRARY_PATH # Linux only
$ export DYLD_LIBRARY_PATH=/opt/mono/lib:$DYLD_LIBRARY_PATH # Mac OS X
$ export PKG_CONFIG_PATH=/opt/mono/lib/pkgconfig
$ export MONO_PATH=/opt/mono/lib
```

Download Gtk# source code from *http://gtk-sharp.sourceforge.net/*. Compiling Gtk# is somewhat more involved than Mono and is not covered here. If you are able to install the prerequisite libraries for compilation from source, it is likely that you have enough skill to handle the compilation process. You should refer to Gtk#'s release notes for compilation guidelines.

If you want to compile a development version of Mono from source code, see "Run a Development Version of Mono" in Chapter 8.

What about ...

...Using the Windows compatibility assemblies? The purpose of these assemblies is to smooth the migration of Microsoft .NET applications onto the Linux platform. The Windows.Forms user interface APIs will only work on x86 Linux, because of their dependence on the WINE system (*http://www.winehq.com*). WINE provides a compatibility layer to enable Windows-native code to execute on a Linux machine.

Although this book does not cover the compatibility assemblies in depth, you may quite reasonably want to install them. Packages can be downloaded from the Mono web site, marked as part of the "Microsoft .NET stack". Details on compiling them from source are available in the release notes.

Explore Mono

The addition to class assemblies and documentation, the Mono distribution contains a variety of tools for creating and executing Mono programs. This lab takes you through a guided tour of the most important tools.

Now you have Mono installed, what's in the box?

How do I do that?

To get going with Mono, you must learn how to use the various command-line tools, especially mcs (the Mono C# compiler) and mono (the Mono virtual machine).

mcs

mcs is the Mono C# compiler. You can compile, embed resources, and link Mono programs by using mcs. Try compiling the Hello World example from "Say "Hello" to the World" in Chapter 2 with `mcs Hello.cs`. The result should be a file called *Hello.exe*.

mcs doesn't compile programs into directly executable code; rather, it compiles into an intermediate bytecode called *Common Intermediate Language* (CIL).

mono

The mono command executes a compiled Mono program in the virtual machine. mono uses a just-in-time compiler (JIT) to translate the compiled CIL bytecode to machine code for execution. The *Hello.exe* program can be run with `mono Hello.exe`.

Find out which version of Mono is installed by running `mono --version`. The output will look something like this:

```
Mono JIT compiler version 0.91, (C) 2002-2004 Novell, Inc
and Contributors. www.go-mono.com
        TLS:          NPTL
        GC:           Included Boehm (with typed GC)
        SIGSEGV     : altstack
        Globalization: ICU
```

Include this version information if you need to ask questions in any of the forums listed in "Join the Mono Community."

mint

Not every platform on which Mono runs has the JIT compiler implemented yet. A slower alternative to mono is available in the form of mint, which interprets the CIL bytecode in real-time as the program is executing.

monodoc

Monodoc is the Mono documentation viewer, through which official Mono API documentation is available. It can be run with the command monodoc. As well as the official Mono APIs, any third-party assembly may also install its documentation so it can be viewed from Monodoc. One of Monodoc's neat features is that it allows anyone to submit changes and additions to the documentation. These are sent to a central server and a human editor merges them into the official documentation repository. Figure 1-2 shows Monodoc in action.

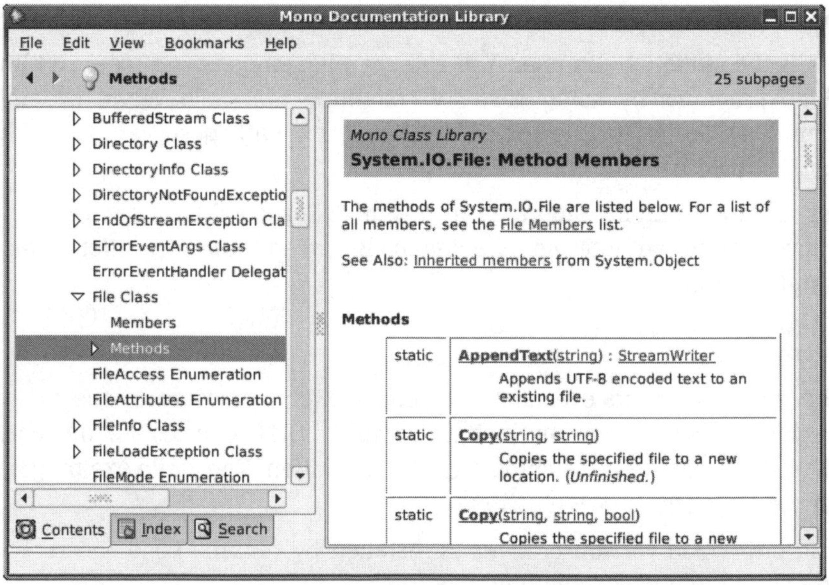

Figure 1-2. The Monodoc documentation browser

monop

There are times when documentation may not be easy to find for a particular assembly. This is where monop comes in. monop can print out the signatures of any class for which the system has an assembly. For example:

```
$ monop System.Byte
public struct Byte : IComparable, IConvertible, IFormattable {

    public static byte Parse (string s, IFormatProvider provider);
    public static byte Parse (string s,
        System.Globalization.NumberStyles style);
    public static byte Parse (string s,
        System.Globalization.NumberStyles style,
        IFormatProvider provider);
    public static byte Parse (string s);
    public virtual int CompareTo (object value);
    public override bool Equals (object obj);
    public override int GetHashCode ();
    public Type GetType ();
    public virtual TypeCode GetTypeCode ();
    public virtual string ToString (string format,
        IFormatProvider provider);
    public override string ToString ();
    public string ToString (string format);
    public virtual string ToString (IFormatProvider provider);

}
```

If the class you need isn't in the core system assembly, then the assembly name can be given on the command line:

```
$ monop -r:NUnit.Framework NUnit.Framework.AssertionException
```

monop is a really handy tool for when all you need is a quick check on a method signature.

gacutil

To install a system library on a Linux system, you typically place it in */usr/lib* or */usr/local/lib*. On Windows, you put it in *C:\WINDOWS*. With Mono and .NET, system-wide assemblies are stored in the *Global Assembly Cache*, (GAC). gacutil is used to manipulate the contents of the GAC. Information on gacutil can be found in "Package Related Classes with Assemblies" in Chapter 2, but a quick check on things can be made with gacutil -l, which lists all the assemblies stored in a system's GAC. It's another good way of finding version information, which can be very useful in filing bug reports.

What about ...

...The names of the commands? As all Mono programs compile to a file with *.exe* suffix, how come programs such as Monodoc aren't run with mono monodoc.exe?

The answer is that Mono uses wrapper scripts to call the mono runtime program, to make the commands seem more natural in a Unix environment. If you intend to distribute your Mono programs, it's a good idea to create similar scripts to make it easy for users. On some Linux systems,

Some Linux users get very upset to see a "Windows" file extension like .exe on their system!

such as Debian, the Mono packages use a neat trick called *binfmt*. This allows the system to execute Mono *.exe* files directly. If using binfmt, you just need to make a symbolic link to the *.exe* without the suffix.

Where to learn more

To find out more about the command-line applications Mono installs, try these following options. The quickest (but not always the most informative) way is to run the command with the `--help`. This should result in a brief aide-memoir to the program's function being printed to the console.

Mono also ships with manual pages for use with the Unix system manual reader, `man`. For example, the function of the mysterious `soapsuds` command can be discovered by running man soapsuds. If your Mono is installed in a custom directory, such as */opt/mono*, don't forget to add */opt/mono/man* to your `MANPATH` environmental variable.

Run the MonoDevelop IDE

Real men may use vi, but productive ones use an IDE.

MonoDevelop is a port of the SharpDevelop .NET integrated development environment (IDE) to Linux, using the Gtk# user interface toolkit. Both MonoDevelop and SharpDevelop are free, open source applications.

As you work through the labs in this book, you'll need a development environment to work in. While "Fit Mono into Your World" provides hints on how to integrate Mono with an existing setup, this lab shows you how to get up and running with MonoDevelop. For the Mono 1.0 release, MonoDevelop is supported only on Linux, although some members of the Mono community have made it run on Mac OS X. See the "What about" section near the end of this lab for IDE solutions for Windows and Mac OS X.

MonoDevelop provides modern programming aids common to most IDEs, such as class browsing, integrated API documentation, build system, code completion, and support for multiple filetypes. Even if you're a hardened command-line and text editor geek, it's worth giving MonoDevelop a try. The integrated documentation is a great aid in navigating the many new APIs that Mono makes available.

How do I do that?

Source code and precompiled packages of MonoDevelop can be obtained from the project web site at *http://www.monodevelop.com*. If possible, use precompiled packages for installation, because the number of prerequisites required to compile MonoDevelop is a little daunting. Users of the

Debian (unstable) or Gentoo Linux distributions should be able to locate a *monodevelop* package using *apt-get* or *emerge*.

Before taking a tour of MonoDevelop's features, here's a word about how it organizes source code. MonoDevelop *solutions* may contain one or more *projects*. A project contains one or more files, which are compiled and linked to create a target assembly. For small undertakings, such as those in this book, a solution is likely to contain only one project.

As a way of discovering MonoDevelop's major features, this lab will lead you through creating a very simple Gtk# application. Start up MonoDevelop and choose **New Solution/Project** from the **File** menu. You should see a dialog similar to that shown in Figure 1-3. Navigate to the options for C#, and click on Gtk# Project. Name the project and choose a location in your home directory for it. Then click New to create the MonoDevelop solution.

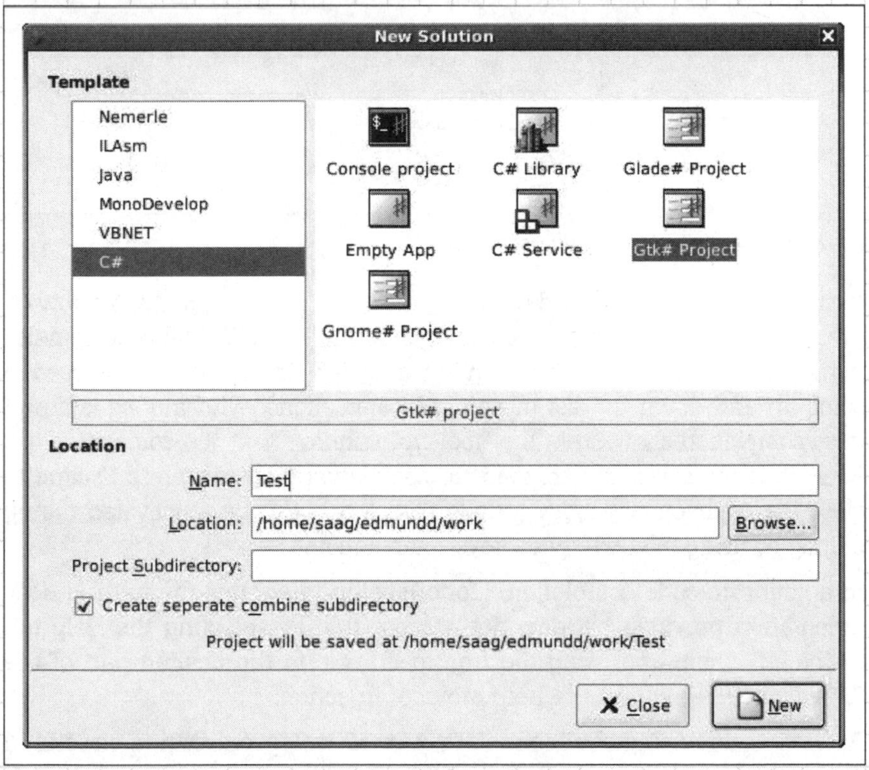

Figure 1-3. Creating a solution in MonoDevelop

When you tell it to create a new solution, MonoDevelop creates several files: *AssemblyInfo.cs*, which contains metadata about your project and is described in more detail in "Package Related Classes with Assemblies" in Chapter 2, *Main.cs*, containing the main function of the program; and

MyWindow.cs, containing the application window class. Navigate to *MyWindow.cs* using the solution viewing panel, shown in Figure 1-4, and double-click on *MyWindow.cs* to make its source appear in the source code window.

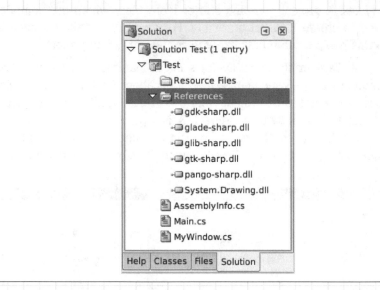

Figure 1-4. MonoDevelop's solution browser

Position the cursor at the end of the this.ShowAll ( ) line in *MyWindow.cs*, press **Enter** to create a new blank line, and type this.Ti. The code completion window will appear, as shown in Figure 1-5. The mouse can be used to scroll up and down the list of possible completions, with the signature of each completion showing in the "tool-tip" window near the completion list. Press **Enter** to select the this.Title completion (you can press **Escape** to close the completion window). Code completion can be reactivated during editing by using the **Ctrl-space** keys combination.

In addition to code completion, MonoDevelop integrates the full API documentation provided by Monodoc. Access this by selecting the Help tab in the left panel and using the tree to browse to the desired part of the APIs. Figure 1-6 shows the help browser in action.

As well as browsing the Mono APIs, MonoDevelop presents a structured view of the classes in each project. Click on the Classes tab in the left panel, and expand the tree to explore the classes in your project. The view should look something like Figure 1-7. Double-clicking on a definition will move the cursor to the corresponding point in the source code.

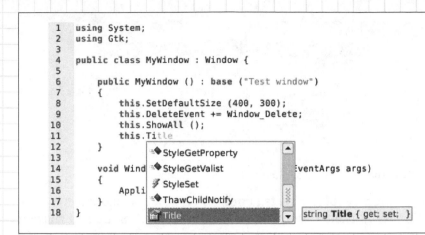

```
1    using System;
2    using Gtk;
3
4    public class MyWindow : Window {
5
6        public MyWindow () : base ("Test window")
7        {
8            this.SetDefaultSize (400, 300);
9            this.DeleteEvent += Window_Delete;
10           this.ShowAll ();
11           this.Title
12       }
13
14       void Wind                              ventArgs args)
15       {
16           Appli
17       }
18   }
```

| StyleGetProperty |
| StyleGetValist |
| StyleSet |
| ThawChildNotify |
| Title |

string **Title** { get; set; }

Figure 1-5. Code completion in MonoDevelop

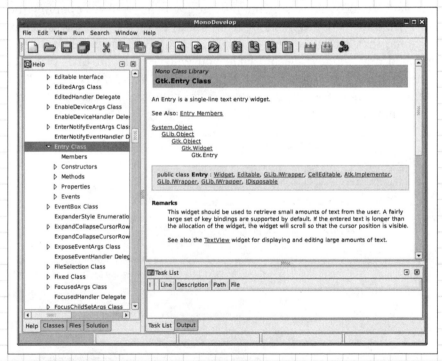

Figure 1-6. Integrated API documentation in MonoDevelop

MonoDevelop has an internal build system that will recompile any source code changed since the last build. The easiest way to access this is by using the compile-and-run ("gears") button on the toolbar. This will compile and then run the project currently being edited. Any errors will show up in the task list window, visible at the bottom of Figure 1-6.

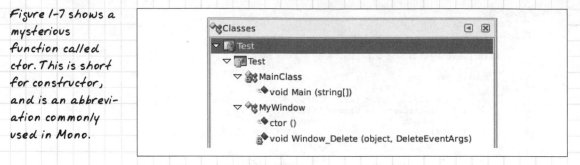

Figure 1-7. MonoDevelop's class browser

Try inserting a deliberate syntax error, and hit the compile-and-run button. The result should be similar to that in Figure 1-8. Double-clicking on the error report positions the cursor at the offending line in the source code. Finally, when you correct all the errors, press compile-and-run and MonoDevelop will run the program. As well as opening the Gtk# window MyWindow, MonoDevelop opens a console window to show anything that is printed to the standard output. Because would not have supplied any window closing code you will need to hit **Ctrl+C** in the console window to terminate the program. (See "Write a Basic Gtk# Program and Handle Events" in Chapter 4" for details of how to add code to close the window)

```
1   using System;
2   using Gtk;
3
4   public class MyWindow : Window {
5
6       public MyWindow () : base ("Test window")
7       {
8           this.SetDefaultSize (400, 300);
9           this.DeleteEvent += Window_Delete;
10          this.ShowAll ();
11          this.Ti
12      }
13
14      void Window_Delete (object o, DeleteEventArgs args)
15      {
```

!	Line	Description	Path	File
−	12	Expecting `;'(CS1002)		MyWindow.cs

Task List | Output

Figure 1-8. Errors during compilation in MonoDevelop

What about ...

...IDEs for Windows or Mac OS X? Windows users need to look only as far as SharpDevelop, mentioned in the introduction to this lab. SharpDevelop can be configured to compile programs with Mono. MonoDevelop can load SharpDevelop projects and solutions directly. More information can be found at the SharpDevelop web site at *http://www.sharpdevelop.com/*.

The situation is a little less straightforward for Mac OS X users. Some members of the Mono community have been able to compile MonoDevelop for OS X, and in time it is likely that precompiled packages will be published. Additionally, work is ongoing in creating the necessary files to configure *XCode*, the IDE that Apple ships with OS X, for use with Mono projects. Visit *http://www.druware.com/* for more information on XCode integration. Also, keep an eye out for details of Mac OS X IDE support on the mailing lists and news sites described in "Join the Mono Community."

You can build a MonoDevelop project from the command line with make by downloading prj2make from http://forge.novell.com and creating a makefile from the MonoDevelopment project's prix file.

Fit Mono into Your World

Everybody has their preferred development environment, whether it's just a text editor or a full-blown IDE. While Mono has a great IDE in the form of MonoDevelop, there may be many reasons for continuing with your current environment.

This lab shows how Mono can be integrated with some of the more common tools used by Linux and Java developers.

Development environments are a near-religious issue. Mono won't make you abandon your favorite tools.

How do I do that?

If you are an old-school geek, you probably prefer to write your code with a text editor such as *Emacs* or *Vim*. Support for editing in C# ships as part of Vim 6.2, which can be found at *http://www.vim.org/*. Emacs users should install Brad Merrill's C# mode, available from *http://www.cybercom.net/~zbrad/DotNet/Emacs/*.

Unix geeks will also be familiar with using *make* to build their programs. It's simple to use *make* to control the building of Mono programs. The most obvious difference from C and C++ is that Mono doesn't need intermediate object files, so all the source files must be given to the compiler at once. Example 1-1 shows an example makefile that can be used as a starting point. The accompanying source files used by this makefile are available from the book's web site.

Brad Merrill has worked on .NET at Microsoft since 1999, so he's had plenty of time to refine his Emacs C# mode!

Example 1-1. Using make with Mono: 04-integrate/Makefile

```
# 01-tooling/04-integrate
MCS = mcs

ifdef DEBUG
MCSFLAGS = -debug
endif

.PHONY: clean all

all: SimpleMain.exe Main.exe FatMain.exe Library1.dll

# default way to make executables
%.exe: %.cs
	$(MCS) $(MCSFLAGS) -target:exe -out:$@ $(filter %.cs,$^) \
	  $(foreach dl,$(filter %.dll,$^),$(addprefix -r:,$(dl)))

# default way to make libraries
%.dll: %.cs
	$(MCS) $(MCSFLAGS) -target:library -out:$@ $(filter %.cs,$^) \
	  $(foreach dl,$(filter %.dll,$^),$(addprefix -r:,$(dl)))


# SimpleMain.exe is automatically built from its sole
# source file, SimpleMain.cs

# Main.exe has two source files and links with Library1.dll
Main.exe: Main.cs Sprockets.cs Library1.dll

# Library1.dll is automatically built from its sole
# source file, Library1.cs

# FatMain.exe has some resources, and links against Library1.dll
# define them in variables, let make do the walking
FATMAIN_RESOURCES = monkey.png readme.txt
FATMAIN_SOURCES = Main.cs Sprockets.cs Widgets.cs
FATMAIN_LIBS = Library1.dll

FatMain.exe: $(FATMAIN_SOURCES) $(FATMAIN_RESOURCES) $(FATMAIN_LIBS)
	$(MCS) $(MCSFLAGS) -target:exe -out:$@ \
	  $(foreach res,$(FATMAIN_RESOURCES), \
	    $(addprefix -resource:,$(res))) \
	  $(foreach dl,$(FATMAIN_LIBS),$(addprefix -r:,$(dl))) \
	  $(FATMAIN_SOURCES)

clean:
	rm -f *.exe *.dll
```

Running make with the makefile in Example 1-1 yields the following output:

```
$ make
mcs  -target:exe -out:SimpleMain.exe SimpleMain.cs \
```

You can have the best of both worlds, of course. The MonoDevelop IDE generates makefiles for its projects.

```
Compilation succeeded
mcs  -target:library -out:Library1.dll Library1.cs
Compilation succeeded
mcs  -target:exe -out:Main.exe Main.cs Sprockets.cs \
        -r:Library1.dll
Compilation succeeded
mcs  -target:exe -out:FatMain.exe \
          -resource:monkey.png  -resource:readme.txt \
          -r:Library1.dll \
        Main.cs Sprockets.cs
Compilation succeeded
```

Developers coming from the Java world are more likely to be familiar with the *Ant* build tool than with *make*. The Mono and .NET world has a similar tool, called *NAnt*. You can download NAnt from the web at *http://nant.sourceforge.net/*. Be sure to read the accompanying documentation for Mono-specific notes on building and installing NAnt.

NAnt supports many .NET-specific build tasks, such as running unit tests with NUnit (see "Test Your C# Code" in Chapter 3). Examples and further documentation are available on the NAnt Wiki, linked from the project's web site. Example 1-2 shows a NAnt build configuration that performs the same tasks as the makefile from Example 1-1 when invoked with mono */path/to/NAnt.exe* (adjust the path to wherever you installed NAnt).

For best results with Mono, use NAnt version 0.85 or better.

Example 1-2. Using NAnt with Mono: 04-integrate/monodn.build

```
<project name="monodn" default="all">
    <target name="all">
        <call target="SimpleMain" />
        <call target="Library1" />
        <call target="Main" />
    </target>

    <target name="SimpleMain">
        <csc target="exe" output="SimpleMain.exe">
            <sources>
                <includes name="SimpleMain.cs" />
            </sources>
        </csc>
    </target>

    <target name="Library1">
        <csc target="library" output="Library1.dll">
            <sources>
                <includes name="Library1.cs" />
            </sources>
        </csc>
    </target>
```

Example 1-2. Using NAnt with Mono: 04-integrate/monodn.build (continued)

```
        <target name="Main" depends="Library1">
            <csc target="exe" output="Main.exe">
                <sources>
                    <includes name="Main.cs" />
                    <includes name="Sprockets.cs" />
                </sources>
                <references>
                    <includes name="Library1.dll" />
                </references>
            </csc>
        </target>

        <target name="FatMain" depends="Library1">
            <csc target="exe" output="FatMain.exe">
                <sources>
                    <includes name="Main.cs" />
                    <includes name="Sprockets.cs" />
                    <includes name="Widgets.cs" />
                </sources>
                <references>
                    <includes name="Library1.dll" />
                </references>
                <resources>
                    <includes name="readme.txt" />
                    <includes name="monkey.png" />
                </resources>
            </csc>
        </target>
</project>
```

Many Java users will also be familiar with the *Eclipse* IDE. A C# editing and compilation plugin is available for Eclipse, from a company called Improve. The plugin is open source and can be downloaded from Improve's web site at *http://www.improve-technologies.com/*. After downloading and installing the plugin, configure it with the path of the Mono C# compiler. To find this setting, select the **Preferences** from the **Window** menu, and select the **C# Preferences** section.

Improve's C# plugin, shown in Figure 1-9, offers syntax highlighting, code indentation, and compilation. The C# editing features are not as advanced as in MonoDevelop (described in "Run the MonoDevelop IDE"). For instance, code completion and API documentation is lacking. However, if your environment of choice is Eclipse, the C# plugin is a good start. And not to be forgotten is the variety of Eclipse's other handy features, such as wealth of editor plugins and CVS source code repository support.

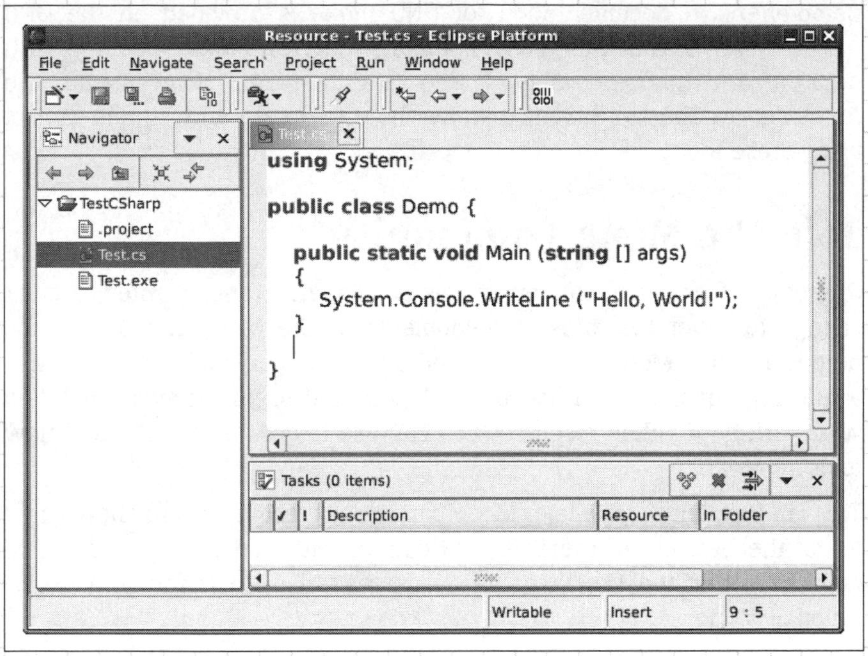

Figure 1-9. C# editing in Eclipse

What about …

…Windows developers who don't want to use IDEs? After all, many Mono projects don't come in a form that fits nicely into SharpDevelop or Eclipse. All is not lost! For many years now the cygwin project has provided ports of the GNU developer toolchain and command-line tools to the Windows platform. Cygwin is impressively comprehensive, including (among other things) the *bash* shell, used throughout this book, the *make* build tool, and the *XFree86* windowing system. Cygwin can be downloaded and installed from *http://www.cygwin.com/*. With a little bit of care, a developer on the Windows-Cygwin environment can perform all the same command-line and compilation tasks that Linux and Mac OS X developers can.

Where to learn more

As Mono grows in popularity, more resources will become available for using it in both traditional Unix environments and integrated with Mac OS X and Windows. To learn of new resources, keep an eye on the forums described in "Join the Mono Community," as well as some Microsoft-focused ones such as *http://blogs.msdn.com/*.

Comprehensive documentation for GNU *make* is provided on the GNU project's web site at *http://www.gnu.org/software/make/*. Users of GNU *autoconf* and *automake* should read "Maintain Your Sources with the Autotools" in Chapter 8, which shows how to create an example project using these tools.

Join the Mono Community

One of the few disadvantages of this book is that, once printed, it can't change to cover the latest developments in the Mono world. Happily, help is at hand. Mono is a vibrant and evolving open source project, with a growing community of active developers and users. As such, there's a wide variety of online resources you can use to get news, help, and new tools for Mono.

This lab introduces the major Mono community resources and shows how to get the best out of them. As you continue to read through this book, familiarity with the Mono's online resources will help you in your exploration of Mono.

How do I do that?

Before jumping into forums or mailing lists with questions, it's a good idea to make yourself as familiar as possible with Mono, its documentation, and recent developments. The first stopping-off point is the Web, where news, answers to common questions, and a variety of tutorials can be found.

Mono web site

Available at *http://www.go-mono.com/*, the Mono web site is the authoritative source for information on Mono. As well as a host of documentation, the Mono web site publishes the latest news about the project. The comprehensive list of frequently asked questions is a good resource for answering questions technical and commercial alike about Mono. The API documentation that ships with Monodoc is also available on the Web, by following the "Documentation" link.

MSDN

As the originators of .NET and the Common Language Runtime, Microsoft obviously has a lot to say on the topic. The Microsoft Developer Network, *http://msdn.microsoft.com*, contains a wealth of reference material and tutorials on using C#, and the APIs common to both Mono and the Microsoft .NET framework.

Don't struggle on your own, there's a world of help out there!

O'Reilly Network

An online magazine run by the publishers of this book, the O'Reilly Network regularly publishes articles for developers on development with .NET, keeping up with the latest happenings in the Mono and .NET world. You can access the O'Reilly Network at *http://www.oreillynet.com/*.

Monologue

Many from the team of developers responsible for maintaining Mono, including project founder and leader Miguel de Icaza, regularly update their weblogs. These are aggregated online at a site called Monologue, which you can find at *http://www.go-mono.com/ monologue/*. Reading Monologue is a good start if you wish to get involved with the Mono project yourself, care about the internal details of its implementation, or are interested in the sometimes amusing and off-beat reflections of its developers.

Mailing lists are a popular way of receiving peer support for technologies. There are several mailing lists that Mono users should consider joining in order to receive (and give!) help and find release announcements for Mono-related software. A full list of mailing lists is available linked from the Mono home page. Here are the ones most useful for developers starting out with Mono.

mono-announce

The Mono announcement list is a low-volume mailing list, carrying news of new Mono releases and important community events. It is a moderated forum, so any posts to it must be approved by Mono project staff before they are distributed. Subscription information for mono-announce is available from *http://lists.ximian.com/mailman/ listinfo/mono-announce-list*.

mono-list

The Mono list is the main forum for developers who are building programs using Mono. Anybody can participate in this list. Before posting to the list, it's a good idea to look through the archives to see if somebody else has posted the same question before. Subscription information is available from *http://lists.ximian.com/mailman/listinfo/ mono-list*.

gtk-sharp-list

The gtk-sharp-list is focused on issues surrounding development with, and the development of, the Gtk# user interface assemblies for Mono. Subscription information is available from *http://lists.ximian.com/ mailman/listinfo/gtk-sharp-list*.

Do your homework
first and you'll get
the best out of
the Mono
development
community.

Software inevitably has bugs, and despite the quality of its developers, it's possible you will come up against a bug in Mono. Often, there's a good chance somebody else has this problem too. For this reason, Mono has a bug tracking database, implemented using the popular bugzilla system. By accessing the bugzilla at *http://bugzilla.ximian.com/* you can search to see if your problem has already been reported. If it hasn't been reported, you can use bugzilla to file a new problem report. Although some bugs will inevitably get discussed on the mailing lists, the Mono developers vastly prefer to get bug reports in bugzilla as it enables them to track and organize the bugs more effectively.

When reporting bugs, the more information you can give, the better. Ensure you include:

- Your operating system, distribution, kernel version if appropriate, and CPU family.

- The version of Mono for which the bug occurs. Obtain this by running `mono --version`. If the problem is with Gtk#, find out the version by running `pkg-config --version gtk-sharp`.

- What makes the bug occur, and how to reproduce it. Where appropriate report what you expected to happen, and what actually did happen.

- A test case. You may not always be able to create one, but a small program that demonstrates the problem is very helpful.

As a developer, one of the ways in which you can learn is by looking at the source code of, and possibly getting involved with, open source projects that use Mono. Additionally some of these projects might be code libraries that will prove useful in your own projects. Some useful resources and projects include:

Novell Forge

A collection of projects rather than an individual project, Novell Forge is a community site where Novell and others release open source software. Many of these projects use Mono, including the iFolder file-sharing system, LDAP libraries for directory services, and a multicast DNS responder. Novell Forge's URL is *http://forge.novell.com/*.

F–Spot

F–Spot is an open source photo management program for the GNOME desktop platform. Its source code uses both C and C#, and is available from the GNOME CVS repository at *http://cvs.gnome.org/*.

Dashboard

Dashboard performs a continuous search of your personal information space, showing results relevant to the current desktop activity. For instance, if you are reading an email from your friend Jane Doe, Dashboard will show the recent instant messaging conversions that you have had with Jane, a summary of the most recent emails she has sent you, Jane's contact details, a list of documents written by or mentioning Jane, and so on. Dashboard is a multithreaded application using Gtk# for the user interface and completely implemented in C#. Dashboard has quite a broad community of contributors, and its own mailing list. More information is available at the Dashboard home page, *http://nat.org/dashboard*.

Finally, should you wish to engage in real-time chat with Mono users and developers, there is an Internet Relay Chat (IRC) channel for talking about Mono. Configure your IRC client for the *irc.gimp.org* server, channel #*mono*. As with any forum, there are rules of etiquette for IRC. It's a good idea just to "lurk," that is keep quiet and listen, for a while to determine the conventions of the channel. If you don't receive answers to your questions, don't keep repeating them ad nauseam, it's just likely that others are busy with other things.

Getting Started with C#

C# (pronounced *see-sharp*) is a powerful, modern, object-oriented language whose syntax will be familiar for developers who have used C, C++, or Java. C# takes the simplicity of Java, with its automatic garbage collection, monolithic inheritance, and standard class library, and adds a number of advanced features, such as properties, delegates, and attributes.

This chapter will get you up to speed on C# syntax, the Common Language Infrastructure types, and some features unique to C#. To run the labs in this chapter, you must have a working Mono installation as described in Chapter 1.

Say "Hello" to the World

This lab introduces some basic features of C# and the Framework Class Library (FCL). You'll see how to write and compile a simple "Hello, world!" program in C# and learn how C# is similar to other modern, object-oriented computer languages, as well as some of the keywords and language features unique to C#. Choosing from among the Choosing from among the panoply of Mono IDEs and installing your IDE of choice is discussed in Chapter 1.

How do I do that?

Fire up your editor or IDE of choice, and create the file *Hello.cs*. Enter the following code (see Example 2-1) in your editor.

Example 2-1. 01-languagebasics/Hello.cs

```
// 02-csharp/01-languagebasics

public class HelloWorld {
  public static void Main (string [] args) {
    if (args.Length != 1) {
      System.Console.Error.WriteLine("You must tell me your name.");
      System.Environment.Exit(-1);
    }
    string name = args[0];
    System.Console.WriteLine ("Hello, {0}!", name);
  }
}
```

The traditional first exercise when learning a new language is the "Hello, world!" program.

Now you have a simple C# source file. To compile it using Mono, type the following command at your command prompt:

```
$ mcs Hello.cs
```

And to run it, type this command line:

```
$ mono Hello.exe Niel
```

You'll want to use your own name, unless you want to confuse your computer.

You'll see the following output on your screen:

```
Hello, Niel!
```

How it works

The class `HelloWorld` is small; it only contains the `Main( )` method. Any class may have a `Main( )` method; if more than one class passed to *mcs.exe* does have a `Main( )` method, you can specify which one contains the method for a given executable at compile time with the `-main:`*classname* command-line switch.

Command-line arguments are passed to a C# program through the `Main( )` method's parameter, an array of `string` objects. `System.Environment.Exit( )` is used to end the program and send a return code to the shell. A return code of 0 will be sent to the shell if control passes to the end of the program without calling `Environment.Exit( )`. `System.Environment` is a class that contains numerous convenient static methods and properties that you can use.

There's also a Console.Out that you just used without knowing it. Console.WriteLine( ) is an alias for Console.Out.WriteLine( ).

`System.Console` is a class that represents the command-line interface to a program. Its `WriteLine( )` method simply writes a line of text to the standard output. `Console.Error` can be used to write text to standard error. Similarly, `Console.In` can be used to read from standard input.

The source file is named *Hello.cs* and the class defined within it is named `HelloWorld`. Java programmers will find this strange, because a Java

Unsafe code is any code that uses pointers and foregoes the built-in garbage collection. You have to use the unsafe keyword in your code and the --unsafe command-line argument to mcs.exe when compiling unsafe code.

class must have the same name as the file containing it. There is no such restriction in C#; in fact, any number of classes (and structs and interfaces) may be defined in the same source file. You may wish to limit your use of this feature, however, as mismatched file and class names can be confusing.

C# has a few curve balls to throw at C and C++ programmers as well. Like Java, there are no header files in C#. Instead, the task of discovering public classes and members is accomplished at runtime via introspection. Class members are referenced using the . operator. The C++ :: operator is meaningless in C#, and the C/C++ -> operator is reserved for unsafe code.

C# *does* use preprocessor symbols such as #define and #if, although they are more limited in scope than in C.

In this example, the name of System.Console is fully specified (namespace plus class name), but the using directive can be used to import a namespace; Java programmers will recognize this functionality as similar to the import directive. Example 2-2 shows *Hello.cs* with the fully specified Hello.World namespace and the using statement for the System namespace.

Namespaces are used to group classes with similar functionality and to help disambiguate classes with similar names but different functions.

Example 2-2. 01-languagebasics/Hello2.cs

```
// 02-csharp/01-languagebasics
using System;

public class HelloWorld {
  public static void Main (string [ ] args) {
    if (args.Length != 1) {
      Console.Error.WriteLine("You must tell me your name.");
      Environment.Exit(-1);
    }
    string name = args[0];
    Console.WriteLine ("Hello, {0}!", name);
  }
}
```

You can even use the using statement to import a namespace, like System, then refer to namespaces within it using a partial namespace. For example, to use the class System.Drawing.Color, you can import System and then just refer to it as Drawing.Color.

What about ...

...Defining your own namespaces? The C# namespace concept is similar to Java's packages. Unlike Java, however, a C# class need not be located in a physical directory matching its namespace. You may wish to limit your use of this feature by making your physical directory structure match your namespace structure, but it's not necessary. Namespace declarations may be nested, or they may be fully specified using dot notation. The two statements that follow are equivalent:

```
namespace OReilly {
  namespace DevelopersNotebook {
    public class HelloWorld {
      ...
    }
  }
}

namespace OReilly.DevelopersNotebook {
  public class HelloWorld {
    ...
  }
}
```

You can now refer to the class HelloWorld just as HelloWorld, if you're in a class in the namespace OReilly.DevelopersNotebook; as OReilly.DevelopersNotebook.HelloWorld from some other namespace; or use the using statement to import OReilly.DevelopersNotebook and refer to the class simply as HelloWorld.

Where to learn more

Standard ECMA-334: the C# Language Specification can be found at *http://www.ecma-international.org/publications/standards/Ecma-334.htm.* The standard, freely available as an Adobe PDF file, is the ultimate resource when it comes to C# language issues. ECMA-334's sister standard, *Standard ECMA-335: Common Language Infrastructure (CLI)* is available at *http://www.ecma-international.org/publications/standards/Ecma-335.htm.*

The C# Programming Language, by Anders Hejlsberg, Scott Wiltamuth, and Peter Golde (Addison-Wesley), contains information about C# from the language's architect and design team members. It also includes detailed information about some features of C# Version 2.0 (expected to arrive in Mono 1.2 in late 2004; see *http://www.mono-project.com/about/mono-roadmap.html* for the Mono roadmap). More information may be found at *http://www.awprofessional.com/bookstore/product.asp?isbn=0321154916.*

Microsoft maintains a C# Developers Center at *http://msdn.microsoft.com/vcsharp/team/language/default.aspx.* Look to this web site for the latest information about C# from the source, as well as an FAQ page, "Ask A Language Designer," and interviews with the C# design team.

The Usenet newsgroup *microsoft.public.dotnet.languages.csharp* provides a forum for questions and answers about the C# language. This newsgroup is populated by Microsoft employees as well as experienced C# developers. Beware: you will find many of these discussions biased towards Microsoft's implementation of C#!

For more Mono-specific language discussions, the mailing list *mono-list@go-mono.com* is an excellent resource. All the Mono mailing lists are listed on the Mono web site at *http://www.mono-project.com/*.

Model the Behavior of Real-World Things

C# provides a rich set of reference types, including classes, interfaces, arrays, and delegates.

The C# language takes a number of its language features from C++. Java developers will already be familiar with the class and interface types. C# adds array and delegate types. In this lab you'll see how they work.

How do I do that?

The third reference type, interface, is discussed in this section. The fourth reference type, delegate, is complex enough that it merits its own lab. See "Define Function Pointers."

Example 2-3 shows the contents of a file called *Beverage.cs*, which demonstrates two of the four reference types. The Beverage class represents a beverage, about which certain properties can be queried. Every beverage is assumed to have a brand name, and every beverage is assumed to have a volume in fluid ounces. It is also assumed to contain some amount of caffeine—we're programmers, right?

Example 2-3. 02-reftypes/Beverage.cs

```
// 02-csharp/02-reftypes
using System;

public class Beverage {
  private string brand;
  private double volume;
  private double percentCaffeine;

  public Beverage(string brand, double volume,
      double percentCaffeine) {
    this.brand = brand;
    this.volume = volume;
    this.percentCaffeine = percentCaffeine;
  }

  public string Brand {
    get {
      return brand;
    }
```

Example 2-3. 02-reftypes/Beverage.cs (continued)

```
  }

  public double Volume {
    get {
      return volume;
    }
  }

  public double PercentCaffeine {
    get {
      return percentCaffeine;
    }
  }

  public override string ToString( ) {
    return Volume + " oz " + Brand +
      " with " + PercentCaffeine + "% caffeine";
  }
}

public class BeverageTester {
  public static void Main(string [ ] args) {
    Beverage [ ] beverages = new Beverage [2];

    Beverage jolt = new Beverage("Jolt", 12.0, 0.25);
    beverages[0] = jolt;

    Beverage coke = new Beverage("Coca-Cola", 12.0, 0.125);
    beverages[1] = coke;

    foreach (Beverage beverage in beverages) {
      Console.WriteLine(beverage);
    }
  }
}
```

Compile and run this program to see the following results:

```
$ mcs Beverage.cs
$ mono Beverage.exe
12 oz Jolt with 0.25% caffeine
12 oz Coca-Cola with 0.125% caffeine
```

The members Brand, Volume, and PercentCaffeine are called properties. Properties are a shorthand way of writing accessor methods.

How it works

Reference types are variables that refer to the location in memory where an object instance is stored. The test program in Example 2-3 contains a number of reference types. The first type is a class called Beverage. A class is a reference type that derives from System.Object.

You'll notice the this keyword sprinkled throughout the code. The this keyword indicates a reference to the current object instance, so this.brand is a reference to the current Beverage instance's brand field. The same keyword is used in C++ and Java for the same purpose, although in C++ the syntax would be this->brand.

Because classes all derive from System.Object, they have a few public *virtual methods*. A virtual method is one which may be overridden in a derived class. This term will be familiar to C++ programmers. This behavior differs from Java, however, where all nonfinal methods are treated as virtual.

System.Object's virtual methods include Equals( ), GetHashCode( ), and ToString( ); these will be familiar to Java programmers, as they serve the same purpose as Java's equals( ), getHashCode( ), and toString( ) methods. We've overridden ToString( ) in Beverage in order to provide a more meaningful string representation of a Beverage instance.

The second reference type in Example 2-3 is an array of Beverage instances. An array is also a reference type, which derives from the System.Array class. The syntax for declaring an empty array of Beverage objects is as follows:

```
Beverage beverages [] = new Beverage [] {};
```

In BeverageTester, however, we're declaring an array with exactly two elements, by calling the constructor new Beverage [2]. The array declaration allocates space for the array itself, but not for the object stored in each of its elements. Each individual element must be declared. This can either be done separately, as in Example 2-3, or inline in the array declaration, as follows:

```
Beverage beverages [] = new Beverage [] {
        new Beverage(), new Beverage(), new Beverage()
};
```

That declaration would allocate space for an array with three elements, as well as the actual object instances for each of those elements.

There are better ways to handle string concatenation in C#. Wait for "Manage String Data" in Chapter 3.

System.Array implements an interface called System.Collections.IEnumerable, which allows you to use the foreach statement to iterate over its members.

What about ...

...Multiple inheritance, the ability for a single class to extend more than one parent class? Strictly speaking, C# does not allow multiple inheritance. It does, however, allow *interfaces*. An interface is about as close as C# comes to having C-style header files. An interface represents a contract that a class must satisfy, but the interface itself does not provide any implementation for the members that it declares. An interface is similar to a pure abstract class in C++, and is identical in semantics to the interface type in Java.

We can declare an IBeverage interface that Beverage implements, as shown in Example 2-4.

Example 2-4. 02-reftypes/IBeverage.cs

```
// 02-csharp/02-reftypes
using System;

public interface IBeverage {
  string Brand { get; }
  double Volume { get; }
  double PercentCaffeine { get; }
}
```

IBeverage.cs defines the interface named IBeverage.

Any class that implements IBeverage has to provide implementations for IBeverage's members. These methods are not marked with the virtual keyword, because they are part of an interface, not virtual methods of a base class.

If Beverage were to implement IBeverage, its declaration would begin like this:

```
public class Beverage : IBeverage {
        // the rest of the code remains the same as Example 2-3...
}
```

Time for another forward reference. The System.Collections namespace is discussed in "Manage Collections of Data" in Chapter 3.

By convention, the names of interfaces in C# begin the name with a capital letter I.

Avoid Overhead While Passing Data

In addition to the reference types in "Model the Behavior of Real-World Things," C# also includes two *value types*. Value types can be used to model objects that are based mostly on data rather than behavior. In this lab, you'll see how to work with the struct and enum types.

How do I do that?

Example 2-5 shows *ValueTypes.cs*, which demonstrates the use of the C# value types.

Example 2-5. 03-valuetypes/ValueTypes.cs

```
// 02-csharp/03-valuetypes
using System;

public enum Units {
  Ounces,
  Liters,
```

Example 2-5. 03-valuetypes/ValueTypes.cs (continued)

```
    Pints
}

public struct BeverageSize {
  private double volume;
  private Units units;

  public BeverageSize(double volume, Units units) {
    this.volume = volume;
    this.units = units;
  }

  public override string ToString( ) {
    return volume + " " + units;
  }
}

public class ValueTypesTester {
  public static void Main(string [] args) {
    BeverageSize size = new BeverageSize(12.0, Units.Ounces);
    Console.WriteLine(size);
  }
}
```

Compile and run Example 2-5 with the following commands to see the results:

```
$ mcs ValueTypes.cs
$ mono ValueTypes.exe
12 Ounces
```

How it works

ValueTypes.cs demonstrates how to define value types in C# using the enum and struct keywords. All value types, like all other CLI types, ultimately derive from System.Object, but they have an additional intermediate base class, System.ValueType. Value types differ from reference types in that a variable of value type contains the actual object data. Compare this to reference type variables, which, you will remember, contain a reference to the location of the object data. Additionally, value types are allocated on the stack, as opposed to reference types, which are allocated on the heap. Value types may not be null.

The first value type demonstrated in Example 2-5 is an enum. enum declares an enumeration type that derives from System.Enum. In addition to the C/C++-like behavior you would expect from an enumeration type, the System.Enum has a few advanced features. For example, enum values may be of any integral type except `char`. The base type defaults to `int`, or you can explicitly set it with the following declaration:

```
enum Units : byte {
    ...
}
```

This gives you the ability to control how many distinct values an `enum` has room to enumerate.

`enum`s may be converted to and from other types, and may override the virtual methods from `System.Object` (like `ToString()`). You can also parse a string value to determine its equivalent `enum` value, using the `Enum.Parse()` method. The code below parses the string "Ounces" and assigns the value `Units.Ounces` to the variable `units`:

```
Units units = (Units)Enum.Parse(typeof(Units), "Ounces");
```

The second value type is `struct`. `struct`s are useful for objects with a small number of relatively static fields. C++ developers will be familiar with a type called `struct`, which is nearly identical to a class, except for the default scope of its members. The C# `struct` is nothing at all like that.

The `Enum.Parse()` method can parse any enum, but it needs to know what specific type it's working with. That's why you pass in the Type and cast the return value.

A C# `struct` is similar to a C# `class`, except for a few points:

- A `struct` is a value type, unlike a `class`, which is a reference type.
- The default value for a field of a `struct` type is 0, false, or '\0', while the default value for a field of `class` type is null.
- A `struct` cannot explicitly declare a parameterless constructor. The default constructor implicitly sets all instance variables to their default values.
- As a value type, assigning the value of one `struct` to another creates a copy of the original.
- If a `struct` does declare a constructor, all instance variable values must be explicitly set before the constructor can return.
- A `struct`'s instance fields may not have initializers.
- A `struct` (a value type) is allocated on the stack, whereas a `class` (a reference type) is allocated on the heap.

The fact that `struct`s are created on the stack rather than the heap makes them ideal for use as lightweight data structures. In fact, all of the CLI primitive types, from `bool` to `float`, are value types.

`struct`s also make excellent types for immutable values such as `string`s.

What about ...

...Wrapping value types in a reference and unwrapping value types? Referred to as *boxing*, value types are converted into reference types when they need to be treated as references. And they are *unboxed* to convert them back. For example, in order to store a value type in a collection, a reference to the object instance must actually be stored.

Java developers will be familiar with the int primitive type and the Integer object type. To add an int to a collection, you have to construct a new Integer instance with the int's value. And you have to call the Integer's toInt( ) method to convert it back to an int, as in Example 2-6 demonstrates C#'s automatic boxing and unboxing. In C#, a value type is automatically boxed when you add it to a collection, and you can unbox it by casting to its original type when you retrieve it.

Example 2-6. 03-valuetypes/BoxUnbox.cs

```
// 02-csharp/03-valuetypes
using System;
using System.Collections;

public class BoxUnbox {
  public static void Main(string [] args) {
    ArrayList h = new ArrayList( );
    int i = 1;
    h.Add(i); // box
    int j = (int)h[0]; // unbox
  }
}
```

Since boxing is a copying operation, you can't change the original value by doing something to the boxed value:

```
int i = 1;
object o = i; // boxing
o = 10; // i is still 1
int j = (int)o; // j is a copy of i
```

Handle Unexpected Errors

Many languages contain the concept of *exceptions*, a way to report errors and short-circuit processing. The C# System.Exception class and the try...catch...finally syntax are first-class members of the language, and are easy to understand and use. You can catch exceptions thrown by class libraries, rethrow them, clean up before moving on, and even declare and throw your own custom exceptions.

How do I do that?

Example 2-7 shows a class called `FileFinder` which handles some errors that might arise while opening a file.

Example 2-7. 04-exceptions/FileFinder.cs

```
// 02-csharp/04-exceptions
using System;
using System.IO;

public class FileFinder {

  public static void Main(string [] args) {
    string filename = null;
    try {
      // will throw IndexOutOfRangeException if the
      // filename is not specified
      filename = args[0];

      // will throw FileNotFoundException if the file
      // does not exist
      using(StreamReader reader = File.OpenText(filename)) {
        string contents = reader.ReadToEnd();
      }

    } catch (IndexOutOfRangeException e) {
      Console.Error.WriteLine("No filename specified.");
      Environment.Exit(1);

    } catch (FileNotFoundException e) {
      Console.Error.WriteLine("File \"{0}\" does not exist.",
        filename);
      Environment.Exit(2);

    } catch (Exception e) {
      Console.Error.WriteLine(e);
      Environment.Exit(3);

    } finally {
      Console.WriteLine("Done");
    }
  }
}
```

Compile Example 2-7 with this command:

```
$ mcs FileFinder.cs
```

FileFinder.exe can be run with several different scenarios to produce different results. For example, run it without a parameter to catch the `IndexOutOfRangeException` and print an error message:

```
$ mono FileFinder.exe
```

```
No filename specified.
```

Then run it with a nonexistent filename as the parameter, to catch the FileNotFoundException:

```
$ mono FileFinder.exe foo
File "foo" does not exist.
```

Finally, run it with the name of a file that exists, and the program will run to the end successfully.

In each of these cases, the error condition could also be handled proactively. For example, rather than catching an IndexOutOfRangeException when checking for parameters, you could just check the value of args. Length. Similarly, instead of catching the FileNotFoundException, you could use the static method Exists() of the File class to see if the file exists. The way you choose to handle exceptions is mostly a matter of style and personal preference.

How it works

The C# language includes a try...catch...finally syntax to handle exceptions that have been thrown, as well as the throw statement, which allows exceptions to be *thrown*, or propagated up the call stack until the first appropriate catch statement can handle it. Example 2-7 demonstrates declaring, throwing, and catching exceptions.

The Main( ) method of FileFinder starts by declaring a string variable to hold the filename and assigning it a value from the args parameter array. If there is no 0th element of the parameter array—if, in other words, no filename was passed on the command line—an IndexOutOfRangeException will be thrown. If this exception is thrown, it will be caught at the end of the method and the program will print an error message and exit.

You can also have a try and finally without the catch. Any exceptions are just passed up to the next available catch statement after executing any code in the finally statement. Remember that the finally statement is *always* executed, whether an exception is caught or not.

Next, the program attempts to read from the file. This will throw a FileNotFoundException if the file does not exist. Again, this exception will be caught at the end of the try...catch...finally statement.

At the end of the Main( ) method, several catch statements are ready to handle different exceptions. In this example, IndexOutOfRangeException and FileNotFoundException merit their own individual catch statements, each of which prints out an appropriate error message. Then any other exceptions are caught with the fallback catch (Exception e), which will catch any exception not caught by a more specific catch statement.

If you want to bewilder your users, you can print an entire stack trace to help you debug the code that caused the exception. Every exception has a StackTrace property that returns a string containing the contents of the call stack when the exception was thrown.

Unlike Java, C# does not require a throws statement on every method that does not catch all possible exceptions internally. This may take a little getting used to, but you will eventually find it liberating.

What about ...

...Defining your own exceptions? An exception is actually just a regular class that derives from System.Exception. To create a new exception type, you simply declare a class that extends System.Exception or one of its subclasses. For your application, you should extend System.ApplicationException to meet your needs. For example, Example 2-8 declares MyException as a subclass of System.ApplicationException, and two subclasses, MyException1 and MyException2.

Example 2-8. 04-exceptions/Exceptions.cs

```
// 02-csharp/04-exceptions
using System;

public class MyException : ApplicationException {
  public MyException(string message) : base(message) {
  }
}

public class MyException1 : MyException {
  public MyException1(string message) : base(message) {
  }
}

public class MyException2 : MyException {
  public MyException2(string message) : base(message) {
  }
}
```

The syntax for throwing an exception is quite simple:

```
    throw new MyException1("Error!");
```

You instantiate an exception just you would any other class. The constructor can take parameters as needed. The key is that only System.

You can throw any exception that has a public constructor, not just the ones you declare.

Sometimes you know you need to take action, but you'd rather let someone else decide exactly what action to take.

Exception and classes that derive from System.Exception are eligible to be thrown.

Define Function Pointers

Delegates fill the same role in C# that function pointers fill in C/C++, a role that is not filled at all in Java. They allow you to define a method signature but defer the assignment of an actual method until runtime. Delegates play a large role in the FCL and Mono class libraries, through the event mechanism, which we describe in this lab.

How do I do that?

Example 2-9 shows the contents of the file *WatchDirectory.cs*. The class WatchDirectory demonstrates the general concepts of delegates and events, as well as giving a preview of one of the classes in the System.IO namespace, FileSystemWatcher.

Example 2-9. 05-delegates/WatchDirectory.cs

```
// 02-csharp/05-delegates
using System;
using System.IO;

public class WatchDirectory {

  private static void OnFileSystemEvent (object sender,
      FileSystemEventArgs e) {
    Console.WriteLine("Something happened to {0}", e.Name);
  }

  private static void OnChanged (object sender,
      FileSystemEventArgs e) {
    Console.WriteLine("{0} changed", e.Name);
  }

  private static void OnCreated (object sender,
      FileSystemEventArgs e) {
    Console.WriteLine("{0} created", e.Name);
  }

  private static void OnDeleted (object sender,
      FileSystemEventArgs e) {
    Console.WriteLine("{0} deleted", e.Name);
  }

  private static void OnRenamed (object sender,
      RenamedEventArgs e) {
    Console.WriteLine("{0} renamed to {1}", e.OldName, e.Name);
```

Example 2-9. 05-delegates/WatchDirectory.cs (continued)

```
  }

  public static void Main(string [ ] args) {
    string path = (string)args[0];
    FileSystemWatcher watcher = new FileSystemWatcher(path);
    watcher.Filter = "*";

    watcher.Changed += new FileSystemEventHandler(OnChanged);
    watcher.Created += new FileSystemEventHandler(OnCreated);
    watcher.Deleted += new FileSystemEventHandler(OnDeleted);
    watcher.Renamed += new RenamedEventHandler(OnRenamed);

    FileSystemEventHandler onFileSystemEvent =
      new FileSystemEventHandler(OnFileSystemEvent);
    watcher.Changed += onFileSystemEvent;
    watcher.Created += onFileSystemEvent;
    watcher.Deleted += onFileSystemEvent;

    watcher.EnableRaisingEvents = true;
    Console.WriteLine("Enabled watcher on {0}; " +
      "hit return to terminate.", path);

    Console.ReadLine( );

    watcher.EnableRaisingEvents = false;

    watcher.Changed -= new FileSystemEventHandler(OnChanged);
    watcher.Created -= new FileSystemEventHandler(OnCreated);
    watcher.Deleted -= new FileSystemEventHandler(OnDeleted);
    watcher.Renamed -= new RenamedEventHandler(OnRenamed);

    watcher.Changed -= onFileSystemEvent;
    watcher.Created -= onFileSystemEvent;
    watcher.Deleted -= onFileSystemEvent;

    Console.WriteLine("done");
  }
}
```

Do the familiar compile-and-run dance, passing in a pathname as a
parameter to *WatchDirectory.exe*. Then create, change, delete, and
rename a few files in that path, and watch the fun happen. For example,
if you were to create a file named *foo*, rename it to *bar*, edit its contents,
then delete it, you would see something like the following:

```
$ mcs WatchDirectory.cs
$ mono WatchDirectory.exe /Users/niel
Enabling watcher on /Users/niel; hit return to terminate.
/Users/niel/foo created
Something happened to /Users/niel/foo
/Users/niel/bar created
```

```
Something happened to /Users/niel/bar
/Users/niel/foo deleted
Something happened to /Users/niel/foo
/Users/niel/bar changed
Something happened to /Users/niel/bar
/Users/niel/bar deleted
Something happened to /Users/niel/bar
```

The Renamed event is not raised in Mono. Instead, you'll see that the Created event is raised for the new filename, followed by the Deleted event for the old filename. As of this writing, `FileSystemWatcher` has a managed implementation by default, although it will use `libfam` if it's available. Either way, it's a known issue having to do with the underlying filesystem on various platforms.

How it works

If you've got access to the Mono source code, look for those event handler source files in the directory mcs/class/System/System.IO.

The class `WatchDirectory` in Example 2-9 begins by defining five private static members to handle events that will be raised by `System.IO.FileSystemWatcher`. Each method simply reports to the console that something happened to a file. These methods must match the delegates declared in `FileSystemWatcher`. From the Mono *FileSystemEventHandler.cs* and *RenamedEventHandler.cs* source files, respectively, these are:

```
public delegate void FileSystemEventHandler (object sender,
FileSystemEventArgs e);
public delegate void RenamedEventHandler (object sender, RenamedEventArgs e);
```

A delegate declaration defines an instance of a class descended from `System.Delegate`. In `FileSystemWatcher`, then, `FileSystemEventHandler` is an implicit subclass of `System.Delegate`.

After that, the `Main( )` method is defined. It takes the pathname passed in on the command line and constructs a new `FileSystemWatcher` to monitor it. The `Filter` property is set so that the `FileSystemWatcher` will watch all files; the default is `"*.*"`, which won't match all files in a Unix filesystem, although it should work fine in Windows. We override it by supplying `"*"` as the argument, which will match everything except dotfiles.

Note that the OnFileSystemEvent can't be used to handle the FileRenamed event, because the delegate signatures are different. The compiler will complain about this error.

Now each of the four event handler methods is added to the appropriate event's invocation list. The `+=` operator does this.

Next, we construct a new delegate of type `FileSystemEventHandler`, and use the `+=` operator to add it to each of the `FileSystemWatcher`'s `FileSystemEventHandler` events. This demonstrates that a delegate instance can be treated much like any other variable, and that a particular delegate instance can be used to handle multiple events.

Having handled all the events, we set the `FileSystemWatcher`'s `EnableRaisingEvents` flag to `true` to start it. The `while` loop will wait for the `return` key to be pressed on the console, allowing the program to handle events as they happen.

When a file is created, changed, deleted, or renamed, an event is raised. Each delegate instance in the appropriate event's invocation list is called, in order, with the same parameter list.

After the `return` key is pressed, the delegate's instances are removed from the event's invocation list. While this step is not strictly necessary in this simple example, it does demonstrate how to remove a delegate. You'll notice that the delegate instance being removed is created with the `new` operator; strictly speaking, it would seem that the delegate being removed is *not* the same as the one that we added earlier. It still works, though, and this makes sense when you remember that a delegate acts somewhat like a function pointer; delegate instances are considered equal and identical if they refer to the same method and object instance.

Add Metadata to Your Types

Sometimes you need to specify additional information about a class or member, but until now most programming languages lacked built-in language constructs to express these details. Developers have been reduced to using interfaces as "markers" or hacking together special preprocessors to fill this need.

No more marker interfaces, no more preprocessor junk in comments. Attributes do all that and much, much more!

C# addresses the need for custom declarative information with the concept of *attributes*. Attributes are classes derived from `System.Attribute` that may be placed on any C# language feature. Attributes add information about, and functionality to, the language features to which they are applied.

How do I do that?

Attributes appear throughout the CLI. `System.SerializableAttribute` is one attribute that shows up quite often; it's used to mark a class which can be serialized, which is necessary for remoting and XML serialization (see "Serialize Objects to XML" in Chapter 6). Example 2-10 shows a class which uses the `SerializableAttribute` attribute.

The naming standard for attribute types is to use Attribute as a suffix. However, when applying an attribute, the Attribute suffix may be omitted.

Example 2-10. 06-attributes/SerializableClass.cs

```
// 02-csharp/06-attributes
using System;
```

Example 2-10. 06-attributes/SerializableClass.cs (continued)

```
[Serializable]
public class SerializableClass {
    // ...
}
```

If you do need a class to implement its own serialization functionality, there is an ISerializable interface that you can implement.

It's important to note that attributes are not normally used by the class or member that they are applied to. Instead, they are accessed via reflection at runtime by some other class that needs information about the object in question. `SerializableAttribute` is a perfect example; a class that is marked with the `Serializable` attribute does not implement any special methods or add any particular fields or properties. Instead, the `System.Xml.Serialization.XmlSerializer` class uses reflection to look inside a serializable class and determine how to serialize it.

What about ...

...Creating your own attributes? Attributes may be applied to many different language features. Valid targets include assemblies, classes, constructors, delegates, enums, events, fields, interfaces, methods, modules, parameters, properties, return values, and structs, and any combination thereof—in other words, pretty much anything that can be declared. When declaring an attribute, you actually *use* an attribute, `AttributeUsageAttribute`, to specify the target. The `AttributeTargets` enum is a parameter to the `AttributeUsageAttribute` constructor.

Just like any other class, attributes may have constructors, properties, and methods. Attributes may also have named parameters as well as the usual positional parameters. This allows you to apply an attribute specifying only a few parameters as necessary. The positional parameters are declared in the attribute class' constructor and the named parameters are simply the read-write properties of the attribute. The parameters may only be of one of the primitive types, `System.Object`, `System.Type`, or enum.

Example 2-11 shows the declaration of an attribute named `MethodAttribute`. You can see from the code that `MethodAttribute` may only be applied to methods, and has one `named` parameter and one positional parameter.

Example 2-11. 06-attributes/MethodAttribute.cs

```
// 02-csharp/06-attributes
using System;

[AttributeUsage(AttributeTargets.Method)]
```

Example 2-11. 06-attributes/MethodAttribute.cs (continued)

```
public class MethodAttribute : Attribute {

  private string namedParameter;
  private int positionalParameter;

  public string NamedParameter {
    get {
      return namedParameter;
    }
    set {
      namedParameter = value;
    }
  }

  public MethodAttribute(int positionalParameter) {
    this.positionalParameter = positionalParameter;
  }
}
```

Example 2-11 is not a complete program. You must compile it as a DLL:

```
$ mcs -target:library MethodAttribute.cs
```

To apply the `MethodAttribute` attribute to a method, you would use the following syntax:

```
public class MyClass {
        [MethodAttribute(0, NamedParameter="foo")]
        public void MyMethod( ) {
            ...
        }
}
```

As you can see, the positional parameter comes in order in the attribute's parameters, while the named parameter is specifically assigned. If you save `MyClass` in a file named *MyClass.cs*, you can compile it against the dll with:

```
$ mcs -target:library -lib:. -r:MethodAttribute.dll MyClass.cs
```

Call External Libraries

One of the beauties of Mono is the fact that, as an open source project, it builds on other, existing, open source projects. Most of these other projects, such as the Boehm garbage collector and the IBM ICU library, are written in traditional unmanaged programming languages, such as C and C++, and are linked with the Mono runtime. Others, such as libxslt, are accessed through a technique known as Platform Invocation Services, or P/Invoke.

Don't discard all those open source C libraries just because you're using Mono!

For more information on curses, see Programming with curses by John Strang (O'Reilly).

You can use P/Invoke to invoke external libraries from your own C# code, too, as you'll see in this lab.

How do I do that?

Let's begin with Example 2-12, which shows the file *Curses.cs*. The first class it defines, Curses, is a very rudimentary wrapper around the ncurses terminal-based user interface library.

Example 2-12. 07-pinvoke/Curses.cs

Mac OS X users should replace const string Library = "ncurses"; with const string Library = "libncurses.dylib";.

```
// 02-csharp/07-pinvoke
using System;
using System.Runtime.InteropServices;

public class Curses {
  const string Library = "ncurses";

  [DllImport(Library)]
  private extern static IntPtr initscr();

  [DllImport(Library)]
  private extern static int endwin();

  [DllImport(Library)]
  private extern static int mvwprintw(IntPtr window,
    int y, int x, string message);

  [DllImport(Library)]
  private extern static int refresh(IntPtr window);

  [DllImport(Library)]
  private extern static int wgetch(IntPtr window);

  private IntPtr window;

  public Curses() {
    window = initscr();
  }

  ~Curses() {
    int result = endwin();
  }

  public int Print(int x, int y, string message) {
    return mvwprintw(window, y, x, message);
  }

  public int Refresh() {
    return refresh(window);
  }
```

Chapter 2: Getting Started with C#

Example 2-12. 07-pinvoke/Curses.cs (continued)

```
  public char GetChar() {
    return (char)wgetch(window);
  }
}

public class HelloCurses {
  public static void Main(string [] args) {
    Curses Curses = new Curses();
    Curses.Print(10, 10, "Hello, curses!");
    Curses.Refresh();
    char c = Curses.GetChar();
    Curses = null;
  }
}
```

When we say "rudimentary," we mean it. We've only implemented enough function calls to print a message on the screen and wait for any key to be pressed. The second class in Example 2-12, HelloCurses, is used to test the Curses class by calling its public methods.

Compile and run *Curses.cs* with these commands:

```
$ mcs Curses.cs
$ mono Curses.exe
```

You'll see the screen go blank, and then the message "Hello, curses!" will be displayed 10 lines from the top and 10 characters from the left side of your console. Finally, the program will wait for any key to be pressed and exit.

If you don't happen to have libncurses.so installed on your system, Example 2-12 will compile just fine. But at runtime, you'll see a message akin to the following:

```
Unhandled Exception: System.DllNotFoundException: ncurses
in <0x00053> (wrapper managed-to-native) Curses.Screen:initscr ()
in <0x0001b> Curses.Screen:.ctor ()
in <0x0002a> HelloCurses:Main (string[])
```

P/Invoke uses *late binding*, which means that no checks are done on the function call arguments or even the name of the library until runtime.

How it works

The class Curses in Example 2-12 starts by defining a constant string called Library, which contains the name of the ncurses library. This constant will be used in the System.Runtime.InteropServices. DllImport attribute for each external function being wrapped.

DllImport is applied to a method that also has the extern keyword to indicate that the method is to be imported from an external library. External methods can also be marked static. The positional parameter to DllImport is the name of the library, and its named parameters include EntryPoint, which specifies the name of the external function being invoked, and several others that specify which character set to use, whether a persistent error code should be set, and what calling convention to use.

At runtime, when a P/Invoke method is called, the specified DLL is located and loaded into memory, and the named function is located and invoked. The DLL is only loaded the first time the method is called. Any parameters are marshaled according to the DllImport attribute's parameters.

External libraries do not typically have object-oriented interfaces, so it's common to wrap them in an object-oriented class in the managed environment. That's what happens next in Example 2-12; for each extern method declared, a wrapper method is defined. The first and second, the constructor and destructor, call initscr( ) and endwin( ), respectively, from the ncurses library. The return value from initscr( ) is a pointer to a *WINDOW* structure, which is stored in an instance field of type IntPtr called Window.

IntPtr is a NET type that holds an address. It's roughly equivalent to void * in C/C++.

The next three methods, Print( ), Refresh( ), and GetChar( ), call the extern methods mvwprintw( ), refresh( ), and wgetch( ), respectively, passing in the value of the Window field. Because the Curses class holds on to the Window value, it is able to act as an object-oriented wrapper around the procedural ncurses library.

Finally, the HelloCurses class runs a very simple ncurses "Hello, World" program.

Where to learn more

Microsoft's .NET Framework Developer's Guide contains a section titled *Consuming Unmanaged DLL Functions* that tells you more than you probably ever wanted to know about P/Invoke. Read it online at *http://msdn.microsoft.com/ library/en-us/cpguide/html/cpconconsumingunmanageddllfunctions.asp*.

Package Related Classes with Assemblies

In the olden days of Windows programming, the term *DLL hell* was used to describe the nightmares of deploying a new software application over an existing one. The open source world has similar woes, making dependency checking tools such as RPM and APT *de riguer* to keep your system up-to-date.

In .NET, Microsoft introduced the concept of the *assembly*. An assembly is simply a package of classes and resources, containing a manifest and a signature. The promise of assemblies is the end of DLL hell, allowing each application to bring along the knowledge of its dependencies as well as allowing multiple versions of the same library to coexist to serve those different applications.

Group common functionality together in namespaces, then group common namespaces in assemblies.

How do I do that?

Typically, when we refer to an assembly, we're referring to a DLL compiled with the -target:library command-line argument to mcs. However, you've actually been creating an assembly every time you compile any Mono executable. A Mono library is simply an assembly without a Main( ) method, while a Mono executable is an assembly with a Main( ) entry point.

What makes assemblies distinct is the metadata they contain. The metadata are part of the assembly manifest, and their values can be set both by including classes and resources in the assembly and through assembly-level attributes. The manifest includes the assembly's identity information, including the version and digital signature; a list of files included in the assembly; a list of external assemblies referenced by the assembly; public classes and resources included in the assembly; and any permissions the assembly needs to run.

Although they may be included in any source file, assembly-level attributes by convention are only included in a file called *AssemblyInfo.cs*. Example 2-13 shows the contents of a typical *AssemblyInfo.cs* file.

Example 2-13. 08-assemblies/AssemblyInfo.cs

```
// 02-csharp/08-assemblies
using System;
using System.Reflection;
using System.Runtime.CompilerServices;

[assembly: CLSCompliant(true)]
[assembly: System.Security.AllowPartiallyTrustedCallers]

[assembly: AssemblyTitle("SprocketSet")]
[assembly: AssemblyDescription("Build Sprockets for your widgets.")]
[assembly: AssemblyConfiguration("Release")]
[assembly: AssemblyCompany("Amalgamated Widgets")]
```

Example 2-13. 08-assemblies/AssemblyInfo.cs (continued)

```
[assembly: AssemblyProduct("SprocketSet")]
[assembly: AssemblyCopyright("2004 Amalgamated Widgets. All Rights Reserved.")]
[assembly: AssemblyTrademark("")]
[assembly: AssemblyCulture("en-US")]

[assembly: AssemblyVersion("1.0.*.*")]

[assembly: AssemblyDelaySign(false)]
[assembly: AssemblyKeyFile("SprocketSet.snk")]
[assembly: AssemblyKeyName("")]
```

You can compile *AssemblyInfo.cs* into an assembly by simply including it on the command line with the other source files to be compiled into the assembly. You can also include arbitrary resources in an assembly by specifying a resource file with the -resource:*filename*.resources command line option. Resources are contained in a binary file, but you can create them with a text or XML file using the monoresgen tool. A typical resource file is shown in Example 2-14 in text format.

Example 2-14. 08-assemblies/SprocketSet.txt

```
; 02-csharp/08-assemblies
; this file contains resource for the SprocketSet.dll assembly
resource1 = foo ; some resource
resource2 = bar ; some other resource
```

And Example 2-15 shows an equivalent resource file in XML:

Example 2-15. 08-assemblies/SprocketSet.resx

```
<?xml version="1.0" encoding="utf-8"?>
<!-- 02-csharp/08-assemblies -->
<root>
  <resheader name="resmimetype">
    <value>text/microsoft-resx</value>
  </resheader>
  <resheader name="version">
    <value>1.3</value>
  </resheader>
  <data name="resource1">
    <value>foo</value>
    <comment>some resource</comment>
  </data>
  <data name="resource2">
    <value>bar</value>
    <comment>some other resource</comment>
  </data>
</root>
```

Given a resource file in text or XML, you can translate it into a binary resource file for embedding in an assembly. The monoresgen tool can translate between any of the three formats. So, for a text file, use the following command:

```
$ monoresgen SprocketSet.txt SprocketSet.resources
```

Or, for an XML file, use this command:

```
$ monoresgen SprocketSet.resx SprocketSet.resources
```

The resulting file, *SprocketSet.resources*, can be accessed at runtime from the System.Resources.ResourceManager class.

Putting these all together, you can use the following command line to build an assembly called *SprocketSet.dll* from the source files *AssemblyInfo.cs*, *Sprocket.cs*, and *Widget.cs*, and the resource file *SprocketSet.resources*:

```
$ mcs -out:SprocketSet.dll -target:library \
-resource:SprocketSet.resources AssemblyInfo.cs Sprocket.cs Widget.cs
```

You can also include arbitrary resource files, such as PNG images, icons, and plain text, in an assembly using the -resource:*filename* argument.

What about ...

...Making an assembly available for use in multiple applications? Normally, an executable program may only use assemblies that are in the same directory as the executable. The Global Assembly Cache (GAC) makes assemblies available to any executable on a given system. Think of the GAC as similar to /usr/lib on a Linux system.

Before an assembly can be installed into the GAC, it has to be signed to ensure that the assembly is what it claims to be. The first step in this process is the creation of a hash value for the assembly using the SHA1 algorithm. This hash is stored in the assembly manifest, and is used to ensure that the assembly has not been tampered with. At runtime, the CLR re-computes the hash and compares the two values; if they do not match, the CLR will not load the assembly.

In order to ensure that the hash in the assembly manifest has not been tampered with, it is encrypted with a *strong name*, which is a public key/private key pair. You can generate a key pair with the strong name utility, sn. First, you should create a strong name key, which is a file with the extension *.snk*:

```
$ sn -k key.snk
```

The assembly hash value is computed automatically by the assembly linker.

Your SNK file contains both the private key and public key, and can be used to sign any assembly and make it look like it was signed by you. So keep it safe!

Then, to sign the assembly with that key, you place it in the AssemblykeyFile attribute in *AssemblyInfo.cs* with the following code, using the relative path to the SNK file:

```
[assembly: AssemblyKeyFile("key.snk")]
```

Now when you compile the assembly, it will be signed with your private key. Now that the assembly is signed, you can install it in the GAC. *gacutil.exe* is the tool responsible for installing assemblies in the GAC.s

Install *SprocketSet.dll* into the GAC with the following command line (as root):

```
# gacutil -i SprocketSet.dll
```

Now other assemblies may refer to *SprocketSet.dll* without requiring it to be in the same directory.

Assemblies may also be removed from the GAC using *gacutil.exe*, like so (as root):

```
# gacutil -u SprocketSet.dll
```

Where to learn more

Depending on where Mono is installed, you may need administrator privileges to run gacutil.exe, because it creates files and directories.

The *.NET Framework Developer's Guide: Metadata and Self-Describing Components* contains more information than you'll probably ever need. Read it online at *http://msdn.microsoft.com/library/en-us/cpguide/html/cpconmetadataselfdescribingcomponents.asp.*

The article *The Secrets of Strong Naming* at *http://www.ondotnet.com/pub/a/dotnet/2003/04/28/strongnaming.html* provides a thorough introduction to strong naming, and some of the other features of sn.

## CHAPTER 3

Core .NET

By now you've become familiar with the C# language, and you've seen some of its differences and similarities to Java and C/C++. We've alluded to some of the powerful *Framework Class Library* (FCL) classes, but we haven't really gone into depth on them.

In this chapter, you'll be introduced to the FCL and some of its most commonly used classes, including those that let you work with files, strings, regular expressions, collections, assemblies, process control, and threading. And, as a bonus, you'll get your first look at NUnit, the .NET unit testing framework.

Work with Files

File I/O is an important part of any class library, and the FCL contains a complete and powerful set of file access classes. In this lab, you'll see how to manipulate files and directories with Mono.

How do I do that?

You need to learn three basic classes in the FCL to manage files. They are File, TextReader, and TextWriter. Example 3-1 shows the source for a class that uses these three classes to create a file, write to it, read from it, and set some of the file's attributes.

Example 3-1. 01-files/FileCreator.cs

```
// 03-keyfunc/01-files
using System;
using System.IO;

public class FileCreator {
```

In this chapter:
- *"Work with Files"*
- *"Manage String Data"*
- *"Search Text with Regular Expressions"*
- *"Manage Collections of Data"*
- *"Work with Assemblies"*
- *"Start and Examine Processes"*
- *"Multitask with Threads"*
- *"Test Your C# Code"*

Reading, writing, and 'rithmetic may be elementary skills, but Mono makes them even easier.

Example 3-1. 01-files/FileCreator.cs (continued)

```
public static void Main(string [] args) {
  string file = args[0];

  if (File.Exists(file)) {
    Console.WriteLine("File {0} exists with attributes {1}," +
      "created at {2}", file, File.GetAttributes(file),
      File.GetCreationTime(file));
  } else {
    using (TextWriter writer = File.CreateText(file)) {
      writer.WriteLine("Greetings from Mono!");
    }
    File.SetAttributes(file,
      File.GetAttributes(file) | FileAttributes.ReadOnly |
      FileAttributes.Temporary);
  }

  using (TextReader reader = File.OpenText(file)) {
    Console.WriteLine(reader.ReadToEnd());
  }
}
}
```

There are attributes, attributes, and attributes. In "Add Metadata to Your Types" in Chapter 2, we told you about attributes in C#. In Chapter 6 we'll talk about XML attributes. This lab features file attributes, indicating metadata such as whether the file is to be archived, and whether it's compressed, encrypted, hidden, and others.

You should always remember to close any files you open. Luckily, TextReader and TextWriter both implement IDisposable, so you can wrap them in the using statement to make sure they get closed. This using is different than the one used to import namespaces. Here's how using works in this context: classes that implement IDisposable have a Dispose method. In Example 3-1, this code:

```
using (TextReader reader = File.OpenText(file)) {
  Console.WriteLine(reader.ReadToEnd());
}
```

translates into:

```
{
  TextReader reader = File.OpenText(file);
  try {
    Console.WriteLine(reader.ReadToEnd());
  } finally {
    if (reader != null) {
      ((IDisposable)reader).Dispose();
    }
  }
}
```

Most classes that use system resources implement IDisposable, and care should be taken to always use the using statement to guarantee a timely release of those resources.

How it works

The File class, which you previously saw in Example 2-7 of Chapter 2, contains methods that you can use to access files and information about them. Another class, Stream, lets you access any resource (including files, memory, and network sockets) as a stream of bytes. Finally, TextReader and TextWriter let you read and write files as text.

Some of the more useful methods of File are Exists( ), Create( ), and Delete( ), and several methods to open a file. Table 3-1 describes the file-creating and file-opening methods, their parameters and return values, and what they do.

Table 3-1. Methods to create and open files

Method	Parameters	Returns	Description
Create( )	string, int	FileStream	(Two overloads) Creates the file with the given buffer size for reads and writes.
CreateText( )	string, int	StreamWriter	Creates the file.
Open( )	string, FileMode, FileAccess, FileShare	FileStream	(Three overloads) Opens the file for reading and/or writing, depending on the FileMode and FileAccess parameters. Other processes' access to the file is limited by the FileShare parameter.
OpenRead( )	string	FileStream	Opens the file for reading.
OpenText( )	string	StreamReader	Opens the file for reading.
OpenWrite( )	string	FileStream	Opens the file for writing.

In addition to the methods listed in Table 3-1, the GetAttributes( ) method returns a FileAttributes enum, which contains information about the file. And the SetAttributes( ) method sets the file's attributes. There are also GetLastAccessTime( ) and SetLastAccessTime( ), GetLastWriteTime( ), SetLastWriteTime( ), and others. See monodoc for more information.

The FileAttributes enum was designed to map to the Windows filesystem, so some of its values don't make sense in a Linux or Mac OS X Mono context. You can use the Syscall class from the Mono.Posix namespace to manipulate file permissions through the chmod( ) and chown( ) methods, as shown in Example 3-2.

Mono.Posix. FileMode is a completely different class from System.IO. FileMode, described in Table 3-1. Don't get them confused!

Example 3-2. 01-files/Syscall.cs

```
// 03-keyfunc/01-files
using Mono.Posix;

public class ChmodTest {
  public static void Main(string [ ] args) {
    string file = args[0];
    Syscall.chmod(file, (FileMode)0x777);

    int uid = Syscall.getuid( );
    int gid = Syscall.getegid( );
    Syscall.chown(file, uid, gid);
  }
}
```

To compile Example 3-2, you must reference the Mono.Posix DLL with the following command line:

```
$ mcs -r:Mono.Posix Syscall.cs
```

Syscall's methods map very closely to the POSIX functions with the same name. chmod( ) and chown( ) do exactly what their POSIX (and command line) namesakes do. And there are other POSIX functions available, like open( ), close( ), and creat( ), in addition to getuid( ) and getegid( ).

The code in Example 3-2 takes a filename on the command line and changes its permissions to 0x777 (rwxrwxrwx), full read, write, and execute access, and changes its owner to the current process's user ID and effective group ID.

What about ...

...Reading binary data from a file? TextReader and its subclasses can only be used to read text from files, so you must use a different class. Recall that the File class' Open( ) and Create( ) methods return a FileStream. The Stream class has several subclasses, including FileStream, MemoryStream, and NetworkStream, designed to provide byte-level access to resources.

Stream's methods include Read( ) and Write( ), as well as methods and properties like Seek( ), Flush( ), Position, and Length. These methods use byte arrays as buffers to store data as it is read and written rather than the strings that TextReader and TextWriter use.

There are also two classes analogous to the TextReader and TextWriter. Called BinaryReader and BinaryWriter, respectively, they let you read and write data of a particular type from a binary file. BinaryReader, for example, has methods called ReadByte() and ReadDouble() that read the appropriate amount of data from the underlying Stream and return it in an instance of the appropriate type.

Stream also allows asynchronous access to resources through the BeginRead() and EndRead(), and BeginWrite() and EndWrite() methods.

Where to learn more

Asynchronous I/O is covered in the *.NET Framework Developer's Guide* at *http://msdn.microsoft.com/library/en-us/cpguide/html/ cpconASynchronousFileIO.asp*.

Almost every program has to deal with strings in one way or another.

Manage String Data

Strings are first-class objects in C#. They can be created just like any other type, but you will do well to use them wisely.

How do I do that?

Example 3-3 shows how strings are created and manipulated using the string class.

System.String, like Int32, Byte, Char, and other primitive types in the System namespace, can be referred to by an alias. For String, that's string.

Example 3-3. 02-strings/Strings.cs

```
// 03-keyfunc/02-strings
using System;

public class Strings {
    public static void Main(string [] args) {
        string s1 = "a string!";
        string s2 = @"a string with \escaped characters,
including a carriage return";
        string s3 = new String('a', 4);
        string s4 = s3 + s1;
        string s5 = s4.Replace('a', 'b');

        Console.WriteLine(s1);
        Console.WriteLine(s2);
        Console.WriteLine(s3);
        Console.WriteLine(s4);
        Console.WriteLine(s5);
    }
}
```

Compiling and running this program, here's what you'll see:

```
$ mcs Strings.cs
$ mono Strings.exe
a string!
a string with \escaped characters,
including a carriage return
aaaa
aaaaa string!
bbbbb string!
```

Going over these one at a time, here's how they work. The first string, s1, is assigned to the literal value "a string!". Simple enough.

The second string, s2, is prefixed with the @ character. This @-quoted (literal) string contains an embedded backslash and a carriage return. Special characters such as these typically need to be escaped using the \\ and \n character sequences. By @-quoting the string, any characters that normally need to be escaped can be put in the string literally.

s3 demonstrates one of the string class' overloaded constructors. This one takes a char and an int, and creates a string containing the char value repeated by the int number of times.

s4 demonstrates the concatenation of two strings. In this case, a new string is created containing the concatenated values of s2 and s3.

Finally, s5 shows how you can use the string class' Replace() method to return a new string instance with every instance of the character a replaced with the character b. Notice that the original string is not changed, because the string class is immutable.

Of course, concatenating strings with the + operator is not the most efficient use of memory. Each original string has to be allocated, and then a new string has to be allocated with the concatenated contents of the two strings. And because the string class is immutable, you can't just set some character within the string directly, which means you have to allocate another string to return every time. Wouldn't it be nice to have a way to do these things less expensively?

Sure it would. Enter StringBuilder. A member of the System.Text namespace, StringBuilder provides a way to build strings that you can modify and format on the fly.

We can replace the string s4 with a StringBuilder thus:

```
StringBuilder s4 = new StringBuilder();
s4.Append(s3);
s4.Append(s1);

Console.WriteLine(s4.ToString());
```

Unicode? Of course! Strings in Mono are stored in Unicode internally. To embed a Unicode character within a string, use the format \unnnn, where nnnn is a four-digit number, or \unnnn\unnnn for 8-digit Unicode characters.

Because the StringBuilder is not a string, you must call its ToString() method to get a string representation of it.

Or, you could use one of the `StringBuilder`'s overloaded constructors to condense the code, like this:

```
StringBuilder s4 = new StringBuilder(s3);
s4.Append(s1);
```

And, because the `Append( )` method returns its `StringBuilder` instance, you can chain the various calls like this:

```
StringBuilder s4 = new StringBuilder(s3).Append(s1);
```

What about ...

...Formatting strings? You may be accustomed to `printf( )` and its %s and %d format strings. Mono handles composite formatting with the following syntax:

```
string s = string.Format("{0} {1} {2:C} {3:N4}",
    DateTime.Now, 'a', 5.95, 1);
```

After this assignment, the string s would have the value Saturday, 24 April 2004 12:18:35 a $5.95 1.0000.

The `Format( )` method has the following signature:

```
public static string Format(string format, params object [] args);
```

The `params` keyword is the C# way of indicating a variable argument list. Although the parameter type is `object [ ]`, you don't have to literally instantiate a new array of objects to hold the arguments. Instead, you can just specify them one by one, and the compiler will create an array on the fly to be passed to the method. Each parameter's `ToString( )` method will be called to produce the output.

The string formatting rules are simple. Each element in the `params` array can be referenced by its ordinal, so the format {0} refers to array element 0, {1} refers to array element 1, and so on. In addition to the ordinal, you can specify more detailed formatting rules for individual objects, such as the number of digits.

`StringBuilder` also lets you format strings. The `AppendFormat( )` method has a similar signature:

```
public StringBuilder AppendFormat(string format, params object [] args);
```

Given a `StringBuilder`, you can append a formatted string to it like so:

```
StringBuilder s = new StringBuilder( );
s.AppendFormat("{0} {1} {2:C} {3:N4}", DateTime.Now, 'a', 5.95, 1);
```

The exact string representation of a DateTime value and of numbers formatted with the C currency format specifier, should depend on your locale—and, of course, the date and time that you run the program.

Parse text with
obscure, magical
formulae that
look like a baby
sat down at the
keyboard.

Search Text with
Regular Expressions

Perl and shell programmers have long known the power of *regular expressions,* a language for describing patterns in sometimes excruciating detail. But there's no substitute for a regular expression when you need to separate a fixed- or variable-format chunk of text into its components.

This lab will demonstrate Mono's regular expression support.

How do I do that?

Example 3-4 shows a program that reads a *hosts* file and reports on its contents using regular expressions.

Example 3-4. 03-regex/ParseHosts.cs

```
// 03-keyfunc/03-regex
using System;
using System.Collections;
using System.IO;
using System.Text.RegularExpressions;

public class ParseHosts {
  public static void Main(string [ ] args) {
    string filename;
    if (Environment.OSVersion.ToString( ).StartsWith("Unix")) {
      filename = string.Format("{0}etc{0}hosts",
        Path.DirectorySeparatorChar);
    } else {
      filename = string.Format("{0}{1}drivers{1}etc{1}hosts",
        Environment.GetFolderPath(Environment.SpecialFolder.System),
        Path.DirectorySeparatorChar);
    }

    if (!File.Exists(filename)) {
      Console.Error.WriteLine("{0} does not exist.", filename);
      Environment.Exit(1);
    }

    string text;
    using (TextReader reader = File.OpenText(filename)) {
      text = reader.ReadToEnd( );
    }

    Regex regex =
      new Regex(@"(?<ip>(\d{1,3}\.){3}\d{1,3})\s+(?<name>(\S+))");

    MatchCollection matches = regex.Matches(text);
    foreach (Match match in matches) {
```

The hosts file will
be located in
different places
in different
operating systems.
In Linux, Unix,
and Mac OS X, it
will be in /etc. On
Windows, it will
be in
%WINDIR%\
System32\drivers\
etc. When
constructing a
path, use the
Path.Directory-
SeparatorChar
property, which
gives you the
character that
separates
directories in a
path, / for Unix,
\ for Windows.

Example 3-4. *03-regex/ParseHosts.cs (continued)*

```
    if (match.Length != 0) {
      Console.WriteLine("hostname {0} is mapped to ip address {1}",
        match.Groups["name"], match.Groups["ip"]);
    }
  }
 }
}
```

My *hosts* looks like this:

```
##
# Host Database
#
# localhost is used to configure the loopback interface
# when the system is booting.  Do not change this entry.
##
127.0.0.1       localhost
255.255.255.255 broadcasthost
::1             localhost

# reroute gracenote
64.71.163.204   cddb.cddb.org

# adware blockers
127.0.0.1       207-87-18-203.wsmg.digex.net
127.0.0.1       Garden.ngadcenter.net
127.0.0.1       Ogilvy.ngadcenter.net
...
```

Your hosts file may be very short or completely empty. Ours is full of tricks to keep ads from annoying us when we surf the web.

You can compile and run *ParseHosts.exe* as usual, and see the following output:

```
$ mcs ParseHosts.cs
$ mono ParseHosts.exe
hostname localhost is mapped to ip address 127.0.0.1
hostname broadcasthost is mapped to ip address 255.255.255.255
hostname cddb.cddb.org is mapped to ip address 64.71.163.204
hostname 207-87-18-203.wsmg.digex.net is mapped to ip address 127.0.0.1
hostname Garden.ngadcenter.net is mapped to ip address 127.0.0.1
hostname Ogilvy.ngadcenter.net is mapped to ip address 127.0.0.1
...
```

How it works

The System.Text.RegularExpressions namespace contains a suite of classes that can be used to search text using regular expressions. The main class, Regex, represents a single regular expression and can be used to determine whether a given string matches the expression, and if it does, returns a collection of Match instances.

Example 3-4 demonstrates the use of the Regex, Match, and Group classes. First, some housekeeping must be done to find the *hosts* file based on the operating system and to read the file into a string called text. Then, the regular expression work begins. We create an instance of the Regex class for a particular regular expression.

The C# regular expression language is similar to others that you may be familiar with, although there are a few details unique to C#. This pattern, `(?<ip>(\d{1,3}\.){3}\d{1,3})\s+(?<name>(\S*))`, will match a host entry from the *hosts* file. The pattern breaks down like this:

`(?<ip>(\d{1,3}\.){3}\d{1,3})`

Match a group of one to three decimal digits (`\d{1,3}`) followed by a . (`\.`), repeated three times (`{3}`), and then one to three additional decimal digits (`\d{1,3}`). The `?<ip>` notation and the outer parentheses indicate that the whole thing should be grouped and called ip.

`\s+`

Match one or more whitespace characters, and throw them away.

`(?<name>(\S+))`

Match any number of any nonwhitespace character. Group the whole thing and call it name.

The Matches() method returns a MatchCollection. This collection contains a Match instance for each line in the text variable that matches the regular expression.

Ok, this is not a perfect regular expression for a host entry. We haven't considered that each piece of the dotted-decimal IP address can be no greater than 255, and that there are further limitations based on whether it's a class A, B, or C address, but we're just trying to get the point across.

The Match class has a Groups property that returns a GroupCollection. The GroupCollection contains an instance of Group for each group in the regular expression. To obtain each group, the program iterates over all the Match instances, retrieves the Groups by name ("name" and "ip"), and then prints a message about the host entry to standard output.

Where to learn more

A good reference for regular expressions in general is *Mastering Regular Expressions* by Jeffrey E. F. Friedl (O'Reilly). For .NET regular expressions, which are slightly different, the MSDN documentation is available at *http://msdn.microsoft.com/library/en-us/cpguide/html/cpconCOMRegularExpressions.asp*.

There's a static version of Matches() that you can use if you're only going to call it once. The version we used in the example may be more efficient if you're going to call it multiple times.

A group is anything that has parentheses around it, not just if it's got a name. We're only interested in the named groups here, though.

Manage Collections of Data

Because you can never have too much of a good thing.

Collection types in the .NET Framework are very powerful. Besides the array type we introduced in "Model the Behavior of Real-World Things" in Chapter 2, there is a whole slew of more complex and specialized types to handle almost every case where you need a collection of objects. And you can extend a base class to make your own custom collection.

In this lab, we'll introduce the many ways of working with collections in Mono.

How do I do that?

Example 3-5 shows a class that uses some of the many .NET collection types.

Example 3-5. 04-collections/PrintEnvironment.cs

```
// 03-keyfunc/04-collections
using System;
using System.Collections;

public class PrintEnvironment {
  public static void Main(string [] args) {
    IDictionary variables = Environment.GetEnvironmentVariables();
    Console.WriteLine(variables.GetType());

    ICollection variableNames = variables.Keys;
    Console.WriteLine(variableNames.GetType());

    foreach (string variableName in variableNames) {
      Console.WriteLine("{0}={1}", variableName, variables[variableName]);
    }
  }
}
```

If you compile and run *PrintEnvironment.exe*, you should see something like this:

```
$ mcs PrintEnvironment.cs
$ mono PrintEnvironment.exe
MANPATH=/sw/share/man:/usr/share/man:/usr/local/man:/usr/X11R6/man
VISUAL=/usr/bin/vi
TERM_PROGRAM=Apple_Terminal
TERM_PROGRAM_VERSION=100
OLDPWD=/Users/niel
__CF_USER_TEXT_ENCODING=0x1F5:0:0
XML_CATALOG_FILES=/sw/etc/xml/catalog
INFOPATH=/sw/share/info:/sw/info:/usr/share/info
LOGNAME=niel
TERM=xterm-color
```

This output comes from the bash shell on Mac OS X 10.3. Your mileage may vary, especially if you're running on Windows.

```
USER=niel
PERL5LIB=/sw/lib/perl5:/sw/lib/perl5
_=/usr/local/bin/mono
SGML_CATALOG_FILES=/sw/etc/sgml/catalog
PWD=/Users/niel/Documents/Mono Developers Notebook/monodn
SHELL=/bin/bash
SECURITYSESSIONID=210970
HOME=/Users/niel
PATH=/sw/bin:/sw/sbin:/bin:/sbin:/usr/bin:/usr/local/bin:/usr/sbin:/usr/
X11R6/bin:/usr/local/bin
SHLVL=1
```

How it works

There are four main interfaces in the System.Collections namespace
that all collection types may choose to implement. They are:
ICollection, the basic interface that indicates a class contains a collection of object instances; IEnumerable, which means that the class can be
enumerated using the foreach statement; IList, which means the class
contains an ordered list of object instances; and IDictionary, which
means the class has a collection of keys and a collection of values.

The System.Collections namespace contains classes that can be used
for the most common types of collections: ArrayList, an ordered list of
objects; BitArray, a positional list of bits; Hashtable, a set of key-value
pairs; Queue, a FIFO collection; SortedList, a collection of key-value
pairs, kept ordered by keys; and Stack, a LIFO collection.

There's also the System.Collections.Specialized namespace, which
contains more specialized collection types, like the ListDictionary,
which is like a Hashtable, but is optimized for less than ten entries; and
HybridDictionary, which uses a ListDictionary if the number of items
is small, but switches to a Hashtable as the collection grows in size.
There are also three collection types customized to work with strings
rather than objects: NameValueCollection, a dictionary whose keys and
values are strongly typed as strings; StringCollection, a collection of
strings; and StringDictionary, a dictionary whose keys are strings but
whose values may be any object.

Many namespaces contain other collection types, usually implementing
one or more of the collection interfaces or extending one of the collection base types, such as CollectionBase or DictionaryBase. Quite often,
you can deal with any concrete collection type as just an interface.

Example 3-5 deals with two of the collection interfaces, IDictionary
and ICollection. Environment.GetEnvironmentVariables() returns an
IDictionary; although it just happens to be a Hashtable under the

---

hood, you don't really need to know that. Similarly, the IDictionary interface defines a Keys property that returns an ICollection; in this case, the class under the hood is a private inner class of Hashtable, but it looks just like any other ICollection as far as we're concerned.

What about ...

...Creating your own collection types? The System.Collections namespace contains two handy classes that you can extend to build your own specialized collection types, CollectionBase and DictionaryBase. These two classes provide all the basic functionality needed to create your own specialized collection type.

For example, Example 3-6 shows the source code for a collection of DateTime objects. Descriptive comments are included in this listing.

Example 3-6. 04-collections/DateTimeCollection.cs

```
// 03-keyfunc/04-collections
using System;
using System.Collections;

public class DateTimeCollection : CollectionBase {

  // returns the object at the given index
  public DateTime this[int index] {
    get {
      return (DateTime)List[index];
    }
    set {
      List[index] = value;
    }
  }

  // adds the given object at the end of the collection
  public int Add(DateTime value) {
    return List.Add(value);
  }

  // returns the index of the object with the given value
  public int IndexOf(DateTime value) {
    return List.IndexOf(value);
  }

  // inserts the given value at the given index
  public void Insert(int index, DateTime value) {
    List.Insert(index, value);
  }

  // removes the object with the given value
  public void Remove(DateTime value) {
```

If you built your Mono installation with the right magical incantation, you'll have C# generics enabled. Generics provide typesafe collections at compile time, so you don't need to write the code to do it yourself. See "Use Generics" in Chapter 8 for more information on generics.

Example 3-6. 04-collections/DateTimeCollection.cs (continued)

```csharp
    List.Remove(value);
  }

  // returns true if the the collection contains an object
  // with the given value
  public bool Contains(DateTime value) {
    return List.Contains(value);
  }

  // called before the object is inserted
  protected override void OnInsert(int index, object value) {
    Console.WriteLine("OnInsert({0},{1})", index, value);
    if (value.GetType() != typeof(DateTime)) {
      throw new ArgumentException(
        "value to be inserted must be of type System.DateTime",
        "value");
    }
  }

  // called before the object is removed
  protected override void OnRemove(int index, object value) {
    Console.WriteLine("OnRemove({0},{1})", index, value);
    if (value.GetType() != typeof(DateTime)) {
      throw new ArgumentException(
        "value to be removed must be of type System.DateTime",
        "value");
    }
  }

  // called before the value at the given location is changed
  protected override void OnSet(int index, object oldValue,
      object newValue) {
    Console.WriteLine("OnSet({0},{1},{2})", index, oldValue, newValue);
    if (newValue.GetType() != typeof(DateTime)) {
      throw new ArgumentException(
        "new value must be of type System.DateTime",
        "NewValue");
    }
  }

  // called when the object is validated
  protected override void OnValidate(object value) {
    Console.WriteLine("OnValidate({0})", value);
    if (value.GetType() != typeof(DateTime)) {
      throw new ArgumentException(
        "value must be of type System.DateTime",
        "value");
    }
  }

  // test method
  public static void Main(string [] args) {
```

Example 3-6. 04-collections/DateTimeCollection.cs (continued)

```
    DateTimeCollection collection = new DateTimeCollection();
    collection.Add(DateTime.Now);
    collection.Add(new DateTime(2004,1,1));
    // new instance of the same date/time value
    collection.Remove(new DateTime(2004,1,1));
    collection[0] = new DateTime(2001,12,31);
  }
}
```

Voila! A collection class just for DateTime objects. Most of the members are fairly obvious, but the last four methods bear a little explanation.

The first three On*() methods are called before the value is actually inserted, removed, or set. By overriding them in the DateTimeCollection, you get a chance to check the value being passed before it is actually processed. The OnValidate() method is called before OnInsert(), OnRemove(), or OnSet(), so you get several chances to check the type of the object in question.

Compile and run *DateTimeCollection.exe* with these commands:

```
$ mcs DateTimeCollection.cs
$ mono DateTimeCollection.exe
OnValidate(Wednesday, 19 May 2004 00:21:08)
OnInsert(0,Wednesday, 19 May 2004 00:21:08)
OnValidate(Thursday, 01 January 2004 00:00:00)
OnInsert(1,Thursday, 01 January 2004 00:00:00)
OnValidate(Thursday, 01 January 2004 00:00:00)
OnRemove(1,Thursday, 01 January 2004 00:00:00)
OnValidate(Monday, 31 December 2001 00:00:00)
OnSet(0,Wednesday, 19 May 2004 00:21:08,Monday, 31 December 2001 00:00:00)
```

Work with Assemblies

As was already mentioned in "Package Related Classes with Assemblies" in Chapter 2, the assembly is the basic unit of deployment of a Mono library or application. In that lab, you saw how to create an assembly, how they are named, and how to store them in the GAC.

Everything's an assembly. What's in an assembly?

In this lab, you'll see how to examine the internal organization of assemblies.

How do I do that?

You can use the *monodis.exe* tool to view the CIL for any assembly. For example, the *SprocketSet.dll* assembly, which you'll remember from "Package Related Classes with Assemblies" in Chapter 2, is made up of the classes Sprocket and Widget, along with attributes from *AssemblyInfo.cs* and resources from *SprocketSet.resources*. The contents of *Sprocket.cs* are:

```
public class Sprocket {
}
```

and *Widget.cs* contains this:

```
public class Widget {
        public Sprocket Sprocket;
}
```

Common Intermediate Language is the equivalent of assembly language for the .NET framework.

Run monodis SprocketSet.dll to view the results in Example 3-7.

Example 3-7. 05-assemblies/SprocketSet.il

```
.assembly extern mscorlib
{
  .ver 1:0:5000:0
}
.assembly 'SprocketSet'
{
  .custom instance void class [mscorlib]'System.Reflection.
AssemblyKeyNameAttribute'::.ctor(string) =  (01 00 00 00 00 ) // .....

  .custom instance void class [mscorlib]'System.Security.
AllowPartiallyTrustedCallersAttribute'::.ctor() =  (01 00 00 00 ) // ....

  .custom instance void class [mscorlib]'System.Reflection.
AssemblyTitleAttribute'::.ctor(string) =  (
    01 00 0B 53 70 72 6F 63 6B 65 74 53 65 74 00 00 ) // ...SprocketSet..

  .custom instance void class [mscorlib]'System.Reflection.
AssemblyDescriptionAttribute'::.ctor(string) =  (
    01 00 21 42 75 69 6C 64 20 53 70 72 6F 63 6B 65    // ..!Build Sprocke
    74 73 20 66 6F 72 20 79 6F 75 72 20 77 69 64 67    // ts for your widg
    65 74 73 2E 00 00                                ) // ets...

  .custom instance void class [mscorlib]'System.Reflection.
AssemblyConfigurationAttribute'::.ctor(string) =  (01 00 07 52 65 6C 65 61 73 65
00 00 ) // ...Release..

  .custom instance void class [mscorlib]'System.Reflection.
AssemblyCompanyAttribute'::.ctor(string) =  (
    01 00 13 41 6D 61 6C 67 61 6D 61 74 65 64 20 57    // ...Amalgamated W
    69 64 67 65 74 73 00 00                          ) // idgets..

  .custom instance void class [mscorlib]'System.Reflection.
AssemblyProductAttribute'::.ctor(string) =  (
    01 00 0B 53 70 72 6F 63 6B 65 74 53 65 74 00 00 ) // ...SprocketSet..

  .custom instance void class [mscorlib]'System.Reflection.
AssemblyCopyrightAttribute'::.ctor(string) =  (
    01 00 2E 32 30 30 34 20 41 6D 61 6C 67 61 6D 61    // ...2004 Amalgama
```

Example 3-7. 05-assemblies/SprocketSet.il (continued)

```
    74 65 64 20 57 69 64 67 65 74 73 2E 20 41 6C 6C   // ted Widgets. All
    20 52 69 67 68 74 73 20 52 65 73 65 72 76 65 64   //  Rights Reserved
    2E 00 00                                        ) // ...

  .custom instance void class [mscorlib]'System.Reflection.
AssemblyTrademarkAttribute'::.ctor(string) =  (01 00 00 00 00 ) // .....

  .custom instance void class [mscorlib]'System.Reflection.
AssemblyCultureAttribute'::.ctor(string) =  (01 00 05 65 6E 2D 55 53 00 00 ) // .
..en-US..

  .custom instance void class [mscorlib]'System.Reflection.
AssemblyDelaySignAttribute'::.ctor(bool) =  (01 00 00 00 00 ) // .....

  .custom instance void class [mscorlib]'System.Reflection.
AssemblyKeyFileAttribute'::.ctor(string) =  (
    01 00 0F 53 70 72 6F 63 6B 65 74 53 65 74 2E 73   // ...SprocketSet.s
    6E 6B 00 00                                     ) // nk..

  .custom instance void class [mscorlib]'System.CLSCompliantAttribute'::.
ctor(bool) =  (01 00 01 00 00 ) // .....

  .hash algorithm 0x00008004
  .ver   1:0:1601:37419
  .locale en-US
  .publickey = (
    00 24 00 00 04 80 00 00 94 00 00 00 06 02 00 00   // .$..............
    00 24 00 00 52 53 41 31 00 04 00 00 11 00 00 00   // .$..RSA1........
    C3 9F ED 12 DB 31 A8 97 5A 3C D6 01 3F E6 09 22   // .....1..Z<..?.."
    76 F8 60 A0 A2 6D 49 DD 81 1C E5 12 FB 92 36 94   // v.`..mI.......6.
    93 D8 EC 6D F8 3F D1 FC 4A 02 21 B7 6F 06 BE 18   // ...m.?..J.!.o...
    56 F0 7C 6B C0 D1 07 1A A8 8F 1E FD 38 5E A6 20   // V.|k........8^.
    FD 36 86 E0 12 BE 91 89 DB C0 C2 D6 4F 5B FD 76   // .6.........O[.v
    E1 47 16 8D 67 A0 E6 00 9E B3 A1 5B 75 09 8C 75   // .G..g......[u..u
    36 07 E8 31 E4 8B F2 6D 3B 12 28 0E 1C CC 75 45   // 6..1...m;.(...uE
    55 3B FD 55 BC 60 8E 7C 93 01 78 C6 3A 77 5E C6 ) // U;.U.`.|..x.:w^.
}
.module 'SprocketSet.dll' // GUID = {F7829D2A-5DAC-5B46-AD1D-D6CD2F7899CE}


  .class public auto ansi beforefieldinit 'Sprocket'
    extends [mscorlib]System.Object
  {

    // method line 1
    .method public hidebysig specialname  rtspecialname
         instance default void .ctor () cil managed
    {
       // Method begins at RVA 0x20ec
 // Code size 7 (0x7)
 .maxstack 8
 IL_0000: ldarg.0
```

Example 3-7. 05-assemblies/SprocketSet.il (continued)

```
IL_0001:  call instance void valuetype [mscorlib]'System.Object'::.ctor()
IL_0006:  ret
  } // end of method Sprocket::instance default void .ctor ()


} // end of type Sprocket

.class public auto ansi beforefieldinit 'Widget'
  extends [mscorlib]System.Object
{
  .field  public   class 'Sprocket' 'Sprocket'

  // method line 2
  .method public hidebysig  specialname  rtspecialname
        instance default void .ctor ()  cil managed
  {
      // Method begins at RVA 0x20f4
// Code size 7 (0x7)
.maxstack 8
IL_0000:  ldarg.0
IL_0001:  call instance void valuetype [mscorlib]'System.Object'::.ctor()
IL_0006:  ret
  } // end of method Widget::instance default void .ctor ()

} // end of type Widget
```

How does it work?

Although there's not enough room in this notebook to explain this IL code in detail, you can see that it contains several sections. First, there's a reference to the external library *mscorlib.dll*, with the version number 1.0.3300.0:

```
.assembly extern mscorlib
{
  .ver 1:0:3300:0
}
```

You may notice that the order of the assembly attributes in the SprocketSet.il is not the same as in AssemblyInfo. cs. It doesn't matter; attributes are not order-sensitive.

Next, the assembly definition begins with these lines:

```
.assembly 'SprocketSet'
{
```

Following that, the assembly attributes begin. You'll recall that these attributes were listed in the file *AssemblyInfo.cs*.

```
.custom instance void class [mscorlib]'System.Reflection.
AssemblyDelaySignAttribute'::.ctor(bool) =  (01 00 00 00 00 ) // .....
...
.custom instance void class [mscorlib]'System.CLSCompliantAttribute'::.
ctor(bool) =  (01 00 01 00 00 ) // .....
```

Then the assembly info finishes up with this, which defines the hash algorithm for signing the assembly, and the version and locale of the assembly:

```
.hash algorithm 0x00008004
.ver   1:0:1578:38317
.locale en-US
```

That's the end of the assembly manifest. The next chunk of information is a *module*, which contains the actual classes for *SprocketSet.dll*. The module contains the classes Sprocket and Widget, including the IL for their data and method members.

If you still have questions about assemblies and IL after looking over Example 3-7, see *Inside Microsoft .NET IL Assembler* by Serge Lidin (Microsoft Press).

What about ...

...Decompiling a Mono assembly? *Decompiling* refers to the process of converting IL code back into the C# source that created it. There are two third-party tools that do just that: Anakrino, by Jay Freeman (*http://www.saurik.com/net/exemplar/*), and Reflector, by Lutz Roeder (*http://www.aisto.com/roeder/dotnet/*).

WARNING

If you decide to use a decompiler to look at Microsoft .NET assemblies, you may be asked *not* to contribute source code to the Mono development effort. The Mono team is very serious about maintaining a strict clean room in their development process.

Both of these tools require *System.Windows.Forms.dll* on your system, either by installing the Microsoft .NET Framework or by enabling winelib for Windows Forms compatibility.

Where to learn more

Look online at *http://msdn.microsoft.com/library/en-us/cpguide/html/cpconMicrosoftIntermediateLanguageMSIL.asp* to learn how to compile code to MSIL.

Start and Examine Processes

Often, a program needs to spawn other processes in order to get a job done. Unix programmers are familiar with the old fork( ) and exec( ) routine. Mono has equivalent functionality, and the same classes can be used to examine the state of other processes currently running.

In this lab, you'll see how to spawn processes, and how to look at the other processes currently running on your machine.

How do I do that?

Example 3-8 shows a program that runs the Unix sleep command, taking the number of seconds to sleep from a command-line argument.

Example 3-8. 06-process/StartProcess.cs

```
// 03-keyfunc/06-process
using System;
using System.Diagnostics;

public class StartProcess {
  public static void Main(string [] args) {
    string sleepTime = args[0];

    ProcessStartInfo startInfo = new ProcessStartInfo( );
    startInfo.FileName = "sleep";
    startInfo.Arguments = sleepTime;
    Console.WriteLine("Starting {0} {1} at {2}",
      startInfo.FileName, startInfo.Arguments, DateTime.Now);
    Process process = Process.Start(startInfo);
    process.WaitForExit( );
    Console.WriteLine("Done at {0}", DateTime.Now);
  }
}
```

Compile and run *StartProcess.cs* with the following command lines:

```
$ mcs StartProcess.cs
$ mono StartProcess.exe 10
Starting sleep 10 at Wednesday, 12 May 2004 21:24:47
Done at Wednesday, 12 May 2004 21:24:58
```

You can see that sleep 10 was called, and that the start and end times were printed to standard output.

Example 3-9 contains another program using the Process class. This program, ListProcesses, lists all processes running on the machine, with their process ID, name, and start time.

Consciousness is a state of awareness of self and environment. Mono's got that.

Example 3-9. 06-process/ListProcesses.cs

```
using System;
using System.Diagnostics;

public class ListProcesses {
  public static void Main(string [] args) {
    foreach (Process process in Process.GetProcesses()) {
      Console.WriteLine("Process {0}: {1} on {2} started at {3}",
        process.Id, process.ProcessName, process.MachineName,
        process.StartTime);
    }
  }
}
```

When you compile and run *ListProcesses.exe*, you'll see something very much like this:

```
$ mcs ListProcesses.cs
$ mono ListProcesses.exe
Process 11687: bash started on localhost at Wednesday, 12 May 2004 21:11:19
Process 11691: bash started on localhost at Wednesday, 12 May 2004 21:12:27
Process 11806: ListProcesses started on localhost at Wednesday, 12 May 2004
21:13:43
```

Your results may be very different if you run on Windows. Unix and its brethren will only show you processes running under your user ID, while Windows will show every process running on the box.

How it works

The System.Diagnostics namespace contains a number of classes that can be used to provide information about the process environment currently in place. Among these is Process, which represents a single system process. The process can either be one that's currently running, one that you want to start, or one that has terminated but for which information still exists.

Example 3-8 shows a common technique for starting processes. The ProcessStartInfo class contains a number of properties that can be used to determine how a process is started, including FileName, the name of the file to be executed; Arguments, the argument list of the executable, as a single string; WorkingDirectory, the initial directory in which the process should be started; others that can be used to redirect standard input, output, and error; and others.

Process has a static method Start() that will take a StartInfo instance and start the corresponding process, returning a new Process instance.

Immediately after starting the process, you can call the Process class' WaitForExit() method to force the main Mono process to sleep until the new process terminates. This method has another overload that takes an int parameter, the maximum number of milliseconds to wait for the process to terminate.

Not all properties of the Process class will always contain data. It depends on how the process was started.

In Example 3-9, the ListProcesses class uses another method of Process. The static GetProcesses() method returns an array of Processes, each one containing information about a running process.

Multitask with Threads

Mono can walk and chew gum at the same time.

In addition to processes, as seen in "Start and Examine Processes," Mono allows you to start and monitor threads within a single process.

In this lab, you'll see how to start threads and ensure data synchronization between running threads.

How do I do that?

Example 3-10 shows a program that uses the thread pool to queue a new work item that prints a line to the standard output at random intervals. The main thread continues to run until a carriage return is read from standard input.

The thread pool is like a big bowl of noodles. When you're hungry, you pull a noodle from the bowl and dip it in the sauce of your choice. Now make the noodle a Thread, the bowl the Thread-Pool, and the sauce a WaitCall-back delegate.

Example 3-10. 07-threading/UseThreadPool.cs

```
// 03-keyfunc/07-threading
using System;
using System.IO;
using System.Threading;

public class UseThreadPool {
    private static Thread thread;

    public static void Main(string [] args) {

        WaitCallback callback = new WaitCallback(Callback);
        Console.WriteLine("Calling QueueUserWorkItem()...");
        ThreadPool.QueueUserWorkItem(callback);

        Console.WriteLine("Hit return to exit.");
        Console.In.ReadLine();

        thread.Abort();

        Console.WriteLine("Done.");
    }

    private static void Callback(object state) {
        thread = Thread.CurrentThread;

        Console.WriteLine("Started thread {0}", thread.GetHashCode());

        Random random = new Random();
        for (int counter = 0; true; counter++) {
```

Example 3-10. 07-threading/UseThreadPool.cs (continued)

```
    try {
      Thread.Sleep(random.Next(10000));
    } catch (ThreadAbortException) {
      Console.WriteLine("Aborting thread");
    }
    Console.WriteLine("{0}: {1}", counter, DateTime.Now);
  }
 }
}
```

Compiling and running *UseThreadPool.exe*, you'll see something like the following output:

```
$ mcs UseThreadPool.cs
$ mono UseThreadPool.exe
Calling QueueUserWorkItem( )...
Hit return to exit.
Started thread 2069958092
0: Thursday, 06 May 2004 03:43:49
1: Thursday, 06 May 2004 03:43:52

Aborting thread
Done.
```

Note that you may see some of the output in a different order, depending on when the Thread is pulled from the ThreadPool and started.

How it works

Most of the time, it's recommended that when you need to start a new thread, you ask for a thread from the ThreadPool, as in Example 3-10.

The ThreadPool class provides access to a pool of Thread instances. By calling QueueUserWorkItem, you can request a Thread from the pool. When a Thread is available, it is started with the WaitCallback delegate that you specify, and the optional state object that you pass in. You don't have any control over when the Thread will become available, however, so this technique is best suited for times when immediate execution is not critical.

Regardless of how you start a thread, there may be times when you must ensure that only a single thread at a time has access to static data. Mono provides three good ways to do this, the Monitor class, the lock keyword, and the System.Runtime.CompilerServices.MethodImpl attribute. Under the hood they each do the same thing, but they provide variously more convenient ways of preventing threads from stepping on each other.

The `Monitor` class provides a way to explicitly synchronize threads. You can call the `Enter()` method, passing in an object to synchronize on, and if you later call the `Enter()` with the same synchronization object, that call will be blocked until the first thread calls `Leave()`. There are other methods to work with the thread lock in different ways, such as `TryEnter()` and `Wait()`.

The `lock` keyword provides the same functionality as `Monitor`, except that it automatically exits the monitor at the end of the block. For example, the following code block:

```
lock (someobject) {
  // ...
}
```

is exactly equivalent to this:

```
try {
  Monitor.Enter(someobject);
  // ...
} finally {
  Monitor.Exit(someobject);
}
```

The final synchronization technique, the `MethodImpl` attribute, synchronizes a thread around an entire method call. So the following method definition:

```
using System.Runtime.CompilerServices;

[MethodImpl(MethodImplOptions.Synchronized)]
public void MyMethod() {
  // ...
}
```

compiles down to the following:

```
using System.Runtime.CompilerServices;

public void MyMethod() {
  try {
    Monitor.Enter(this);
    // ...
  } finally {
    Monitor.Exit(this);
  }
}
```

What about ...

...When you need more control over the `Thread`'s execution? You can instantiate a `Thread`, passing in a `ThreadStart` delegate, and call its `Start()` method directly. Although you can be sure that the new thread will start working immediately this way, the advantage may be mooted by the overhead of creating a new Thread instance. The thread pool keeps track of system utilization and will only create new Thread instances when absolutely necessary.

Example 3-11 shows how you can start a new thread, bypassing the thread pool.

Example 3-11. 07-threading/UseThreadStart.cs

```
// 03-keyfunc/07-threading
using System;
using System.IO;
using System.Threading;

public class UseThreadStart {
  private static Thread thread;

  public static void Main(string [] args) {

    ThreadStart start = new ThreadStart(Start);
    thread = new Thread(start);
    Console.WriteLine("Calling Start()...");
    thread.Start();

    Console.WriteLine("Hit return to exit.");
    Console.In.ReadLine();

    thread.Abort();

    Console.WriteLine("Done.");
  }

  private static void Start() {
    Console.WriteLine("Started thread {0}", thread.GetHashCode());

    Random random = new Random();
    for (int counter = 0; true; counter++) {
      try {
        Thread.Sleep(random.Next(10000));
      } catch (ThreadAbortException) {
        Console.WriteLine("Aborting thread");
      }
      Console.WriteLine("{0}: {1}", counter, DateTime.Now);
    }
  }
}
```

The differences between Example 3-10 and Example 3-11 are small, but important. To begin with, instead of creating a delegate of type WaitCallback, we create a ThreadStart delegate. Then, instead of calling ThreadPool.QueueUserWorkItem(), we instantiate a new Thread object directly, and call its Start( ) method. Rather than waiting for a thread to be returned from the pool, the thread will start immediately.

Since we're creating a Thread instance directly in this program, there's no need for the Start( ) method to set the thread field in this case; we can just assign its value in the Main( ) method. Everything else remains the same.

Test Your C# Code

Does your code work? Does it really, really work?

It's a truism in software development that you can never find every bug. It also seems that just when you fix one bug, two more pop up to replace it. There are ways, however, to help prevent new errors from cropping up while working on new or existing code.

NUnit is a direct descendant of the JUnit Java unit testing framework, although it has taken on the characteristics of a C# framework as well. In this lab, we'll show you how you can use NUnit to test your code.

How do I do that?

Depending on how you installed Mono, you may or may not have NUnit on your system. If you find you do not have it already, you can install it from CVS module mcs/nunit20 (see "Run a Development Version of Mono" in Chapter 8 for information on getting files from CVS). You may either copy *NUnit.Framework.dll* to your working directory, or install it in the GAC (see "Call External Libraries" in Chapter 2 for more information on using *gacutil.exe*).

Example 3-12 shows a test class called MathTest.

Example 3-12. 08-nunit/MathTest.cs

```
// 03-keyfunc/08-nunit
using System;

using NUnit.Framework;

[TestFixture]
public class MathTest {

  private int Zero = 0;
  private int One = 1;

  [SetUp]
  public void SetUp() {
    // do any set up the test requires
  }
```

Example 3-12. 08-nunit/MathTest.cs (continued)

```
[TearDown]
public void TearDown() {
   // clean up any data the test may have affected
}

[Test]
public void ZeroIs0() {
   Assertion.Assert("0 != Zero", 0 == Zero);
}

[Test]
public void OneIsNot0() {
   Assertion.Assert("0 == One", 0 != One);
}

[Test]
public void ZeroPlusZero() {
   Assertion.AssertEquals("0 + 0 != 0", Zero + Zero, Zero);
}

[Test]
[ExpectedException(typeof(DivideByZeroException))]
public void DivideByZero() {
   int i = One / Zero;
}

[Test]
public void NoObject() {
   object nullObject = null;
   Assertion.AssertNull("nullObject is not null", nullObject);
}

[Test]
public void ThisTestFails() {
   // this is designed to fail for demonstration purposes
   Assertion.Fail("This test failed");
}

[Test]
[Ignore("This test is not run at all")]
public void SkipThisTest() {
   // this test will be ignored for demonstration purposes
}
}
```

You'll notice that Example 3-12 has no Main() method. NUnit provides a
test runner, called *nunit-console.exe*, so all you need to write is a suite of
unit tests, not the infrastructure required to run them.

If you were testing another library, you would need to reference it with a -r argument as well.

Compile *MathTest.cs* just as you would any other Mono library. Use the following command line:

```
$ mcs -target:library -r:NUnit.Framework MathTest.cs
```

After compiling *MathTest.dll*, you can run the tests using *nunit-console.exe*. Use the following command line:

```
$ mono nunit-console.exe MathTest.dll
```

If all goes well, you'll see the following output:

```
NUnit version 1.0.5000
Copyright (C) 2002-2003 James W. Newkirk, Michael C. Two, Alexei A.
Vorontsov, Charlie Poole.
Copyright (C) 2000-2003 Philip Craig.
All Rights Reserved.

......F.N
Tests run: 6, Failures: 1, Not run: 1, Time: 0.382437 seconds

Failures:
1) MathTest.ThisTestFails : This test failed
in <0x00020> MathTest:ThisTestFails ()
in (unmanaged) (wrapper managed-to-native) System.Reflection.MonoMethod:
InternalInvoke (object,object[])
in <0x0008c> (wrapper managed-to-native) System.Reflection.MonoMethod:
InternalInvoke (object,object[])
in <0x00104> System.Reflection.MonoMethod:Invoke (object,System.Reflection.
BindingFlags,System.Reflection.Binder,object[],System.Globalization.
CultureInfo)

Tests not run:
1) MathTest.SkipThisTest : This test is not run at all
```

There's also a shell script called nunit-console that wraps the mono nunit-console.exe command.

How it works

Example 3-12 demonstrates how unit tests are written using NUnit. The classes from the NUnit framework are in the namespace NUnit. Framework, so the appropriate using statement is included in the code.

The first thing you'll notice is the TestFixture attribute. This attribute is used to indicate to the NUnit framework that the class MathTest is an NUnit *test fixture*; that is, it contains NUnit tests.

JUnit users will remember that in JUnit, test fixtures have to extend TestCase or implement Test. C# attributes make the same functionality possible without inheritance.

Again, JUnit users will remember that the SetUp() and TearDown() methods must have those exact names in JUnit. In NUnit, you can name them however you want, as long as they have the attribute indicating their usage.

Each method within MathTest that needs to be visible to the NUnit framework is marked with at least one attribute. SetUp, for example, is used to indicate a method that will be called to set up any data for the test, and TearDown is used to indicate a method that will be called to clean up any leftover data from the test.

The tests themselves bear the Test attribute. The NUnit framework uses reflection to discover all the methods with the SetUp, TearDown, and Test attributes.

JUnit users know that the names of test methods have to start with Test for JUnit to discover them.

Two other attributes can be used to further define the test results. ExpectedException is useful for negative tests. It indicates that the method is expected to throw an exception, so that the exception indicates correct passage of the test.

The other attribute is Ignore. This attribute indicates that the test method should not be executed. The attribute has a single positional parameter, which is a string containing the reason why the test should not be run. This attribute is best used for test methods that you expect to fail temporarily, but you don't want the entire test session to show failures.

Within each test method, the Assertion class is used to find errors and report them as test failures. Assertion has a number of methods, with multiple overloads of each:

Assert( )

   Throws an AssertionFailedError exception if the value is false, optionally printing a specific message.

AssertEquals( )

   Throws an AssertionFailedError exception if two values are not equal, optionally printing a specific message.

AssertNotNull( )

   Throws an AssertionFailedError exception if the value is null, optionally printing a specific message.

AssertNull( )

   Throws an AssertionFailedError exception if the value is not null, optionally printing a specific message.

AssertSame( )

   Throws an AssertionFailedError exception if the values are not references to the same object, optionally printing a specific message.

Fail( )

   Causes the test to fail unconditionally, optionally printing a specific message.

When a test fixture is run with *nunit-console.exe*, the output indicates the tests passed, failed, and ignored by printing . for each test method found, F for a failed test, and N for a test not run, followed by a summary of the tests:

```
......F.N
Tests run: 6, Failures: 1, Not run: 1, Time: 0.383369 seconds
```

Following the test summary information, specific information about any ignored and failed tests is printed, including any message passed into the assert method, and a stack trace (for failures):

```
Failures:
1) MathTest.ThisTestFails : This test failed
in <0x00020> MathTest:ThisTestFails ()
in (unmanaged) (wrapper managed-to-native) System.Reflection.MonoMethod:
InternalInvoke (object,object[])
in <0x0008c> (wrapper managed-to-native) System.Reflection.MonoMethod:
InternalInvoke (object,object[])
in <0x00104> System.Reflection.MonoMethod:Invoke (object,System.Reflection.
BindingFlags,System.Reflection.Binder,object[],System.Globalization.
CultureInfo)

Tests not run:
1) MathTest.SkipThisTest : This test is not run at all
```

What about ...

...Controlling the execution and output format of the NUnit test console? There are several ways to customize the output from *nunit-console.exe*. For example, if the test assembly contains more than one test fixture, you can specify which test fixture to run with the /fixture=*classname* argument.

You can also control the output format by requesting output to an XML file with the /xml=*filename* argument, optionally transforming it via an XSLT stylesheet specified in the /transform=*stylesheet* argument; or you may output the XML to the console with the /xmlConsole argument. If the standard text output is acceptable but you don't want the version banner printed, you can specify the /nologo argument.

Where to learn more

The definitive reference for unit testing in all platforms and languages is *http://www.junit.org/*, the home of JUnit.

Documentation on NUnit, where it differs from JUnit, is available at *http://www.nunit.org/*.

Kent Beck's *Test Driven Development: By Example* (Addison-Wesley) is one of the seminal works in test driven development, and should be on the desk of every serious developer.

For a taste of how the Mono team uses NUnit, see the Mono Contributor Howto at *http://www.mono-project.com/contributing/testing.html*.

Gtk#

Gtk# is the Mono wrapper for the GTK+ user interface toolkit. GTK+ was originally created to provide the user interface for the GNU Image Manipulation Program (GIMP), hence the expansion of its acronym: Gimp Tool Kit. These days GTK+ is most closely associated with being the toolkit behind the GNOME desktop platform. Gtk# is the native Linux user interface toolkit of choice for the Mono project.

Mono will eventually implement a complete compatibility layer for the `Windows.Forms` user interface toolkit from Microsoft's .NET platform. `Windows.Forms` should be seen as a migration strategy: Gtk# is the preferred toolkit for Linux.

The labs in this chapter lead you through creating basic GTK+ applications using Gtk# (pronounced *GTK-sharp*), the Mono API to the GTK+ toolkit. You'll discover the event loop concept behind GTK+ applications, how to create windows and use widgets, and how to subclass widgets to customize their behavior.

If you followed the labs in Chapter 1, you should already have the Gtk# assemblies installed on your computer and be able to jump right into these labs. If not, return to "Install Mono" in Chapter 1 to install *gtk-sharp*.

Write a Basic Gtk# Program and Handle Events

Any user interface programming toolkit defines a way for delivering events from the user to the program. Whereas with noninteractive programs the flow of control is under the programmer's direction, interactive programs must respond to the events they receive.

In this chapter:

- *"Write a Basic Gtk# Program and Handle Events"*
- *"Arrange Widgets Using Boxes"*
- *"Make Widgets Interact"*
- *"Make Dialogs by Subclassing"*
- *"Draw Graphics"*
- *"Create Menus"*
- *"Organize Data with TreeView"*
- *"Exchange Data with Drag and Drop"*

Mono wrappers for other Linux toolkits such as Qt are available but not maintained as part of the Mono project.

In Gtk#, the flow of control is governed by a main event loop. The program yields its control to the main loop, which is responsible for processing input events. When events occur that the program is interested in, handlers for those events are called and control is given to the main program.

This lab demonstrates the concept of the Gtk# main loop and handling events.

How to do it

Construct a basic Gtk# program using a window and a button. Both of these raise events and need handlers assigned for those events that the programmer wants to process. Example 4-1 shows the program listing.

Example 4-1. Basic Gtk# application: 01-basics/Main.cs

```
// 04-gtk/01-basics
using System;
using Gtk;

class MainClass {
  public static void Main (string[ ] args)
  {
    Application.Init ( );

    Window w = new Window ("Gtk# Basics");
    Button b = new Button ("Hit me");

    // set up event handling: verbose to illustrate
    // the use of delegates.
    w.DeleteEvent += new DeleteEventHandler (Window_Delete);
    b.Clicked += new EventHandler (Button_Clicked);

    // initialize the GUI
    w.Add (b);
    w.SetDefaultSize (200, 100);
    w.ShowAll ( );

    Application.Run ( );
  }

  static void Window_Delete (object o, DeleteEventArgs args)
  {
    Application.Quit ( );
    args.RetVal = true;
  }

  static void Button_Clicked (object o, EventArgs args)
  {
    System.Console.WriteLine ("Hello, World!");
```

Example 4-1. Basic Gtk# application: 01-basics/Main.cs (continued)

```
  }
}
```

Either create the application as a project inside MonoDevelop, or use a regular text editor to create it in *Main.cs* and compile and run it by hand:

```
$ mcs Main.cs -pkg:gtk-sharp
$ mono Main.exe
```

When you run the application, you will see a window as in Figure 4-1: the button takes up the entire window. Click the button a few times, and you'll see the output on the terminal as shown in Example 4-2.

Figure 4-1. Gtk# window with button

Example 4-2. Terminal output

```
Hello, World!
Hello, World!
Hello, World!
```

How it works

The Gtk namespace is imported with using Gtk. The basic Gtk# tasks of initializing the toolkit are performed by the Application class. Specifically, there are three static methods of interest:

- Init causes the Gtk# library to be initialized. You won't get very far without doing this.

- Run causes the flow of control to enter the main event loop.

- Quit causes the event loop to terminate when control is returned

The creation of the window and its button is a trivial matter: there are more interesting examples in the following labs. What is more relevant here is the hooking up of the event handlers. Every *widget* (a user interface element) in Gtk# is capable of raising a variety of events. Many of these are derived from the basic Widget class, from which all the Gtk# widgets inherit. Typical events include Focused, sent when the widget receives user focus, and DeleteEvent, sent when the widget is deleted.

The -pkg:gtk-sharp option tells the compiler to reference all the Gtk# assemblies. Without it, the compiler wouldn't know where to find the Gtk namespace. In MonoDevelop, you can control this from the References section of the Projects tab.

If you want your application to check whether it can use graphics, use the InitCheck method instead of Init. That way it won't fail horribly and you can fall back to a text interface.

For more information on events as a feature of C#, refer to "Define Function Pointers" in Chapter 2. When an event is raised, the assigned handlers are invoked. Events can have any number of handlers assigned. Example 4-1 shows the handler Window_Delete being added for the event DeleteEvent.

Our Window_Delete handler does two things of interest. First, it instructs the main loop to exit when control is returned to it. Second, it sends *true* back as a return value via the args object. This prevents any subsequent handlers from getting the event.

The handler for the Button is much the same, and is more typical of the general widget event handler. Buttons have some specialized events, of which Clicked is the most useful.

The assignment of the handlers has been shown in full to give some hint as to the underlying implementation. However, it's possible to take a shortcut, and write the two lines as shown:

```
w.DeleteEvent += Window_Delete;
b.Clicked += Button_Clicked;
```

The event handlers need not be static methods if they need to access an object instance. The only difference is to assign them prefixed by the instance.

Where to learn more

An introduction to programming with Gtk# can be found as part of the documentation shipped with Monodoc. Refer to the "Mono for Gnome Applications" section of the *Mono Handbook*, available from the Monodoc table of contents. As ever, another excellent source of reference material is the Gtk# API reference itself in Monodoc. More information on Monodoc can be found in "Explore Mono" in Chapter 1.

To understand more about delegates and events, refer to Chapter 2 of *C# Essentials* by Ben Albahari, Peter Drayton, and Brad Merrill (O'Reilly).

A good introduction to the GTK+ toolkit can be found in the *GTK+ 2.0 Tutorial*, available at *http://www.gtk.org/tutorial/*. Although specific to the C language implementation of GTK+, the tutorial contains a lot of theory about the toolkit that we will only gloss over in this book.

A document outlining the changes available in C# 2.0 can be found linked from Microsoft's C# web site at *http://msdn.microsoft.com/vcsharp/team/language/default.aspx*.

There's an art to packing a suitcase, and the same applies to a user interface.

Arrange Widgets Using Boxes

Most user interface layout in Gtk# is done using *boxes*. These are invisible widgets into which other widgets are *packed*. By packing widgets into boxes, you can create layouts that remain consistent at different window sizes, and orient boxes either vertically or horizontally.

This lab shows how to put boxes together to create a simple user interface design. As well as boxes, you'll learn about widget expansion, borders, and padding.

The rarely used alternative to boxes is table layout. Similar to their HTML cousins, tables provide a very regular grid-like layout structure.

How to do it

Figure 4-2 shows the desired layout: a couple of labels and corresponding text entry boxes. The labels must be left-aligned, and the text entry boxes the available space to the right-hand side of the window. Example 4-3 shows the code needed to achieve this.

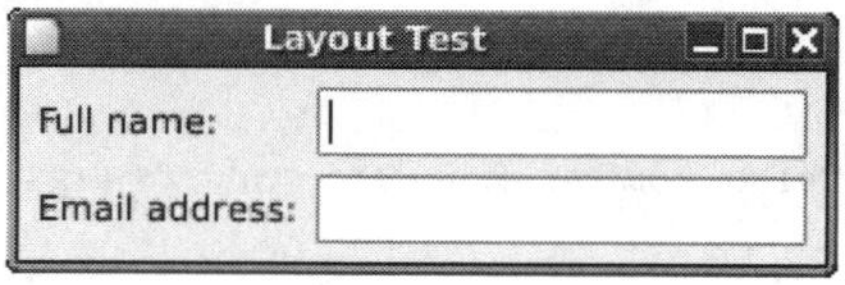

Figure 4-2. Window layout

Example 4-3. Box model layout: 02-layout/Main.cs

```
// 04-gtk/02-layout
using System;
using Gtk;

class MainClass {
  public static void Main (string[ ] args)
  {
    Application.Init ();
    SetUpGui ();
    Application.Run ();
  }

  static void SetUpGui ()
  {
    Window w = new Window ("Layout Test");

    HBox h = new HBox ();
    h.BorderWidth = 6;
    h.Spacing = 6;
    w.Add (h);

    VBox v = new VBox ();
    v.Spacing = 6;
    h.PackStart (v, false, false, 0);

    Label l = new Label ("Full name:");
```

Example 4-3. Box model layout: 02-layout/Main.cs (continued)

```
    l.Xalign = 0;
    v.PackStart (l, true, false, 0);

    l = new Label ("Email address:");
    l.Xalign = 0;
    v.PackStart (l, true, false, 0);

    v = new VBox ();
    v.Spacing = 6;
    h.PackStart (v, true, true, 0);

    v.PackStart (new Entry (), true, true, 0);
    v.PackStart (new Entry (), true, true, 0);

    w.DeleteEvent += Window_Delete;
    w.ShowAll ();
  }

  static void Window_Delete (object o, DeleteEventArgs args)
  {
    Application.Quit ();
    args.RetVal = true;
  }
}
```

As usual, you can either create the application as a project inside MonoDevelop, or compile and run it by hand as demonstrated in "Write a Basic Gtk# Program and Handle Events."

When the application runs, try resizing the window. If you make the window vertically larger, you'll get the effect as shown in Figure 4-3. Try making it wider too, and you should get a result similar to Figure 4-4. In both cases, the labels and text entries remain aligned with each other, and the text entries expand to fill the available space.

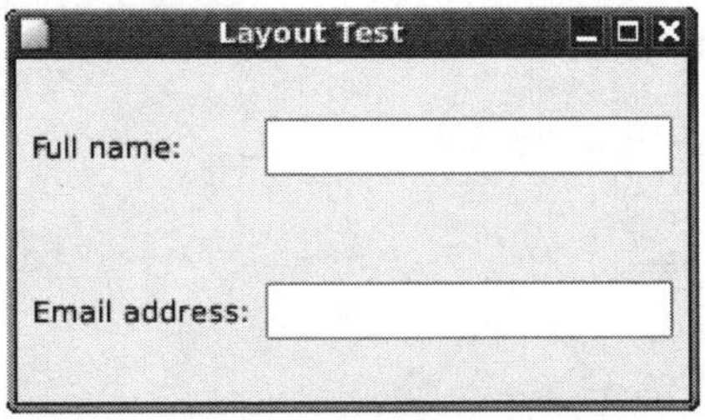

Figure 4-3. Window expanded vertically

Figure 4-4. Window expanded in both dimensions

How it works

To get the box design correct, start from the inside and work out. The left and right edges of the widgets must be aligned. To achieve this, each column is packed inside a VBox. As the two columns must be next to each other, both of the VBox widgets are packed in an HBox. This is then added to the main window.

A box has two useful properties, Spacing and BorderWidth. Spacing dictates the number of pixels to leave between child (contained) widgets. BorderWidth dictates the border in pixels to be placed between the box's contents and its own parent container.

Examine the PackStart method used in the example. It adds widgets to a box with reference to the start of the box. For HBox, the start of the box is the left, for VBox it's the top. A PackEnd method is also available, which packs with respect to the opposite end of the box. PackStart's declaration looks like this:

```
public void PackStart (Widget child, bool expand, bool fill, uint padding)
```

The expand parameter, if true, causes the widget to expand to use all the space available to it. The spare space in a box is shared evenly among all the widgets whose expand parameter is set to true. The fill parameter, if true, causes the widget to use all the space allocated with expand for the widget's rendering. If false then the extra space will be used for padding. The final parameter, padding, allows the addition of spacing pixels around the widget above and beyond the spacing specified by the containing box.

The Add method can be used with boxes, as with the window. The result is the same as using PackStart with the default values for the last three parameters: true, true, 0.

The effects of the choices for expand can be seen in Figures 4-3 and 4-4. Both labels and text entries are set to expand within their VBoxes: you can see that they fill the increased vertical space regularly. As the width of the window increases, however, only the text entries grow in size. This is because the containing VBox of the labels does not have expand set, yet that of the text entries does. Additionally, each text entry is packed with expand and fill, so they grow to fill the available space.

The last thing to note is the alignment of the widgets. By default, a widget's rendering is centered in the space allocated to it. Any widget that can be aligned in different ways implements the Gtk.Misc interface. This interface provides the Xalign and Yalign properties. These are numbers of the float type, whose value can range from 0 (left or top) to 1 (right or bottom). In Example 4-3, the Xalign values are to set 0 in order to left-align the labels. As the text entries are set to expand and fill, their alignment is immaterial.

Where to learn more

For API documentation, refer to the "Gtk" section of the *Gnome Libraries* reference in Monodoc. More tutorial information is available in the "Gtk#: Packing Widgets" section of the *Mono Handbook*, available in Monodoc.

The gold standard for interface layout under GTK is the GNOME Human Interface Guidelines document, or HIG for short. It can be found online at *http://developer.gnome.org/projects/gup/hig/*.

A useful exercise to complete to learn more about layout would be to alter the example in this lab to be conformant to the GNOME HIG: there must be a minimum of 12 pixels between the window border and its contents, and 12 pixels between the labels and the text entries. There's more than one way to do this!

Make Widgets Interact

A user interface not only needs to respond to the user, but to read data from the interface and change the interface in response. In Gtk# this is normally done through the properties of the widgets.

In this lab we extend the user interface developed in "Arrange Widgets Using Boxes" and add an event handler to the text entry widgets. We read and write the text property of text entries, and introduce keyboard shortcuts to focus widgets.

How to do it

Figure 4-5 shows the sort of signup window you might expect to see in an application that subscribes you to an ISP. Because the best applications help and guide the user, we want our application to automatically fill in a suggested email address as the user types his name in.

User activity in one part of the interface often affects another part. Event handlers provide the plumbing.

Notice the underlines by the labels; these mnemonics allow the user to focus a widget by typing Alt and the mnemonic letter.

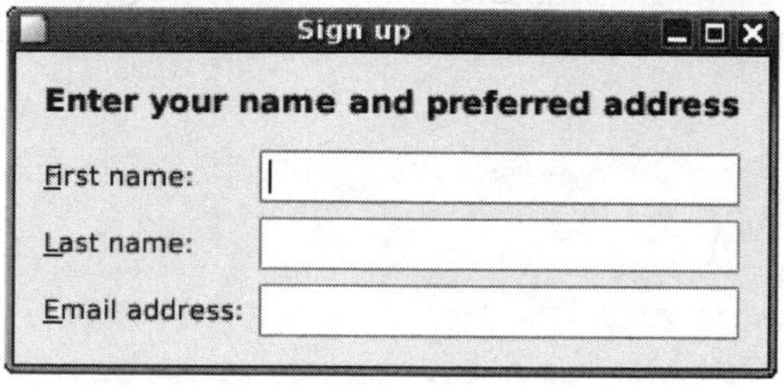

Figure 4-5. Signup window

The listing in Example 4-4 shows the code to do the job. Compile and run the listing, and play around with the interface. When you alter the first and last name fields, the email address will change. Try hitting **Alt-F** to focus the first-name widget.

Example 4-4. Signup window listing: 03-signup/Main.cs

```
// 04-gtk/03-signup
using System;
using Gtk;

class MainClass {
  private static Entry firstname_entry, lastname_entry,
    email_entry;

  public static void Main (string[ ] args)
  {
    Application.Init ();
    SetUpGui ();
    Application.Run ();
  }

  static void SetUpGui ()
  {
    Window w = new Window ("Sign up");

    firstname_entry = new Entry ();
    lastname_entry = new Entry ();
    email_entry = new Entry ();

    VBox outerv = new VBox ();
    outerv.BorderWidth = 12;
    outerv.Spacing = 12;
    w.Add (outerv);

    Label l = new Label ("<span weight=\"bold\" size=\"larger\">" +
      "Enter your name and preferred address</span>");
    l.Xalign = 0;
    l.UseMarkup = true;
    outerv.PackStart (l, false, false, 0);
```

Example 4-4. Signup window listing: 03-signup/Main.cs (continued)

```
        HBox h = new HBox ();
        h.Spacing = 6;
        outerv.Add (h);

        VBox v = new VBox ();
        v.Spacing = 6;
        h.PackStart (v, false, false, 0);

        l = new Label ("_First name:");
        l.Xalign = 0;
        v.PackStart (l, true, false, 0);
        l.MnemonicWidget = firstname_entry;

        l = new Label ("_Last name:");
        l.Xalign = 0;
        v.PackStart (l, true, false, 0);
        l.MnemonicWidget = lastname_entry;

        l = new Label ("_Email address:");
        l.Xalign = 0;
        v.PackStart (l, true, false, 0);
        l.MnemonicWidget = email_entry;

        v = new VBox ();
        v.Spacing = 6;
        h.PackStart (v, true, true, 0);

        v.PackStart (firstname_entry, true, true, 0);
        v.PackStart (lastname_entry, true, true, 0);
        v.PackStart (email_entry, true, true, 0);

        // hook up handlers
        firstname_entry.Changed += Name_Changed;
        lastname_entry.Changed += Name_Changed;
        w.DeleteEvent += Window_Delete;
        w.ShowAll ();
    }

    static void Window_Delete (object o, DeleteEventArgs args)
    {
        Application.Quit ();
        args.RetVal = true;
    }

    static void Name_Changed (object o, EventArgs args)
    {
        string e = firstname_entry.Text.ToLower () +
            "." + lastname_entry.Text.ToLower () +
            "@example.net";
        email_entry.Text = e.Replace (" ", "_");
    }
}
```

How it works

The `Gtk.Entry` widget has a number of interesting properties. The most useful of these is `Text`, which contains the string contents of the text entry box.

Notice that the `Name_Changed` method handles both the first and last name text entries. When either of these change, that method uses simple string manipulation to formulate a new email address. To change the contents of the email address box, the application needs merely to set the `Text` property. If you care which text entry caused the `Changed` event, use the `object` argument to determine which object raised the event:

```
if (o == (object) firstname_entry) {
    // first name changed
}
```

The widget interaction is simple to understand. The creation of the interface using boxes should also be familiar from the previous lab. However, there are some new features introduced that give the user interface a little more polish and are worth noting:

XML Markup

> The first feature of note is the use of XML markup in the label value. The `UseMarkup` property of the label is set correspondingly. Normally, the `<span>` element and its various attributes are used to set styles. Gtk# also borrows some elements from HTML to use as convenient shortcuts: `<b>`, `<big>`, `<i>`, `<s>`, `<sub>`, `<sup>`, `<small>`, `<tt>`, and `<u>`.

Keyboard Shortcuts

> One of letters in each label is rendered as underlined in the interface, indicating that the user can type **Alt** plus that letter to focus the corresponding text entry. The mnemonic letter is indicated by the use of an underscore in the label text. The widget to give focus to is set in the `MnemonicWidget` property of the label.

Where to learn more

To further investigate widget interaction, try linking up some of the other widgets. A good candidate is synchronizing the values of `Gtk.HScale` and `Gtk.VScale` sliders when the `ValueChanged` event is raised, as shown in Figure 4–6.

Other useful properties of GtkEntry include IsEditable and MaxLength. You could use these to change the example so that it limits names to ten characters or prevents the user from changing the email address.

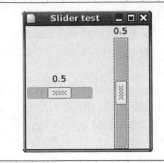

Figure 4-6. Synchronized scale widgets

The Monodoc documentation for `Gtk.Entry` explains in the detail the name and purpose of the various properties, methods, and events the widget provides. Try altering the example to experiment with some of these.

The markup facilities available in the labels are actually implemented by Gtk#'s underlying text rendering library, called Pango. A reference to this markup can be found in the "Basic Pango Interfaces" section of the *Pango Reference Manual*, available from *http://developer.gnome.org/doc/API/2.0/pango*.

Make Dialogs by Subclassing

The *dialog* is a time-honored way of notifying the user of an error, asking them a question or otherwise letting them control the flow of the program. A dialog is a window whose purpose is to deliver a message and optionally return a user response to the calling program.

Dialogs get reused more than many other things. Subclassing is the best way to make this easy.

Gtk# provides a basic `Dialog` class, which is a window with some parts of the user interface already preconfigured. As dialogs often get reused, it makes sense to take advantage of the fact that C# supports inheritance and creates a customized `Dialog` subclass for our own use. Indeed, whenever complex configuration of a widget is required, the recommended course of action in Mono is to subclass it. This keeps the initialization code and contained widgets tidily inside the class that they belong to.

This lab illustrates a simple subclassed dialog, and introduces the use of stock items in the user interface.

How to do it

Figure 4-7 shows a dialog conforming to the GNOME HIG, with typical components: an icon on the left, a heading and subheading, and response buttons.

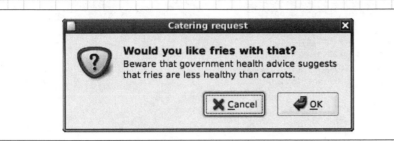

Figure 4-7. Question dialog

Example 4-5 shows the code to create the required dialog, displays it to the user, and takes appropriate action based on her choice. Being encapsulated in the MyDialog class, the insides of the dialog aren't visible from the main program. The implementation of MyDialog is shown in Example 4-6.

Example 4-5. Main program listing: 04-subclass/Main.cs

```
// 04-gtk/04-subclass/Main.cs
using System;
using Gtk;

class MainClass {
  public static void Main (string[] args)
  {
    Application.Init ();
    MyDialog d  = new MyDialog ("Catering request",
      "Would you like fries with that?",
      "Beware that government health advice suggests that " +
      "fries are less healthy than carrots.");
    ResponseType resp = (ResponseType) d.Run ();
    if (resp == ResponseType.Ok) {
      Environment.Exit (0);
    } else {
      Environment.Exit (1);
    }
  }
}
```

Example 4-6. Subclassed dialog: 04-subclass/MyDialog.cs

```
// 04-gtk/04-subclass/MyDialog.cs
using System;
```

Example 4-6. Subclassed dialog: 04-subclass/MyDialog.cs (continued)

```
using Gtk;

public class MyDialog : Dialog {

  public MyDialog (string title, string question,
    string explanation) : base ()
  {
    this.Title = title;
    this.HasSeparator = false;
    this.BorderWidth = 6;
    this.Resizable = false;

    HBox h = new HBox ();
    h.BorderWidth = 6;
    h.Spacing = 12;

    Image i = new Image ();
    i.SetFromStock (Stock.DialogQuestion, IconSize.Dialog);
    i.SetAlignment (0.5F, 0);
    h.PackStart (i, false, false, 0);

    VBox v = new VBox ();
    Label l = new Label ("<span weight=\"bold\" size=\"larger\">" +
      question + "</span>");
    l.LineWrap = true;
    l.UseMarkup = true;
    l.Selectable = true;
    l.Xalign = 0; l.Yalign = 0;
    v.PackStart (l);

    l = new Label (explanation);
    l.LineWrap = true;
    l.Selectable = true;
    l.Xalign = 0; l.Yalign = 0;
    v.PackEnd (l);

    h.PackEnd (v);
    h.ShowAll ();
    this.VBox.Add (h);

    this.AddButton (Stock.Cancel, ResponseType.Cancel);
    this.AddButton (Stock.Ok, ResponseType.Ok);
  }
}
```

Compile and run the application using the following command line:

```
$ mcs Main.cs MyDialog.cs -pkg:gtk-sharp
$ mono Main.exe
```

How it works

All the work of setting up the subordinate widgets that make up the dialog is done in the constructor of MyDialog. In addition to setting some of the properties that dialogs have in common with windows, the HasSeparator setting is set to false. This member controls whether a horizontal line is drawn between the body of the dialog and the bottom row of buttons, known as the *action area*.

A dialog comes with some widgets already constructed. It contains a VBox, referenced by the VBox member, and an HButtonBox referenced by ActionArea. There are convenience methods for adding widgets to the action area. The packing of the HBox that forms the body of the dialog should be familiar territory from earlier labs.

Widget packing always uses the concepts of *start* and *end*, where we in the West might more naturally think of left and right. Not all cultures read left to right though, and Gtk# handles this well. Figure 4-8 shows the example run in a Hebrew locale. Note how all the elements of the user interface that Gtk# controls have been adjusted accordingly. In this locale, start means right and end means left.

Figure 4-8. Dialog run in Hebrew

The text in the buttons was automatically translated because the example uses *stock items*. These are predefined constant images or text with an agreed meaning when used as part of an interface. The rightmost button in Figure 4-7, for example, shows the text "OK" used in conjunction with the curving arrow image. Stock items not only save time for the developer, but they greatly aid the consistency of an interface's look and feel.

To show that the user is being asked a question, the stock "dialog question" image is added to the dialog, using the IconSize.Dialog dimension to get the proper size. Note the use of SetAlignment as a shorthand for setting the Xalign and Yalign properties separately.

Having separator lines everywhere must have seemed a good idea at the time, but they're not used much these days as they add to visual clutter.

GTK+ permits the user to set a themed look-and-feel using the preferences. Stock items automatically change their look to fit the theme.

The final thing to note from the example is the convenience method AddButton, specifically intended as a shortcut for adding stock items to dialogs. This performs the same thing as the following code:

```
Button b = new Button (Stock.Cancel);
this.AddActionWidget (b, ResponseType.Cancel);
```

The Gtk.ResponseType enumeration contains well-known return codes for dialogs, which should be used where applicable. If you need to hook up your own codes, any positive non-zero integer can be used without clashing with these predefined codes.

What about …

…More sophisticated subclassing? Earlier in this lab it was observed that subclassing is the recommended way to encapsulate any non-trivial amount of widget-based code. Study Example 4-7. It implements a button that keeps a count of how many times it has been clicked.

Example 4-7. Subclassed button: 04-button/Main.cs

```
// 04-gtk/04-button
using System;
using Gtk;

class MyButton : Button {
  private int hitcount;

  public MyButton (string text) : base (text)
  {
    hitcount = 0;
  }

  protected override void OnClicked ()
  {
    hitcount++;
    base.OnClicked ();
  }

  public int HitCount {
    get
    {
      return hitcount;
    }
    set
    {
      hitcount = value;
    }
  }
}
```

Example 4-7. *Subclassed button: 04-button/Main.cs (continued)*

```
class MainClass {
  public static void Main (string[ ] args)
  {
    Application.Init ();
    Window w = new Window ("Hit Count");
    MyButton b = new MyButton ("Hit Count");
    b.Clicked += Button_Clicked;
    w.Add (b);
    w.ShowAll ();
    Application.Run ();
  }

  public static void Button_Clicked (object o, EventArgs e)
  {
    MyButton b = (MyButton) o;
    Console.WriteLine ("Click number {0}", b.HitCount);
  }
}
```

One useful feature of subclassing is that the program gets an opportunity to process an event before the delegate handlers are invoked. Compile and run the example program, and observe that the reported hit count starts at 1, demonstrating that the delegate for the clicked event is invoked after the OnClicked method.

Where to learn more

A fuller discussion of subclassing in C# can be found in *C# Essentials* by Ben Albahari, Peter Drayton, and Brad Merrill (O'Reilly).

The *GTK+ 2.0 Reference Manual* has a fine reference, with example graphics, of all the stock items. This can be found online at *http:// developer.gnome.org/doc/API/2.0/gtk/gtk-Stock-Items.html*.

What if the stock items don't cover a program's requirements, but the theming flexibility of stock items is still required? It's possible to register custom stock items, which GTK+ theme designers and other programs can then use. Further information on doing this is available from the Gtk. StockManager and Gtk.StockItem entries in Monodoc.

Draw Graphics

A picture paints a thousand words, and it can often visualize data much better than a thousand widgets too! Handling graphics tends to be done at a lower level than widgets, and a little more work is needed from the programmer to receive results.

An interface with only widgets is dull; a pretty picture brightens up your programs.

In Gtk# graphics are handled using the APIs available in the Gdk namespace. One of the most common uses of Gdk is to handle bitmapped graphics, such as PNG or JPEG files. Gdk calls these Pixbufs. This lab demonstrates how to set up a drawing area and render bitmapped images into it.

How to do it

Although an application could take responsibility for drawing the whole of its window, it would be a large waste of effort. By combining a drawing area with normal widget layout mechanisms the regular Gtk# look and feel can be preserved, while still drawing custom graphics.

Figure 4-9 illustrates a demonstration application window, composed of a drawing area and a regular button widget. The monkey pixbuf is loaded from a PNG graphics file. When the button is clicked the graphic is rendered at a random point on the drawing area, scaled by a random factor between 1 and 3.

Figure 4-9. Monkey madness!

The drawing area is made using the Gtk.DrawingArea widget. This is in reality a blank widget; managing its appearance is left to the application. Because of this, the example code will also give some insight into how widget implementations work.

Compile, link, and run the listing from Example 4-8.

```
$ mcs Main.cs -pkg:gtk-sharp \
    -resource:monkey.png,monkey.png
$ mono Main.exe
```

The -resource option embeds the *monkey.png* file into the assembly. (Not to be confused with the -r, which is short for -reference.) This technique saves the hassle of distributing graphics files separately. The syntax of this option requires two names: the first is where to find the resource and the second is the name to give it in the assembly. For convenience, one of the constructors of Gdk.Pixbuf will load an image directly from an assembly.

You can use your own monkey.png or get the one from this book's web site.

Example 4-8. Collage generator: 05-graphics/Main.cs

```
// 04-gtk/05-graphics
using System;
using Gtk;
using Gdk;

class MainClass {
  private static Gtk.Button add_png;
  private static Gtk.DrawingArea darea;
  private static Gdk.Pixmap pixmap;
  private static Gdk.Pixbuf pngbuf;
  private static Random rand;

  public static void Main (string[ ] args)
  {
    rand = new Random ();
    Application.Init ();

    pngbuf = new Pixbuf (null, "monkey.png");

    Gtk.Window w = new Gtk.Window ("Graphics Demo");

    VBox v = new VBox ();
    v.BorderWidth = 6;
    v.Spacing = 12;
    w.Add (v);

    darea = new DrawingArea ();
    darea.SetSizeRequest (200, 200);
    darea.ExposeEvent += Expose_Event;
    darea.ConfigureEvent += Configure_Event;
    v.PackStart (darea);

    HBox h = new HBox ();
    add_png = new Button ("Add _Primate");
    add_png.Clicked += AddPng_Clicked;
    h.PackStart (add_png, false, false, 0);
    v.PackEnd (h, false, false, 0);

    w.ShowAll ();
    w.Resizable = false;
    w.DeleteEvent += Window_Delete;

    Application.Run ();
```

Example 4-8. Collage generator: 05-graphics/Main.cs (continued)

```
    }

    static void PlacePixbuf (Gdk.Pixbuf buf)
    {
      Gdk.Rectangle allocation = darea.Allocation;
      int width = allocation.Width + 2 * buf.Width;
      int height = allocation.Height + 2 * buf.Height;
      int x = rand.Next (width) - buf.Width;
      int y = rand.Next (height) - buf.Height;
      pixmap.DrawPixbuf (darea.Style.BlackGC,
        buf, 0, 0, x, y,
        buf.Width, buf.Height,
        RgbDither.None, 0, 0);
      darea.QueueDrawArea (x, y, buf.Width, buf.Height);
    }

    static void AddPng_Clicked (object obj, EventArgs args)
    {
      int scale = rand.Next (3) + 1;
      PlacePixbuf (pngbuf.ScaleSimple (pngbuf.Width / scale,
        pngbuf.Height / scale, InterpType.Hyper));
    }

    static void Configure_Event (object obj, ConfigureEventArgs args)
    {
      Gdk.EventConfigure ev = args.Event;
      Gdk.Window window = ev.Window;
      Gdk.Rectangle allocation = darea.Allocation;

      pixmap = new Gdk.Pixmap (window, allocation.Width,
        allocation.Height, -1);
      pixmap.DrawRectangle (darea.Style.WhiteGC, true, 0, 0,
        allocation.Width, allocation.Height);
    }

    static void Expose_Event (object obj, ExposeEventArgs args)
    {
      Gdk.Rectangle area = args.Event.Area;
      args.Event.Window.DrawDrawable (darea.Style.WhiteGC, pixmap,
        area.X, area.Y,
          area.X, area.Y,
            area.Width, area.Height);
    }

    static void Window_Delete (object obj, DeleteEventArgs args)
    {
      Application.Quit ();
      args.RetVal = true;
    }

}
```

How it works

The creation of the user interface follows the regular pattern of boxes and packing. The most interesting aspect of the Main method is the assignment of handlers for the Expose and Configure events for DrawingArea. These events are inherited from the base class, Gtk.Widget, and are not particular to the DrawingArea. The Configure event is raised whenever the widget's window changes size. Expose is raised whenever the widget's window needs redrawing.

The choice of how to redraw the DrawingArea is implementation dependent. One very common choice, employed in Example 4-8, is *double-buffering*. This is the technique of keeping a copy of the desired area in memory, which is simply copied onto the target drawing area on request.

The buffer is set up in the Configure_Event method, by the allocation of a Gdk.Pixmap of the same dimensions as the drawing area, and the graphics characteristics of the parent window. The area is initialized with a solid white rectangle. Drawing the DrawingArea in response to the Expose event is simply a matter of copying the pixmap over.

Were we to allow the user to resize the window, initializing to a white rectangle would be unhelpful. Instead we'd need to preserve the existing image and enlarge it.

The names Pixmap and Pixbuf are unhelpfully similar. While a Pixbuf is an in-memory representation of an image, a Pixmap is an in-memory drawing area with all the necessary additional data structures to support drawing operations.

The final element to the program is the actual drawing of the graphic into the off-screen Pixmap buffer. Given a suitable Pixbuf, the PlacePixbuf method does this. Most of the code in this method is the arithmetic required to compute the random positioning; the drawing itself is quite simple. But as this only affects the off-screen buffer, how is the on-screen drawing area updated? The DrawingArea.QueueDrawArea method is used to cause an Expose event to be raised. Note that the parameters to this method cause only the affected portion of the off-screen buffer to be redrawn. In more complicated applications, this can be an important efficiency saving.

Where to learn more

As ever, Monodoc is the first place to look for references on the Gdk APIs and the Gtk.Pixbuf classes. Further illustrations of their use can also be found in the example programs that ship with the Gtk# source code.

The best way of getting to grips with drawing and basic widget implementation is to try and extend the example. Possibilities include:

- Allowing exact mouse placement of an image by using the `ButtonReleaseEvent` event.
- Drawing lines to join an image with the previously drawn one. See the `DrawLine` method of `Gdk.Drawable`.
- Remembering the placement of each image and permit resizing of the window, where each image keeps its position relative to the window dimensions.

Drawing is not typically the major constituent of a Gtk# application, and even the most generous observer will admit that the API from the `Gdk` namespace is large and complicated. Keeping the class documentation, Google, and a large set of examples nearby is essential!

Create Menus

Menus give users access to the fundamental "verbs" of functionality offered by a program. If a feature is offered in a Gtk# application, then users expect it be accessible via a menu item.

Menus are the time-honored way of giving users access to major program functions.

In Gtk#, there are three important menu classes. `Gtk.MenuItem` represents an item in a menu. `Gtk.Menu` collects items together into a menu. Menus can be submenus of menu items. Finally, `Gtk.MenuBar` collects items together into a widget allowing users to navigate its items and subordinate menus. This is illustrated in Figure 4-10.

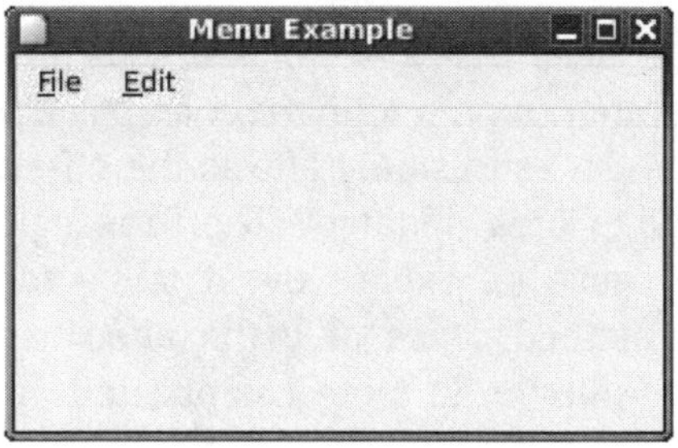

Figure 4-10. The menu bar

To create a set of menus in Gtk#, follow this general procedure.

- Create a menu bar
- Create a menu item for each top-level menu
- For each top-level menu item:
    - Attach a new menu as a submenu of each top-level menu item

- Create each item of the submenu
- Attach the top-level menu item to the menu bar

This lab demonstrates the main features of menu creation in Gtk#, including the use of stock items to add interface consistency.

How to do it

A polished Gtk# application adheres to certain conventions in creating menus to provide a faster and more consistent interface to the user. Mnemonic keys are assigned to each menu item. The menu can be activated by holding down **Alt** and the mnemonic letter. Stock items are used for common menu items, and keyboard accelerators (a fancy name for shortcuts) are provided for rapid access to menu functions.

Figure 4-11 shows a submenu that has been activated either by a mouseclick on the "File" menu item or they use pressing **Alt-F**. It is composed entirely of stock items and has a separator. Figure 4-12 shows a submenu with a further submenu activated. None of the items in these submenus are stock.

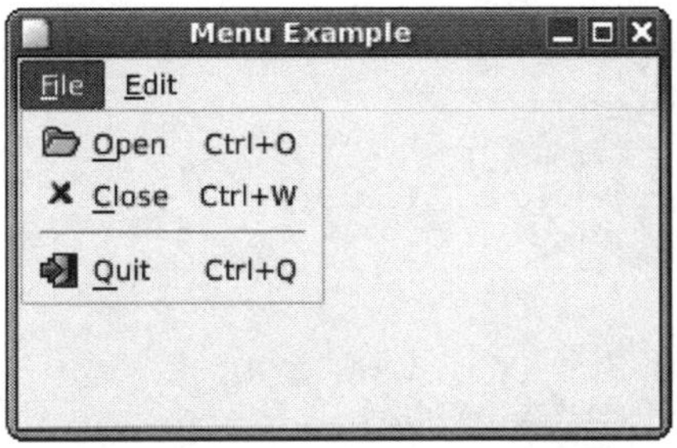

As with all stock items, stock menu items adapt to the current language and theme settings.

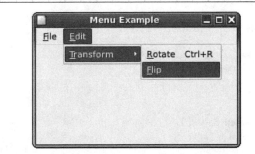

Figure 4-11. The file menu

Figure 4-12. The edit menu

To construct the menus shown in the figures, compile and run the code from Example 4-9:

```
$ mcs Main.cs -pkg:gtk-sharp
$ mono Main.exe
```

Example 4-9. Menu creation: 06-menus/Main.cs

```csharp
// 04-gtk/06-menus
using System;
using Gtk;
using Gdk;

class MainClass {
  static Gtk.Window w;

  public static void Main(string[ ] args)
  {
    Application.Init ();
    w = new Gtk.Window ("Menu Example");
    w.DeleteEvent += Window_Deleted;
    w.SetDefaultSize (260, 150);

    MenuBar mb = new MenuBar ();

    AccelGroup agrp = new AccelGroup ();
    w.AddAccelGroup (agrp);

    // file menu
    Menu file_menu = new Menu ();
    MenuItem item = new MenuItem ("_File");
    item.Submenu = file_menu;
    mb.Append (item);

    item = new ImageMenuItem (Stock.Open, agrp);
    item.Activated += Open_Activated;
    file_menu.Append (item);

    item = new ImageMenuItem (Stock.Close, agrp);
    file_menu.Append (item);

    file_menu.Append (new SeparatorMenuItem ());

    item = new ImageMenuItem (Stock.Quit, agrp);
    item.Activated += Quit_Activated;
    file_menu.Append (item);

    // edit menu
    Menu edit_menu = new Menu ();
    item = new MenuItem ("_Edit");
    item.Submenu = edit_menu;
    mb.Append (item);

    item = new MenuItem ("_Transform");
```

Example 4-9. Menu creation: 06-menus/Main.cs (continued)

```
   Menu transform_menu = new Menu ();
   item.Submenu = transform_menu;
   edit_menu.Append (item);

   item = new MenuItem ("_Rotate");

   // custom accelerator
   item.AddAccelerator ("activate", agrp,
     new AccelKey (Gdk.Key.R, Gdk.ModifierType.ControlMask,
       AccelFlags.Visible));

   item.Activated += Rotate_Activated;

   transform_menu.Append (item);
   item = new MenuItem ("_Flip");
   transform_menu.Append (item);

   VBox v = new VBox ();
   v.PackStart (mb, false, false, 0);
   w.Add (v);
   w.ShowAll ();

   Application.Run ();
}

public static void Open_Activated (object o, EventArgs e)
{
   System.Console.WriteLine ("Open");
}

public static void Rotate_Activated (object o, EventArgs e)
{
   System.Console.WriteLine ("Rotate");
}

public static void Quit_Activated (object o, EventArgs e)
{
   Application.Quit ();
}

public static void Window_Deleted (object o, DeleteEventArgs e)
{
   Application.Quit ();
}
}
```

How it works

Menu construction is verbose but largely straightforward. Example 4-9 follows the simple procedure outlined in introduction to this lab. One key concept to grasp at the outset is the workings of AccelGroup, a class that can accumulate all the required accelerator keys for an application. The group is attached to the widget for which these keys are valid. In most cases, and in Example 4-9, this widget is the window.

Adding stock items is simple. The accelerator group is passed to the constructor so that the stock accelerator keys can be registered with Gtk#. The main event of interest for menu items is Activated. This is raised when the user makes a selection. Example 4-9 implements several handlers for this event. Observe that "Open" is printed to the console either via the manual selection of the menu item or by the pressing of the accelerator **Ctrl-O**.

Where nonstock items are used, you need to do more work to add accelerators. The AddAccelerator method of Gtk.MenuItem performs this function and has the following signature:

```
public void AddAccelerator (string accel_signal,
    AccelGroup accel_group,
    AccelKey accel_key)
```

Modifier keys are those such as Shift, Alt, and Ctrl. Some keyboards have more, but these are the ones you can rely on.

AddAccelerator is inherited from Gtk.Widget and is really a generic mechanism for mapping keyboard accelerators to events on widgets. These events, passed through the accel_signal, are all-lowercase versions of the Gtk# event names. The accel_key parameter controls aspects of the key press: which key to use, what modifiers must be pressed too, and some flags. The most useful flag is AccelFlags.Visible, which controls whether or not the accelerator is rendered on the menu item.

The codes for keyboard keys and modifiers are contained in enumerations in the Gdk namespace. To appreciate the sheer diversity of keys on international keyboards, browse the documentation for Gdk.Key! The corollary of this diversity is that applications should only use accelerators that are universally available.

Want to disable a menu item? Set the Sensitive property, common to all widgets, to false.

It is possible, though not advisable, to place a menu bar anywhere you want in your program window. To get the bar at the top, the example packs it into the start of a VBox, ensuring it won't expand.

This lab has pursued a laborious and error-prone way of constructing menus in order to demonstrate the various concepts and widgets. Rather than repeating code, it would make more sense to create a data structure and use loops to create the desired menus. This is in fact what the Gtk.ItemFactory class is for, although it is in itself quite complex to use. Chapter 5 describes an even easier method of constructing menus, using the *Glade* user interface builder.

What about ...

...More complex menu items? In particular, checkboxes and radio buttons are often used in menus, as shown in Figures 4-13 and 4-14.

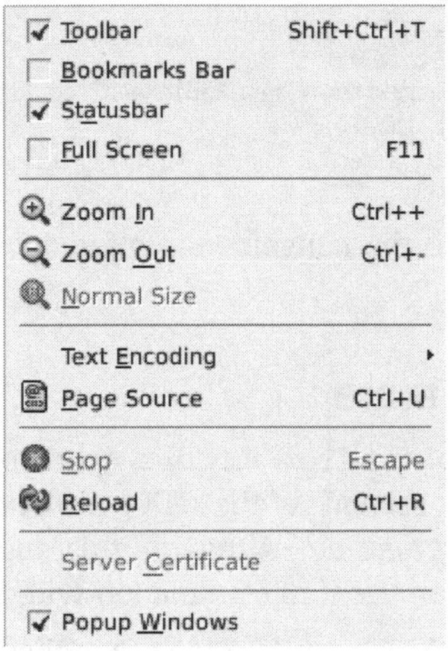

Figure 4-13. Check box menu items, taken from the Epiphany web browser

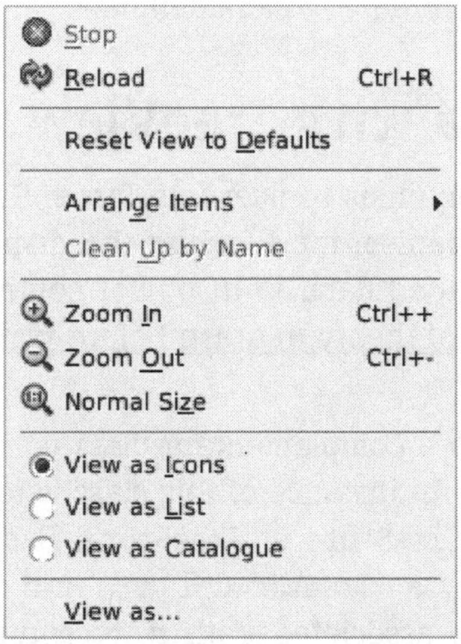

Figure 4-14. Radio button menu items, taken from the Nautilus file manager

Checkbox menu items are implemented by the Gtk.CheckMenuItem class. The state of the box can be read or set using the Active property. The Toggled event is raised when the user changes the state. Otherwise, these menu items can be treated in the same way as any other.

Radio button menu items are implemented by Gtk.RadioMenuItem. Their construction is a little more complex because of the need to express the grouping of menu items:

```
RadioMenuItem item1 = new RadioMenuItem ("Item label");
// add to the menu...
// and create the rest in the group
for (int i = 1; i < 5; i++) {
        RadioMenuItem newitem = new RadioMenuItem (item1,
                "Item label");
    // add the item to a menu...
}
```

This further underlines the convenience offered by tools such as interface builders.

Where to learn more

To find out more about the ItemFactory a good source of information is the "Using ItemFactory section" of the *GTK+ 2.0 Tutorial*, available online at *http://www.gtk.org/tutorial/*. Although this tutorial refers to the C implementation, you can use it in conjunction with Monodoc.

Chapter 4 of the *GNOME Human Interface Guidelines* explains many good conventions for using menus in applications, including standard menu titles and their recommended order. It can be found at *http://developer. gnome.org/projects/gup/hig/1.0/menus.html*.

Organize Data with TreeView

Lists and trees are ubiquitous in user interfaces. Gtk#'s TreeView widget is a very flexible mechanism for allowing the display, sorting, and editing, of list- or tree-shaped data. With power comes responsibility, however, and there's a bit of theory to grasp before you can use the TreeView effectively.

The tree view requires a complementary class containing the data to be displayed in the view. An instance of this class is termed the *model*. Typically this is either a ListStore or TreeStore. Each column in the view must be created as a TreeViewColumn, and have one or more CellRenderer instance associated with it, to control the visual appearance of the data.

Many pages could be written in explanation of the TreeView. This lab demonstrates the basics and shows how to present a slightly more adventurous rendering of data.

How to do it

The first task is the simple case of a list, as shown in Figure 4-15. The data model being displayed is a list where each row is composed of two strings. Setting up the data model requires a `ListStore` object. Its constructor is invoked with the type of each column to be stored.

To create the interface a tree view is constructed. For each visible column, a `TreeViewColumn` is created and its title set. The column acts like a widget container, similar to an `HBox` or `VBox`, except that it must contain `CellRenderer` instances. Basic `CellTextRenderer` instances are created, packed into the column, and attached to the corresponding place in the data model.

Example 4-10 shows the full code to achieve this. It can be compiled and run as usual for Gtk# programs:

```
$ mcs Main.cs -pkg:gtk-sharp
$ mono Main.exe
```

You can control TreeView header behavior with HeadersVisible (as in the example), HeadersClickable (report clicks on headers), and Reorderable (sort view by different columns).

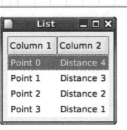

Figure 4-15. Simple list

Example 4-10. Displaying a list: 07-listview/Main.cs

```
// 04-gtk/07-listview
using System;
using Gtk;

class MainClass {
  public static void Main(string[ ] args)
  {
    Application.Init ();
    Window w = new Window ("List");
    w.DeleteEvent += Window_Deleted;
    VBox v = new VBox ();
    v.BorderWidth = 6;
    w.Add (v);

    TreeView tv = new TreeView ();
    tv.HeadersVisible = true;
    v.Add (tv);
```

Example 4-10. Displaying a list: 07-listview/Main.cs (continued)

```
      TreeViewColumn col = new TreeViewColumn ();
      CellRenderer colr = new CellRendererText ();
      col.Title = "Column 1";
      col.PackStart (colr, true);
      col.AddAttribute (colr, "text", 0);
      tv.AppendColumn (col);

      col = new TreeViewColumn ();
      colr = new CellRendererText ();
      col.Title = "Column 2";
      col.PackStart (colr, true);
      col.AddAttribute (colr, "text", 1);
      tv.AppendColumn (col);

      ListStore store = new ListStore (typeof (string), typeof (string));
      tv.Model = store;

      TreeIter iter = new TreeIter ();
      for (int i = 0; i < 4; i++) {
        iter = store.AppendValues ("Point " + i.ToString (),
          "Distance " + (4-i).ToString ());
      }

      w.ShowAll ();
      Application.Run ();
   }

   static void Window_Deleted (object o, DeleteEventArgs e)
   {
      Application.Quit ();
   }
}
```

TreeView has two events that alert the program to use of the triangle-shaped "expanders": RowCollapsed and RowExpanded.

The second major use of TreeView is to display tree-shaped data, as shown in Figure 4-16. To simplify matters, this example uses only one column. Note that there is no difference in the way the view is set up. Only the connected model of data, this time a TreeStore, differs. A TreeStore allows you to store any depth of tree-shaped data.

Example 4-11 demonstrates storing and rendering tree-shaped data.

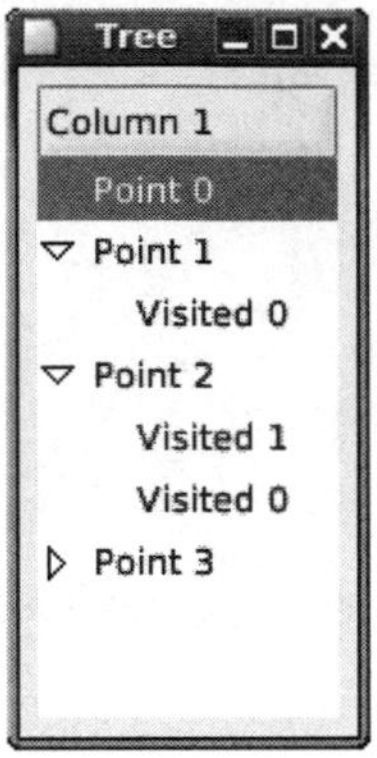

Figure 4-16. Tree view

Example 4-11. Tree view: 07-treeview/Main.cs

```
// 04-gtk/07-treeview
using System;
using Gtk;

class MainClass {
  public static void Main(string[] args)
  {
    Application.Init ();
    Window w = new Window ("Tree");
    w.DeleteEvent += Window_Deleted;
    VBox v = new VBox ();
    v.BorderWidth = 6;
    w.Add (v);

    TreeView tv = new TreeView ();
    tv.HeadersVisible = true;
    v.Add (tv);

    TreeViewColumn col = new TreeViewColumn ();
    CellRenderer colr = new CellRendererText ();
    col.Title = "Column 1";
    col.PackStart (colr, true);
    col.AddAttribute (colr, "text", 0);
    tv.AppendColumn (col);

    // the above can be written more concisely as
    // tv.AppendColumn ("Column 1", new CellRendererText (),
    //                   "text", 0);

    TreeStore store = new TreeStore (typeof (string));
    tv.Model = store;

    TreeIter iter = new TreeIter ();
    for (int i = 0; i < 4; i++) {
```

Example 4-11. *Tree view: 07-treeview/Main.cs (continued)*

```
      iter = store.AppendValues ("Point " + i.ToString ());
      for (int j = i-1; j >= 0; j--) {
        store.AppendValues (iter, "Visited " + j.ToString ());
      }
    }
  }

  w.ShowAll ();
  Application.Run ();
}

static void Window_Deleted (object o, DeleteEventArgs e)
{
  Application.Quit ();
}
}
```

How it works

There are two concepts of particular interest underlying the operation of the TreeView: the creation of and access to the data model, and the linking of renderers to parts of the model.

Iterators become very interesting when you start allowing the editing of data in your TreeView.

The *iterator* provided by the TreeIter class is used heavily in providing access to the data model. An iterator is a pointer into the data model using the data that can be read or written. In relational database terminology, the iterator is a *cursor*.

When adding data into a model, the pattern of use of the iterator varies depending on whether the model is a list or tree. In the simple case of a list, an iterator is returned by the ListStore.AppendValues method. It points to the next empty row in the list. Other methods such as InsertAfter and InsertBefore take such iterators as arguments, and SetValue can be used with an iterator argument to change particular rows in the list.

If the only access required is to append values, as in Example 4-10, then the returned iterator value can be ignored. It becomes more important however where tree-shaped data is concerned. Appending data to a TreeStore follows one of two patterns:

```
iter = store.AppendValues (val1, val2, ...)
child_of_iter = store.AppendValues (iter, val1, val2, ...)
```

The first pattern is similar to that of the list store, and results in a row being added to the top level of tree. The returned iterator is of use as it points to a new child row, not a sibling row. In the second pattern, it can be specified as the first parameter to AppendValues, adding the data as a child. If that *child_of_iter* is then used as a parameter to AppendValues, data will again be added as child of the child, and so on.

Linking renderers to the data model is a matter of setting *attributes* on the renderer. These are not C# attributes, unfortunately, but a term that the Gtk# API uses for this purpose. The `TreeViewColumn.AddAttribute` method links an attribute of a cell renderer with the contents of a certain column in the data model. In Example 4-10, the `text` attribute of the two text cell renderers is linked to three string value contained in each of the columns. The `text` attribute corresponds to the `Text` property of the `CellRendererText` class, which has a host of other interesting properties. Among these is `Editable`. Using this, for example, the editing of individual cells could be controlled by linking the `editable` attribute with a column in the store of type `bool`.

You can store as much data as you need in the model. Only the columns linked to renderers will be displayed.

What about ...

...More visually interesting trees? Using plain old text all the time can make it difficult for the user to pick out the data he requires. One of the simplest and most attractive ways to differentiate data is by the use of images. Figure 4-17 shows a view where the subordinate rows in the tree have been highlighted by the use of a graphical element.

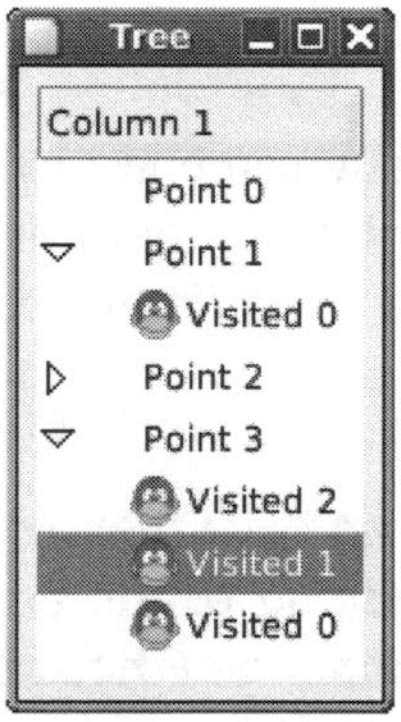

Figure 4-17. Pixbuf renderer

So how is this done? First, the necessary data must be stored in the model. It's not only basic types like `string` that can be stored. `Gdk.Pixbuf` is also a perfectly good type to store:

```
Gdk.Pixbuf monkey = new Gdk.Pixbuf (null, "monkey.png");

TreeStore store = new TreeStore (
    typeof (string),
    typeof (Gdk.Pixbuf));

    ...
```

```
iter = store.AppendValues ("Point 1", null);
store.AppendValues (iter, "Visited 0", monkey);
```

With the images and text stored in the model, what remains is to pack multiple types of cell renderers into the column of the tree. The CellRendererPixbuf provides the necessary functionality when its pixbuf attribute is linked to the Gdk.Pixbuf entries in the model:

```
CellRendererPixbuf pixr = new CellRendererPixbuf ();
col.PackStart (pixr, false);
col.AddAttribute (pixr, "pixbuf", 1);

CellRenderer colr = new CellRendererText ();
col.PackStart (colr, true);
col.AddAttribute (colr, "text", 0);
```

Where to learn more

This lab has only scratched the surface of the possibilities presented by the TreeView. There are other areas of functionality required for successful use, including:

Events
> TreeView raises events for user interactions with the rows in the view.

Searching and sorting
> Rows can be incrementally searched by matching against keyboard input from the user, allowing rapid navigation to the desired row. The view can be sorted by different columns in response to user request.

Editing
> CellRendererText cells can have their Editable set to true, in which case they permit user editing of the contents, stored in the linked model. When an edit is done the Edited event is raised.

A simple first step for further experimentation with the examples in this lab would be to add another column for boolean data, and attach a CellRendererToggle renderer to represent its state as a checkbox.

A comprehensive tree view tutorial can be found online at *http://scentric. net/tutorial/treeview-tutorial.html*. Though aimed at users of the C GTK+ API, the principles are equally applicable to Mono.

Exchange Data with Drag and Drop

Drag and drop is an effective way of allowing the user to manipulate data, both inside an application and between different applications. Although there may not always be a need for advanced drag and drop functionality, most applications find it useful to allow files dropped from the file manager to be interpreted as a "Load file" request.

Gtk# uses media types to control drag and drop. A drag source must describe which types it can provide, and a drop target must describe which types it can accept. If a match is found, then the drag and drop can proceed. Any widget that can generate events can participate in drag and drop.

Despite seeming like a complex feature of mature programs, drag and drop is actually quite simple to implement. It can vastly improve the integration of your program with others on the user's desktop. This lab demonstrates both internal and external drag and drop, showing how to deal with different media types.

Drag and drop is often the easiest interface technique for moving data around the desktop.

Media types are also known as "MIME types". Common ones include text/html or image/jpeg.

How to do it

Study our example program window, shown in Figure 4-18. It contains a drop target on the right to where the user can drag files from the file manager. On the left is a graphical image that can also be dropped on to the target.

Figure 4-18. Program window

Figure 4-19 shows an external drag and drop in action. A file from the *Nautilus* file manager has been dropped onto the target. The target area is automatically outlined by Gtk# to give the user feedback as they hold the file over it. Figure 4-20 shows an internal drag and drop. The graphic item from the left has been picked up by the user and held over the drop target. The application has set the drag icon to the same graphic so the user can easily see what it is they are dragging.

Figure 4-19. Dropping in action

Figure 4-20. Dragging in action

If you're not familiar with URIs, think of them as you do of URLs used in web browsers. It's nearly the same thing.

To have the drop target accept files from the file manager, the media type text/uri-list must be registered as acceptable. When a drop happens, a newline-separated list of Universal Resource Identifiers (URIs) will be sent to the target application. It is this ability to use known media types that enables drag and drop to provide interoperability between programs on the desktop.

The internal drop of the graphic is not concerned with interoperability with other applications, so a private application specific type is invented, application/x-monkey. The drop target must also register that it accepts that type too.

In order to differentiate between the two kinds of drag and drop, the application will print the details of each drop to the console. For text/uri-list, it will print the file URI, and for application/x-monkey it will print some custom data.

Example 4-12 contains the full implementation of both drop target and drag source. Its compilation is in "Draw Graphics."

```
$ mcs Main.cs -pkg:gtk-sharp \
    -resource:monkey.png,monkey.png
$ mono Main.exe
```

Example 4-12. Drag and drop implementation: 08-dragdrop/Main.cs

```
// 04-gtk/08-dragdrop
using System;
using System.Text.RegularExpressions;
using Gtk;
using Gdk;
```

Example 4-12. Drag and drop implementation: 08-dragdrop/Main.cs (continued)

```
class MainClass {
  // the media types we'll accept
  private static Gtk.TargetEntry [] target_table =
    new TargetEntry [] {
      new TargetEntry ("text/uri-list", 0, 0),
      new TargetEntry ("application/x-monkey", 0, 1),
    };

  // the media types we'll send
  private static Gtk.TargetEntry [] source_table =
    new TargetEntry [] {
      new TargetEntry ("application/x-monkey", 0, 0),
    };

  private static Gdk.Pixbuf monkey;

  public static void Main(string[] args)
  {
    Application.Init ();

    monkey = new Pixbuf (null, "monkey.png");
    Gtk.Window w = new Gtk.Window ("Drag & drop");
    w.DeleteEvent += Window_Delete;

    HBox h = new HBox ();
    h.BorderWidth = 6;
    h.Spacing = 6;

    Gtk.EventBox image = new Gtk.EventBox ();
    image.Add (new Gtk.Image (monkey));
    h.Add (image);

    Gtk.Label label = new Gtk.Label ("Drop stuff here");
    h.Add (label);

    w.Add (h);
    w.ShowAll ();

    // set up label as a drop target
    Gtk.Drag.DestSet (label, DestDefaults.All, target_table,
      Gdk.DragAction.Copy);
    label.DragDataReceived += Data_Received;

    // set up image as a drag source
    Gtk.Drag.SourceSet (image, Gdk.ModifierType.Button1Mask,
      source_table, DragAction.Copy);
    image.DragDataGet += Data_Get;
    image.DragBegin += Drag_Begin;
    Application.Run ();
  }

  static void Data_Received (object o, DragDataReceivedArgs args)
```

Example 4-12. *Drag and drop implementation: 08-dragdrop/Main.cs (continued)*

```
{
  bool success = false;
  Gtk.Widget source = Gtk.Drag.GetSourceWidget (args.Context);
  string data = System.Text.Encoding.UTF8.GetString (
          args.SelectionData.Data);

  switch (args.Info) {
    case 0:  // uri-list
      string [] uri_list = Regex.Split (data, "\r\n");
      foreach (string u in uri_list) {
        if (u.Length > 0)
          System.Console.WriteLine ("Got URI {0}", u);
      }
      success = true;
      break;
    case 1: // monkey
      System.Console.WriteLine ("Monkey '{0}' was dropped", data);
      success = true;
      break;
  }

  Gtk.Drag.Finish (args.Context, success, false, args.Time);
}

static void Drag_Begin (object o, DragBeginArgs args)
{
  Gtk.Drag.SetIconPixbuf (args.Context, monkey, 0, 0);
}

static void Data_Get (object o, DragDataGetArgs args)
{
  Atom [] targets = args.Context.Targets;

  args.SelectionData.Set (targets [0], 8,
      System.Text.Encoding.UTF8.GetBytes ("Rupert"));
}

static void Window_Delete (object o, DeleteEventArgs args)
{
  Application.Quit ();
}
}
```

How it works

A more correct example would use an enumeration for the type identifiers rather than 0 and 1.

To receive dragged data the label widget is registered as a drop target with the static method Gtk.Drag.DestSet. A reference to an array of TargetEntry objects is passed as one of the parameters, indicating the acceptable media types. Each of these contains the media type, a flags parameter, and a unique numeric identifier for this type. This identifier is used again when data is received.

The label widget is also assigned a handler for `DragDataReceived`. This is enough to enable it as a recipient of dragged data. When a drag and drop occurs, the event handler is called with its `DragDataReceivedArgs` parameter containing the details of the dropped data. The `Info` property of this object corresponds to the numeric identifier assigned to the media type in the `TargetEntry` table.

The actual data sent by the drop is received as an array of bytes. It is up to the receiving application to interpret these according to the media type. In Gtk#, all text is exchanged using the UTF-8 encoding of the Unicode character set. In the example, a string is derived from the unencoded data for both media types. Our private `application/x-monkey` type is used to send the name of the monkey in UTF-8! The `text/uri-list` is further processed to split the lines up into multiple URIs. More than one URI will be received if the user has grouped multiple files from the file manager and dragged them all at once.

A mature application would trap errors from invalid UTF-8 that would otherwise cause exceptions.

When processing of the dropped data has completed, the handler must call `Gtk.Drag.Finish`. The second parameter to this method is a boolean flag, indicating whether or not the handler was able to process the incoming data successfully.

Setting up the `Image` widget as a source for drag and drops is almost as simple. In the introduction to this lab it was noted that widgets must be capable of raising events in order to participate in a drag and drop. An `Image` does not raise events, so it must be embedded in an `EventBox` first.

The event box is registered as source with `Gtk.Drag.SourceSet`, passing a media type table in a similar way as for the label. The `SourceSet` call also specifies the mouse button to initiate the drag, and the hint that this drag will result in a data copy.

Look at the Gdk. DragAction enumeration for more drag actions such as "move" or "link".

The only handler that must be implemented for a drag to work is for the `DragDataGet` event. This handler, implemented in `Data_Get` converts the data to be transmitted into a byte array. Because the widget in question only sends data of type `application/x-monkey`, the application does not need to perform detection of media types. Otherwise this would be achieved by inspecting the value of `Name` on each member of `targets[]` and providing the appropriate encoded data. In this example, the result of `targets[0].Name` is `application/x-monkey`.

By implementing a handler for the `DragBegin` event, the program is able to set a special icon for the dragged data. Otherwise, a rather generic icon is used by Gtk#. `Gtk.Drag.SetIconPixbuf` sets this icon to the same `Gdk.Pixbuf` used for the image.

It would be prettier to create a translucent version of the image to set as the drag icon.

Where to learn more

As with most of the Gtk# API, it is possible to exert much finer control over the drag and drop process. For instance, you could receive events when a drag is held over a widget before a drop occurs.

Over time the "Mono Handbook" section of Monodoc will cover such topics, but in the meantime tutorials written using C and GTK+ can provide adequate information. A concise but helpful tutorial is available online at *http://wolfpack.twu.net/docs/gtkdnd/*.

Advanced Gtk#

In Chapter 4 the labs were restricted to using the Gtk namespace from the Gtk# user interface toolkit. However, any modern desktop system includes more than windows and widgets. It includes consistent look-and-feel, internationalization, window management, configuration management, and accessibility. This chapter introduces the major topics needed to make your user interfaces full-fledged desktop applications.

Most of the APIs used in this chapter were developed for the GNOME desktop environment, available for Linux and other Unix-like systems. Most of them are available under Windows and OS X. Where this is not the case, it will be noted. If you run Linux but don't run GNOME, don't worry. Applications written with Gtk# and the Gnome namespace will run fine under alternative desktops like KDE.

If you successfully completed the labs in Chapter 4, you have all the assemblies installed that you need for this chapter. Despite its name, the *gtk-sharp* package not only includes the Gtk assembly, but also Gnome and many others used in this book.

Write a Gnome Application

The GTK+ interface toolkit, accessed through the Gtk namespace of Gtk# in Chapter 4, is powerful and expressive. What it does not provide on its own, however, is a framework for graphical applications that preserves consistency of behavior and appearance. The GNOME development platform works in combination with GTK+ to provide higher-level widgets and application services useful to GUI-based programs.

The GNOME APIs, accessible in Gtk# through the Gnome namespace, offer a set of features and widgets that takes Gtk# from being an interface

In this chapter:
- *"Write a Gnome Application"*
- *"Design Interfaces with Glade"*
- *"Store Configuration with GConf"*
- *"Guide the User with Druids"*
- *"Perform Asynchronous Operations"*
- *"Render HTML"*
- *"Provide Help Files"*
- *"Translate Your Programs"*

Nobody likes a messy interface. The Gnome API helps you make a good-looking program.

toolkit to a desktop development platform. That said, users do not need to run GNOME as their primary environment to run programs that use the GNOME APIs, but it will ensure that they get the best results out of them.

This lab introduces the basic framework of GNOME programs, the Gnome.Program and Gnome.Application classes. Gnome.Program provides identification of the program to the desktop, and location of related resources. Gnome.Application provides an application window, enhanced with the screen furniture required by most document-based GUI programs.

How do I do that?

Figure 5-1 shows a basic GNOME application window. In addition to the menu bar familiar from "Create Menus" in Chapter 4, a *toolbar* can be seen at the top of the window. A toolbar is a special container for other widgets that can be moved around the window by the grab bar, seen at the left side. It can even be "ripped" off and placed as a standalone window. Complex GNOME applications, such as the *AbiWord* word processor, make good use of toolbars.

At the bottom of the window is the *appbar*, composed of a progress meter on the left and a status bar on the right. A window icon (top-left) helps provide a common identity for all windows belonging to this application.

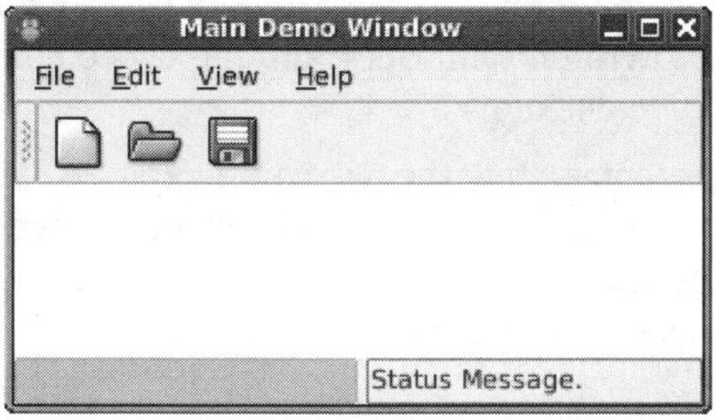

Window icons are also shown in the system window list and window switching dialogs.

Figure 5-1. GNOME program window

Compiling applications using the Gnome namespace requires that you specify the *gnome-sharp* package of assemblies to be specified on the compile line. Compile and run the listing in Example 5-1 with the following commands:

```
$ mcs Main.cs -pkg:gnome-sharp -pkg:gtk-sharp \
              -resource:monkey.png,monkey.png
$ mono Main.exe
```

Example 5-1. Gnome# skeleton program: 01-gnomeapp/Main.cs

```
// 05-advdesktop/01-gnomeapp
using System;
using Gtk;
using Gdk;
using Gnome;

public class MainClass
{
  public static void Main (string[ ] args)
  {
    new MyProgram (args);
  }
}

public class MyProgram
{
  public MyProgram (string [ ] args)
  {
    Program program = new Program ("gnome-demo", "0.1", Modules.UI, args);
    App app = new App ("gnome-demo", "Main Demo Window");
    app.SetDefaultSize (400, 300);
    app.DeleteEvent += Window_Delete;

    app.Icon = new Gdk.Pixbuf (null, "monkey.png");
    app.Statusbar = new AppBar (true, true, PreferencesType.Never);
    app.Toolbar = MakeToolbar ();
    app.Menus = MakeMenubar ();

    app.ShowAll ();
    program.Run ();
  }

  private void Window_Delete (object o, DeleteEventArgs args)
  {
    Application.Quit ();
  }

  private Toolbar MakeToolbar ()
  {
    Toolbar t = new Toolbar ();
    // ... initialization
    return t;
  }

  private MenuBar MakeMenubar ()
  {
    MenuBar m = new MenuBar ();
    // ... initialization
    return m;
  }
}
```

The code in the example won't produce a window exactly as in Figure 5-1 because the menu and toolbars are not initialized. You can bring in menu initialization code from "Create Menus" in Chapter 4. Toolbar initialization can be complex and is best performed with time-saving tools, demonstrated in "Design Interfaces with Glade."

How it works

The Gnome.Program object is how the application announces itself to the rest of the system. Its first two arguments specify the program name and version. The other two arguments can be taken as boilerplate. Passing the args ensures that the command-line options are sent to the Gnome libraries.

Try running **mono Main.exe --help**. Thanks to the passing of args, a host of GNOME-related command-line options are available The Modules.UI argument to the Program constructor adds in the "GNOME GUI Library" set of options. Note also on the first line of the help output that the program name is specified. If you're running the GNOME desktop, use the screen-shot facility (**Take Screenshot...** from the panel's **Action** menu). Note that the screenshot is named with the name of the program. Finally, note that the event loop cycle is started with Program.Run rather than the familiar Application.Run.

Gnome.App is a subclass of Gtk.Window that accommodates a menubar, toolbar, and appbar. Its constructor not only takes a window title, but also the program name. This is so the window manager can intelligently group windows belonging to the same application.

Though AppBar's status bar can be interactive, it is rarely used in this way.

The AppBar indicates the status of a program to the user. It can be constructed with one or both of a progress meter and status bar. Most programs make use of the status bar. Some use the progress meter, such as web browsers or programs with long-running computations. For status bar access, AppBar simplifies the rather cumbersome Gtk.StatusBar API, offering simple AppBar.Push and AppBar.Pop methods for setting and removing messages.

What about adding widgets into the main area of the application window? Using app.Add won't work as expected, because there are already widgets in the window. Instead the App.Contents property can be used. Typically an application would create an HBox or VBox and assign it to the Contents property.

Where to learn more

Although "Design Interfaces with Glade" demonstrates how to use an interactive interface builder to create toolbars and menus, there are programmatic ways too. Gnome.App has a selection of methods such as CreateMenus and CreateToolbar that can be used to create menus and toolbars from data structures, avoiding manually constructing each widget individually. API documentation for these methods can be found in Monodoc. A good source of tutorial information is the *Java-GNOME Tutorial*, available online linked from *http://java-gnome.sourceforge.net/*. Although covering the Java bindings for the GNOME libraries, the principles apply well enough to Gtk#'s Gnome libraries.

Design Interfaces with Glade

While creating user interfaces from code is a good way of understanding how the Gtk# toolkit works, it can quickly become laborious and verbose. *Glade* is an interactive user interface designer program that takes a lot of the hard work out of interface creation. Not only that, but it can enable programmers and interface designers to work in parallel on the same application. *Glade* can be downloaded from *http://ftp.gnome.org/pub/GNOME/sources/glade/* and is also available in most Linux distributions.

Separating interface definition from the main code makes life easier.

Glade works by generating an XML description of a user interface. Using APIs in the Glade namespace from Gtk#, programs can dynamically create widgets straight from the XML description. In Mono applications, the interface description can be linked as a resource into the assembly or be distributed as a separate file.

This lab covers the basics of designing and deploying a user interface with *Glade*.

How do I do that?

This lab uses *Glade* to generate the skeleton of an image viewing application, using the Gnome APIs from "Write a Gnome Application." After installing *Glade*, start it up (run glade-2 from a terminal window, or launch it from a menu). When Glade appears:

1. Choose **New** from the **Project** menu.
2. A dialog appears, asking which kind of project you want. Choose New GNOME Project to obtain access to the widgets from the Gnome namespace in addition to those from Gtk. You won't notice any substantial change except for a New Project created message in the main window status bar.

3. Switch to the Palette window, select the Gnome widget category and click the first widget, which is a basic Gnome.Application window.

4. The new window appears, labeled *app1*. Select the new window from the list in the main Glade window, and use the Properties window to change the name to viewer and its title to Picture Viewer. The Properties window allows access to all the properties of the widget being edited. Figure 5-2 shows the state of the interface so far.

If the Properties window isn't there, activate it using the Show Property Editor option from the View menu.

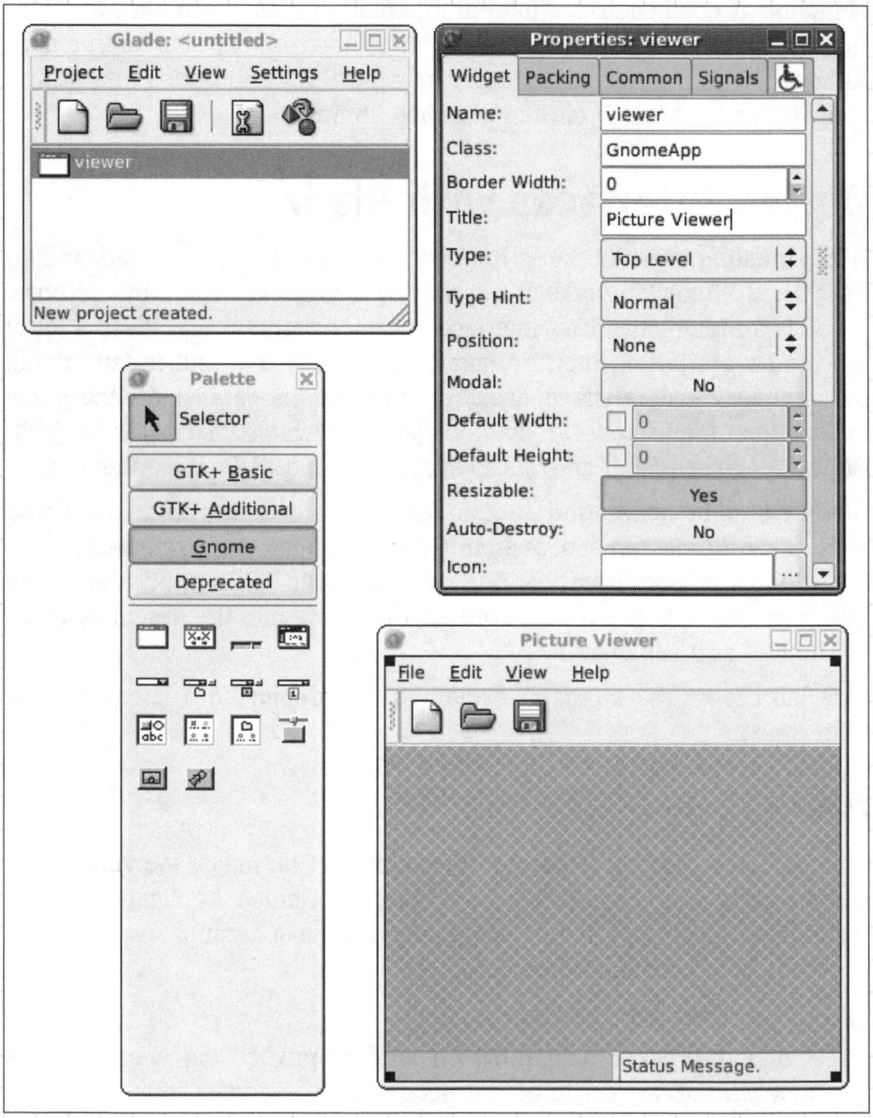

Figure 5-2. Editing an interface with Glade

Chapter 5: Advanced Gtk#

To make a picture viewer, you must add an Image widget. In case the image is larger than the window, the image should be in a scrollable window. Switch the Palette to GTK+ Basic, and click the Scrolled Window widget (at the bottom of the palette). Click on the empty space in the new picture viewer window to add the scrolled window.

Repeat the same process with the Image widget (also from the GTK+ Basic palette), and add it to the newly created Scrolled Window widget. The interface thus far can be seen in Figure 5-3. The hierarchy of contained widgets is displayed in Widget Tree, which you can activate from the Glade main window's **View** menu. This tree helps to navigate to widgets that can't explicitly be clicked on, such as HBox or VBox containers.

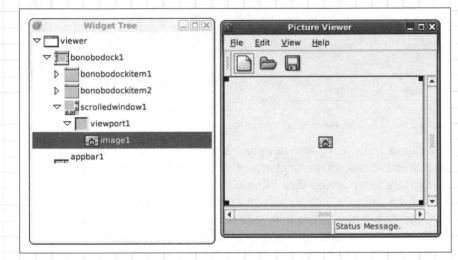

Don't worry about the curiously named "bonobodock" items; these are part of the setup that allows the toolbar to be ripped off and moved around.

Figure 5-3. Glade's widget tree

That's it for building the interface. But *Glade* offers more than just arranging a tree of widgets. As can be seen from the tabs in the Properties window, it allows control over the *signals* (called events in Gtk#) for each widget. Select the viewer application window in the widget tree, and then go to the signals tab in the Properties window. In the same way as the familiar Window.DeleteEvent handler is set up in code, adding a handler for delete_event in *Glade* will hook up a handler function when an interface is loaded and connected. Choose delete_event from the Signal menu, as shown in Figure 5-4, and accept the default handler name. Click Add to add it to the viewer widget.

When *Glade* created the menu bar at the top of the application window, it automatically set up handlers for each menu item's Activate event. Verify this by inspecting the Properties window for a menu item.

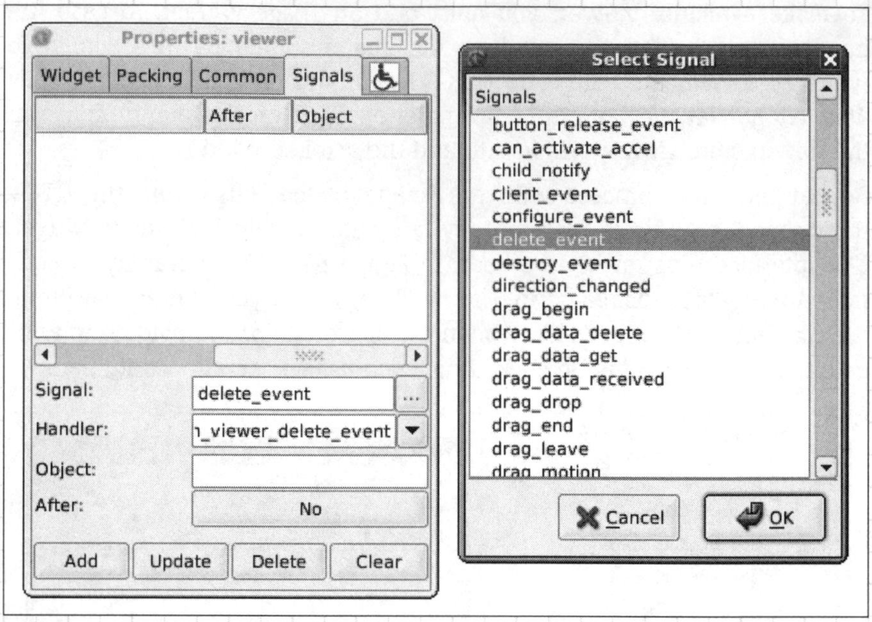

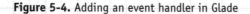

Figure 5-4. Adding an event handler in Glade

However an image viewer does not need the full complement of standard menu items. In particular any of those required for editing (Cut, Paste, Clear) and saving files (New, Save, Save As) are redundant. Delete these from the interface by selecting them and using the **Delete** option from the **Edit** menu of the main window. If you do not delete these, you will receive error messages about unhandled signal handlers when you run the program. Keep Open and Copy, as these are still useful for a read-only image viewer.

Finally, save the interface (choose **Save** from the **Project** menu). The *Glade* save dialog is a little complex. Aside from setting the project directory and program name (set it to "viewer"), it is acceptable to accept the defaults. Take a look inside the *.glade* file just saved. An extract is shown in Example 5-2, describing the Image widget added to the scrolled window.

Example 5-2. Image widget extract from viewer.glade file

```
<widget class="GtkImage" id="image1">
    <property name="visible">True</property>
    <property name="xalign">0.5</property>
    <property name="yalign">0.5</property>
    <property name="xpad">0</property>
    <property name="ypad">0</property>
</widget>
```

Example 5-3 shows code to display and use the interface. It is similar to the Gnome application from "Write a Gnome Application." Compile and run the code using:

```
$ mcs Main.cs -pkg:gtk-sharp -pkg:gnome-sharp \
    -pkg:glade-sharp -resource:monkey.png,monkey.png \
    -resource:viewer.glade,viewer.glade
$ mono Main.exe
```

Adjust the viewer.glade path to reflect the location of the *.glade* file, to -resource:*path/to/viewer.glade*,viewer.glade. Leave the second "viewer.glade" alone, the program will use that name to access the file. When run, the program opens a window similar to that shown in Figure 5-5. The *.glade* file is embedded into the *Main.exe* assembly, so you must recompile the assembly each time you make any changes to the Glade project.

Example 5-3. Basic Gnome program using Glade: 02-glade/Main.cs

```
// 05-advdesktop/02-glade
using System;
using Gdk;
using Gtk;
using Glade;
using Gnome;

public class GladeApp
{
  [Widget] Gtk.Image image1;
  [Widget] Gnome.App viewer;
  [Widget] Gnome.AppBar appbar1;

  private static string [] authors = { "Edd Dumbill" };
  private static string progversion = "1.0";
  private static string progname = "simple-viewer";

  private Gdk.Pixbuf monkey;

  public static void Main (string[ ] args)
  {
    new GladeApp (args);
  }

  public GladeApp (string[ ] args)
  {
    Program program = new Program (progname,
      progversion, Modules.UI, args);

    monkey = new Gdk.Pixbuf (null, "monkey.png");

    Glade.XML gxml = new Glade.XML (null, "viewer.glade",
      "viewer", null);
```

```
    gxml.Autoconnect (this);

    appbar1.Push ("Ready.");
    image1.Pixbuf = monkey;

    program.Run ();
  }

  public void on_viewer_delete_event (object o, DeleteEventArgs args)
  {
    Application.Quit ();
  }

  public void on_open1_activate (object o, EventArgs args)
  {
  }

  public void on_quit1_activate (object o, EventArgs args)
  {
    Application.Quit ();
  }

  public void on_copy1_activate (object o, EventArgs args)
  {
  }

  public void on_properties1_activate (object o, EventArgs args)
  {
  }

  public void on_preferences1_activate (object o, EventArgs args)
  {
  }

  public void on_about1_activate (object o, EventArgs args)
  {
    new Gnome.About (
        "Viewer", "1.0",
        "(C) 2004 Edd Dumbill",
        "A simple picture viewer.",
        authors, null, null, monkey).Run ();
  }
}
```

How it works

The initialization of the Gnome.Program follows the familiar pattern from the previous lab. The user interface description is contained in a Glade.XML. One form of Glade.XML's constructor allows the description to be loaded from a resource in the assembly, in a similar way to that of Gdk.Pixbuf.

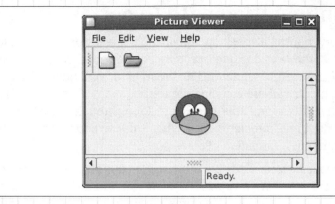

Figure 5-5. Simple image viewer interface

The other important argument given to the constructor is the name of the top-level widget. All widgets contained in this top-level widget will be constructed as the interface is loaded.

The most striking new concept in the example is the use of the [Widget] attribute on the declarations of image1, viewer, and appbar. When the Autoconnect method of Glade.XML is called, these members are automatically assigned to the corresponding widgets in the interface. Additionally, the event handlers named in the interface description are automatically connected. If a handler method isn't found for a particular event, then an exception is thrown. An application must either catch and ignore this exception, or provide "stubbed-out" empty handlers as in the example.

Example 5-3 also illustrates two other aspects of the Gnome API. First, the AppBar.Push method is used to send the Ready message to the status bar. Second, an "About" dialog is hooked up to the **About** item on the **Help** menu. This convenience method constructs a pleasant-looking dialog giving a description of the program, and credit to its authors and translators.

Where to learn more

Tutorials on *Glade* can be found on the GNOME Developer Documentation web site, at *http://developer.gnome.org/doc/tutorials/*. Although at first sight, *Glade* appears to be a somewhat fearsome application, most of the features and properties map directly to the properties of widgets in Gtk#, so as ever a close perusal of the API documentation in Monodoc will help.

Widget.Show is called on each widget when an interface is loaded. To prevent the window or other widget from displaying immediately, set the Hidden property on the Glade Properties editor.

Store Configuration with GConf

Practically every nontrivial desktop application must store user preferences. Of course, the best designed programs make good default choices and keep the number of preferences down to a minimum. However, there's always a point where some configuration needs to be stored. Traditionally in the Unix world this has been done through so-called "dot files" in a user's home directory: files whose name begins with . and contain configuration information of some sort.

The GConf system aims to clear up the mess of dot files, and provide a structured system for user- and system-wide configuration information. It's flexible enough to permit configuration to be stored on a remote server as well as a local machine, enabling the Linux desktop to scale on a network level. For those familiar with the Microsoft Windows registry, GConf has some similarities, but is simpler and more focused in purpose.

GConf provides a a tree-structured repository of keys and values. Data types that can be stored include integers, strings, floating point numbers, boolean values, and lists of any one of these types. Client applications may get and set these values. Additionally, they can register to be alerted of changes in the values. This way, the GNOME desktop system is "instant apply" with regard to system preferences. Rather than requiring restarts, changes in preferences are shown immediately in applications.

This lab demonstrates the main concepts in working with GConf, including the provision of *GConf schemas* for documenting the keys that an application uses. GConf is not available under Windows or Mac OS X.

How do I do that?

A useful tool when writing applications that interact with GConf is *gconf-editor*, a graphical tool that allows interactive viewing and editing of settings. Figure 5-6 shows *gconf-editor* being used to view some of the settings from the *Epiphany* web browser. Start up *gconf-editor* and browse around some of the settings in the system.

There is also a command line tool, *gconftool-2*, that offers complete control over GConf. Example 5-4 shows the command line equivalent of Figure 5-6. Note that lists are shown in square brackets.

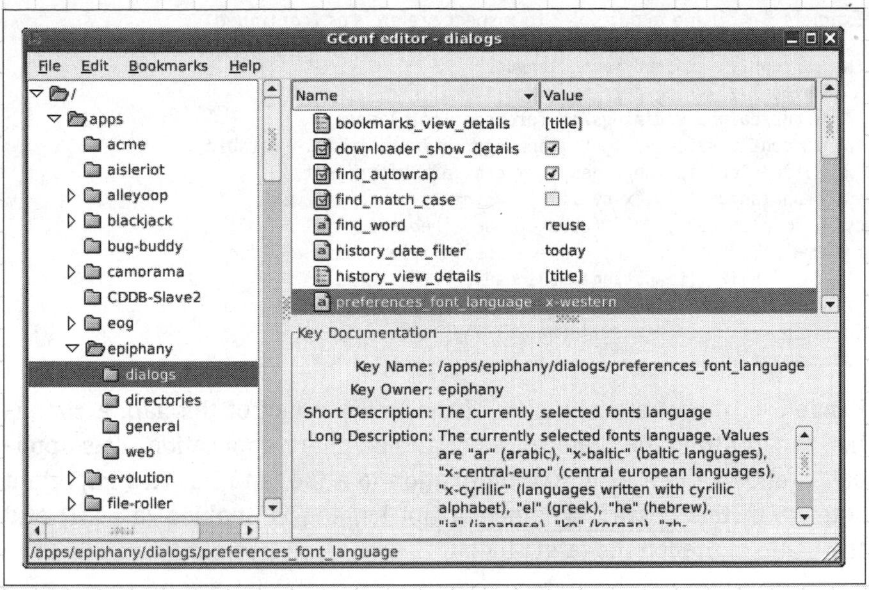

Figure 5-6. Editing preferences with gconf-editor

Example 5-4. Using gconftool-2 to inspect preferences

```
$ gconftool-2 -a /apps/epiphany/dialogs
 find_match_case = false
 print_file = /home/saag/edmundd/grid.ps
 print_on = 0
 print_date = false
 print_orientation = 0
 print_all_pages = 0
 print_page_url = false
 print_right_margin = 10
 find_autowrap = true
 print_top_margin = 10
 print_page_title = false
 history_view_details = [title]
 bookmarks_view_details = [title]
 preferences_font_language = x-western
 print_left_margin = 10
 print_bottom_margin = 10
 history_date_filter = today
 print_color = 0
 print_page_numbers = false
 print_paper = A4
 downloader_show_details = true
 print_printer = lpr
 print_from_page = 1
 print_to_page = 1
 find_word = Edd
$ gconftool-2 --short-docs \
    /apps/epiphany/dialogs/preferences_font_language
```

Example 5-4. Using gconftool-2 to inspect preferences (continued)

```
The currently selected fonts language
$ gconftool-2 --long-docs \
    /apps/epiphany/dialogs/preferences_font_language
The currently selected fonts language. Values are "ar" (arabic),
"x-baltic" (baltic languages), "x-central-euro" (central
european languages), "x-cyrillic" (languages written with
cyrillic alphabet), "el" (greek), "he" (hebrew), "ja"
(japanese), "ko" (korean), "zh-CN" (simplified chinese), "th"
(thai), "zh-TW" (traditional chinese), "tr" (turkish),
"x-unicode" (other languages), "x-western" (languages written
in latin script), "x-tamil" (tamil) and "x-devanagari"
(devanagari).
```

Figure 5-7 shows a screenshot of the end-product of this lab, a simplified excerpt from the preferences of an imaginary application. This application allows the user to log information to a file, and has two important settings in this regard: whether or not logging is enabled (a bool) and the name of the log file (a string).

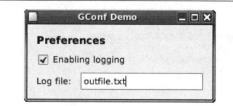

Figure 5-7. GConf client application

Create the interface from Figure 5-7 using *Glade*:

1. Create a new GTK+ project. Add a new Window from the GTK+ Basic palette. All the widgets will be from this palette.

2. Add a vertical box (VBox) to the new window. Set the number of rows to 3. Using the Widget Tree, select the new vertical box, and use the Properties editor to change the spacing to 6 and border width to 12. Select the Packing tab and set Expand to No.

3. Add a new label to the top space in the vertical box. Use the Properties editor to set the label to <span size="larger" weight="bold"> Preferences</span>. Set Use Markup to "Yes", and X Align to 0.0.

4. Add a new check button to the middle space in the vertical box. Use the Properties editor to change its name to logging and its label to "Enable logging"

5. Add a new horizontal box to the bottom space in the vertical box. Set the number of columns to 2. Select the horizontal box using the Widget Tree, and use the Properties editor to change the spacing to 12.

6. Add a new label to the left side of the new horizontal box, adjusting its X Align to 0.0 and label to "Log file:". To the right side, add a new text entry. Use the Properties editor to name the text entry filename.

7. Finally, hook up the event handlers. Select the check button, and navigate to the Signals tab of the Properties editor. Click the ... button by the Signal entry and select the toggled signal. The text on_logging_toggled will appear in the Handler entry. Click Add to register the handler. Repeat the same process for the filename text entry, this time choosing the activate signal. Save your Glade project.

The Activated event on a text entry is raised when a user hits enter.

The code to create the interface and manage the communication with GConf is shown in Example 5-5. Compile and run it, including as a resource the *.glade* file used for the interface and bringing in the *gconf-sharp* package for the GConf namespace.

```
$ mcs Main.cs -resource:demo.glade,demo.glade \
    -pkg:gtk-sharp -pkg:gconf-sharp -pkg:glade-sharp
$ mono Main.exe
```

Example 5-5. GConf client program: 03-gconf/Main.cs

```
// 05-advdesktop/03-gconf
using System;
using Gtk;
using Glade;
using GConf;

class GConfTest {
  GConf.Client client;
  static string KEY_BASE = "/apps/monodn-demo";
  static string KEY_FILENAME = KEY_BASE + "/filename";
  static string KEY_LOGGING = KEY_BASE + "/logging";

  [Widget] Gtk.Entry filename;
  [Widget] Gtk.CheckButton logging;

  public static void Main(string[] args)
  {
    new GConfTest (args);
  }

  public GConfTest (string[] args)
  {
    Application.Init ();
    Glade.XML gxml = new Glade.XML (null, "demo.glade",
      "window1", null);
    gxml.Autoconnect (this);
```

Example 5-5. GConf client program: 03-gconf/Main.cs (continued)

```
    client = new GConf.Client ();
    GuiFromGConf ();
    client.AddNotify (KEY_BASE,
        new NotifyEventHandler (GConf_Changed));
    Application.Run ();
}

void GuiFromGConf ()
{
    try {
        filename.Text = (string) client.Get (KEY_FILENAME);
        logging.Active = (bool) client.Get (KEY_LOGGING);
    } catch (GConf.NoSuchKeyException e) {
        // insert reasonable default here
    } catch (System.InvalidCastException e) {
        // restore sanity
    }
}

public void on_window1_delete_event (object o, EventArgs args)
{
    Application.Quit ();
}

public void on_logging_toggled (object o, EventArgs args)
{
    client.Set (KEY_LOGGING, logging.Active);
}

public void on_filename_activate (object o, EventArgs args)
{
    client.Set (KEY_FILENAME, filename.Text);
}

public void GConf_Changed (object sender, NotifyEventArgs args)
{
    GuiFromGConf ();
}
}
```

Don't forget, all the examples are available from the book's web site.

While running the example, start up *gconf-editor* and navigate to the keys used by the example, as shown in Figure 5-8. Toggle the text box and alter the file name text entry. The changes are reflected in the *gconf-editor* window. Try doing it the other way round. Changes are then reflected in the example program window.

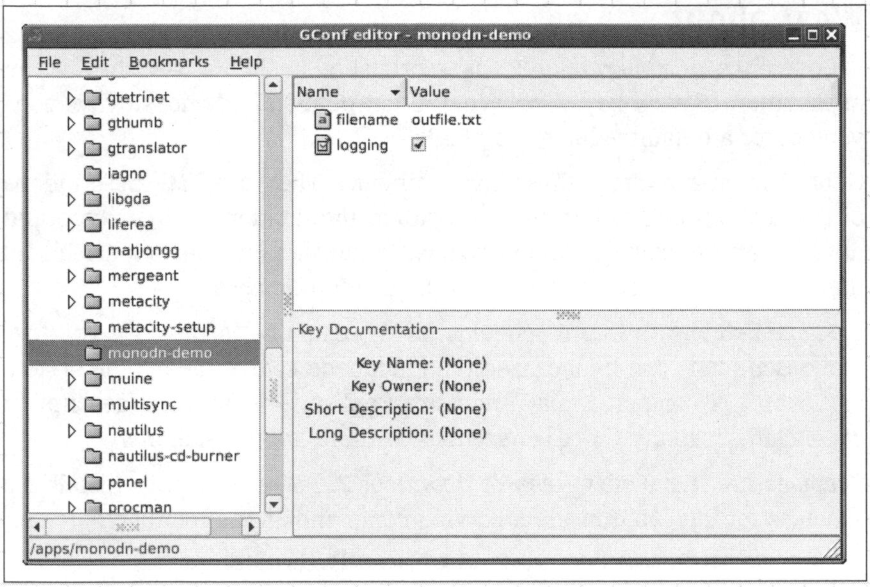

Figure 5-8. Preferences in gconf-editor

How it works

The GConf.Client class provides all the functionality needed to interact with GConf. Specifically, the Set method can be used to set a key, with its second parameter being of one of the types GConf can store. If the type to be stored is a list, then an array should be used. For example, to set an array of strings:

```
client.Set (MY_KEY, new string[ ] {"a", "b", "c" });
```

Using Get to retrieve key values is equally straightforward. The return type is object, so a cast must be used to obtain the desired type. Beware that, because GConf is an open system and any application can change its contents, there is the possibility that the type returned will not be the type expected. In this case a System.InvalidCastException exception will be thrown. The other possible exception, System.InvalidCastException, should also be expected and catered for.

Receiving notifications from GConf is set up through the AddNotify method. This sets up a notification event to be raised whenever the specified subtree is changed. Example 5-5 sets up the notification for the /apps/monodn-demo subtree. One notification is sent per change. The NotifyEventArgs contains the new key and value. Example 5-5 is lazy in that it updates the entire interface when a change happens, rather than simply the part affected by the change.

GConf lists can only contain the same type. They're more like arrays, really.

What about ...

...Preference documentation? The screenshot in Figure 5-6 showed an explanation of each key. Also, what about defaults? It's not always convenient for a default value to be blank.

GConf schemas address these two problems. They are XML descriptions of the keys an application uses, providing information on their type and defaults, and human readable documentation. Applications should install their GConf schemas as part of their installation process.

Example 5-6 shows GConf schemas for the example in this lab. The textual descriptions can be localized. The language code C means the system locale and is conventionally American English. The schema description can include as many <locale> sections as there are translations.

Schemas are installed by use of *gconftool-2*. For example, to install the schemas for this lab, run the following command as the root user:

```
# GCONF_CONFIG_SOURCE="" gconftool-2 --makefile-install-rule \
    monodn-demo.schemas
```

This will install the schemas to the system's default GConf installation. Run *gconf-editor* again, and the documentation will appear, as in Figure 5-9. To restore the default value specified in the schema, right-click on the key, and select **Unset key** from the menu that appears.

Example 5-6. Example GConf schemas: 03-gconf/monodn-demo.schemas

```
<gconfschemafile>
  <schemalist>
    <schema>
      <key>/schemas/apps/monodn-demo/filename</key>
      <applyto>/apps/monodn-demo/filename</applyto>
      <owner>monodn-demo</owner>
      <type>string</type>
      <default>logfile.txt</default>
      <locale name="C">
        <short>Filename of log file</short>
        <long>Debugging and informational messages
        are written to the file named by this
        key.  Logging is controlled by the
        'logging' key.</long>
      </locale>
    </schema>

    <schema>
      <key>/schemas/apps/monodn-demo/logging</key>
      <applyto>/apps/monodn-demo/logging</applyto>
      <owner>monodn-demo</owner>
      <type>bool</type>
      <default>0</default>
```

Example 5-6. Example GConf schemas: 03-gconf/monodn-demo.schemas (continued)

```
      <locale name="C">
        <short>Logging enabled.</short>
        <long>If set to true, this key enables
        logging of debugging and informational
        messages to the file specified by the
        'filename' key.
        </long>
      </locale>
    </schema>
  </schemalist>
</gconfschemafile>
```

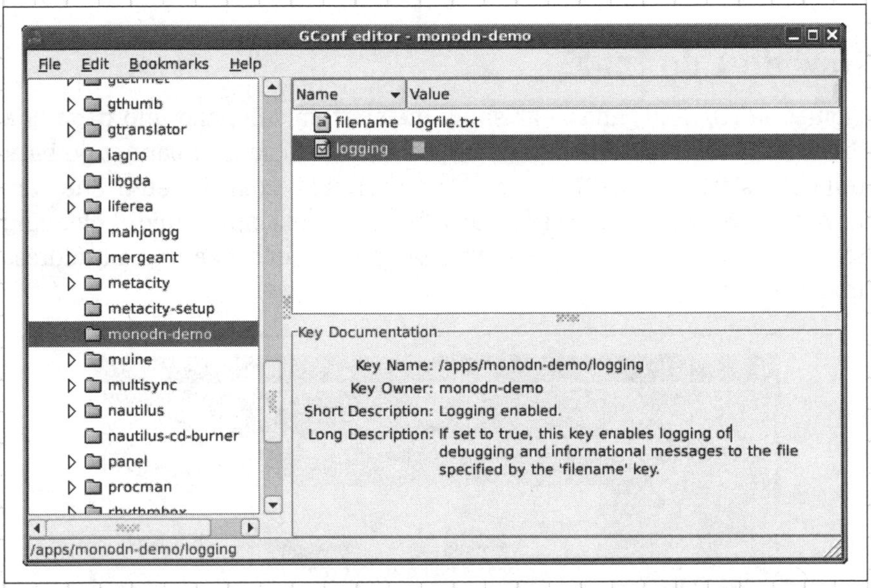

Figure 5-9. Schema documentation in gconf-editor

Guide the User with Druids

When a program is used for the first time it often needs to collect configuration information from the user. A popular technique for doing this is a succession of dialogs, presented in the same window, with explanatory text. On the Microsoft Windows platform, these are known as "wizards." The Gnome API offers similar functionality, called "druids."

It's poor word play on "wizards," but druids are handy for user-friendly configuration.

Every druid has a beginning, middle, and end. The first page of a druid welcomes the user, explaining the process she is about to work through. The final page tells her that she is free to go and thank you for configuring the application. The intermediate pages are where the work gets done. They contain a variety of questions and widgets into which the user inputs the responses. By using the Back and Forward buttons, the user can revisit any page in the druid.

To aid the creation of a consistent interface, the druid APIs have convenience methods for constructing druid pages. This means less code to write, and a more familiar look-and-feel for the user. Druid pages are customizable for color and artwork, so an application can still provide its own branding.

This lab creates a simple druid and demonstrates ways in which an application can validate a user's responses.

How do I do that?

Figures 5-10, 5-11, and 5-12 show the start, middle, and end page of a druid. Note the differences between each stage. The user cannot go back from the start, and neither can she go forward from the end! She can, however, cancel the process at any time. The example druid, belonging to some hypothetical email-sending program, requests an email address from the user.

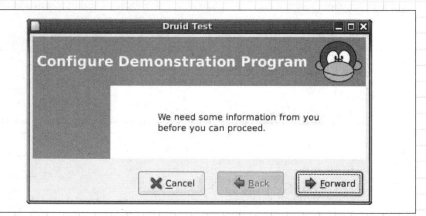

Figure 5-10. The start page of the druid

The Gnome.Druid class itself is a container for Gnome.DruidPage classes. The subclasses Gnome.DruidPageEdge provides implementation of the first and final pages, and Gnome.DruidPageStandard of the intermediate pages. Example 5-7 shows the code necessary to implement the example druid. Compile and run it with:

```
$ mcs Main.cs -pkg:gtk-sharp -pkg:gnome-sharp \
                -resource:monkey.png,monkey.png
$ mono Main.exe
```

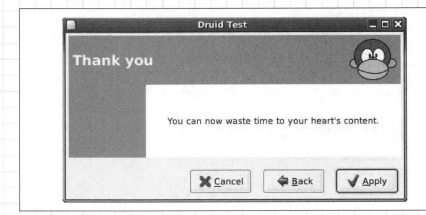

Figure 5-11. Intermediate druid page

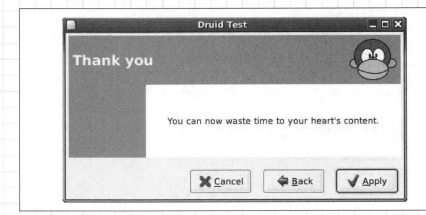

Figure 5-12. The finish page of the druid

Example 5-7. Druid program: 04-druids/Main.cs

```
// 05-advdesktop/04-druids
using System;
using Gtk;
using Gdk;
using Gnome;

class DruidDemo {
  Gnome.Druid druid;
    DruidPageEdge page1, page3;
    DruidPageStandard page2;

  Gdk.Pixbuf monkey;
  Gtk.Entry email;
  Gnome.App druidapp;

  public static void Main(string[ ] args)
```

Example 5-7. Druid program: 04-druids/Main.cs (continued)

```csharp
  {
    new DruidDemo (args);
  }

  public DruidDemo (string[] args)
  {
    Gnome.Program program = new Gnome.Program ("druid-demo", "0.1",
      Modules.UI, args);
    monkey = new Gdk.Pixbuf (null, "monkey.png");
    druid = new Druid ();
    page1 = new DruidPageEdge (
      EdgePosition.Start, true,
      "Configure Demonstration Program",
      "We need some information from you\nbefore you can proceed.",
      monkey, null, null );

    page2 = new DruidPageStandard (
      "Email configuration", monkey, null);

    email = new Gtk.Entry ();
    page2.AppendItem ("_Email address:",
      email,
      "The address you want us keep on file for you.");

    page2.Prepared += Page_Prepared;
    email.Changed += Entry_Changed;

    page3 = new DruidPageEdge (
      EdgePosition.Finish, true,
      "Thank you",
      "You can now waste time to your heart's content.",
      monkey, null, null );

    page3.FinishClicked += Finish_Druid;

    druid.AppendPage (page1);
    druid.AppendPage (page2);
    druid.AppendPage (page3);

    druidapp = new Gnome.App ("druid-demo", "Druid Test");
    druidapp.Contents = druid;
    druidapp.ShowAll ();

    druid.Cancel += Cancel_Druid;
    druidapp.DeleteEvent += Window_Deleted;

    program.Run ();
  }

  void SetButtons ()
  {
    if (email.Text.Length == 0) {
```

Example 5-7. Druid program: 04-druids/Main.cs (continued)

```
      druid.SetButtonsSensitive (true, false, true, false);
    } else {
      druid.SetButtonsSensitive (true, true, true, false);
    }
  }

  void Entry_Changed (object o, EventArgs args)
  {
    SetButtons ();
  }

  void Page_Prepared (object o, PreparedArgs args)
  {
    SetButtons ();
  }

  void Cancel_Druid (object o, EventArgs args)
  {
    System.Console.WriteLine ("Cancelled.");
    Application.Quit ();
  }

  void Finish_Druid (object o, FinishClickedArgs args)
  {
    druidapp.Hide ();
    System.Console.WriteLine ("Got email address {0}", email.Text);
    Application.Quit ();
  }

  void Window_Deleted (object o, DeleteEventArgs args)
  {
    Application.Quit ();
  }
}
```

Run the example and work through the druid. Note that, as shown in Figure 5-13, the Forward on the middle page is grayed out until data is actually entered into the email address box. Exercise the code paths in the example by using the Cancel button, as well as by following the druid through to the end.

How it works

Each druid "edge" (start and finish) page has a set of fixed visual characteristics: title, logo at the top-right, and two "watermark" images that can be used at the top-left and bottom-left of the druid inside the colored border. Intermediate pages only have the logo and bottom-left watermark. All of these are set with the constructor for each druid page. Other

The watermark images look best when feathered into the background border color.

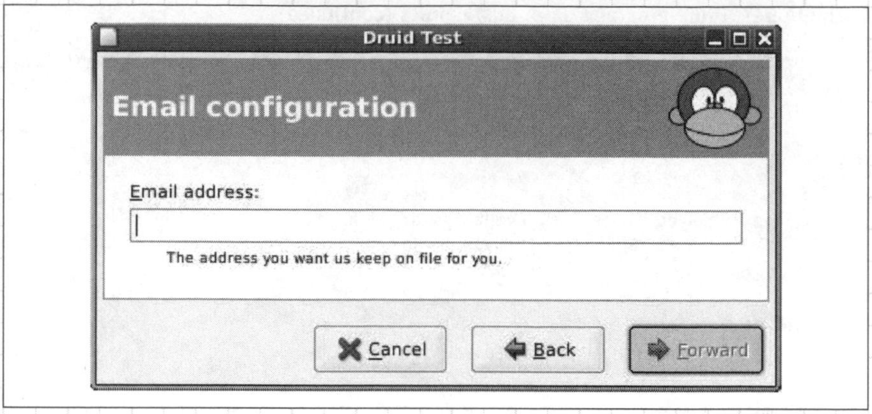

Figure 5-13. Intermediate druid page with grayed out Forward button

visual characteristics can be accessed as properties of the druid page object. Once constructed, add each page to the druid with Druid. AppendPage.

There is little more to creating the edge pages than calling the DruidPageEdge constructor. For the intermediate pages, DruidPageStandard, widgets must be added in order to get useful input from the user. The widget layout of DruidPageStandard creates an internal VBox into which you can add subordinate widgets. Use the AppendItem method to add each widget, accompanied by the question text and an explanatory description. The example uses a simple text entry, but more complex widgets such as a set of radio buttons or treeview would also work.

The Druid.ShowHelp property controls the appearance of the Help button.

The application exerts control over the druid completion process by handling particular events. The Druid class has two events for features that are constant over every page: Cancel and Help (not used in the example.) The rest of the events must be handled for each constituent DruidPage. These can be one of BackClicked, CancelClicked, FinishClicked, NextClicked and Prepared. All of these should be self-explanatory, apart from Prepared, which is raised immediately prior to the druid page being shown. It can be used for any custom initialization that you require.

Validate early, validate often. It's always better not to let the user make a mistake than to waste your time and his by telling him later.

The sensitivity of each of the buttons at the bottom of the druid page is controlled by the Druid.SetButtonsSensitive method. By using this together with the Prepared event on the page2 page, the example application prevents the Next button being used until the email address is filled in. Clearly, more complex validation is possible using this technique.

What about ...

...Configuration processes that aren't linear? Consider that some choice the user makes dictates the appropriateness of subsequent druid pages. For instance, if a user indicates he doesn't want a program to send email on his behalf, the email configuration druid page can be skipped. This can be implemented by subclassing the DruidStandardPage and overriding the Next method. This method normally causes the next page to be displayed. Nonlinear behavior can be created by using the overridden Next to set the required page using the Druid.Page property and returning true to indicate that it has handled the change of pages. A similar approach must also then be taken to the Back method to make sure the interface doesn't get into an inconsistent situation.

Perform Asynchronous Operations

Keep the interface responsive by performing long-running operations asynchronously.

All of the Gtk# labs so far have involved very little computation that occurs within the main loop of the program. Consider what would happen if an application had to perform a 5-second long computation in response to a button click. The obvious way to do this would be to call the computation from the handler for the Gtk.Button.Clicked event. While the computation was taking place, the user interface would be unresponsive, because control would not have yet returned to the main loop. Furthermore, if the window needed redrawing, this would be delayed too. The result is ugly and unprofessional.

So how to solve this problem? There are two possible approaches. If the operation can be broken down into small enough steps without tangibly affecting the responsiveness of the interface, a method can be added which is called periodically by the main loop. If an operation doesn't break down so easily, it can be executed in an alternate thread.

There are advantages and drawbacks to each approach. Avoiding the gratuitous use of threads is always a good idea, as they introduce new possibilities for bugs, such as deadlock, and can generally increase the complexity of the debugging process. On the other hand, breaking up computation into slices small enough to execute in idle moments on the main thread can make code much more complex to read and write.

This lab introduces both approaches, demonstrating how to set up the execution of code on the main event loop, and how to use Mono's threads and still play nice with Gtk# toolkit.

*Calling
Application.Run or
Gnome.Program.
Run turns over
control to the
main event loop.*

How do I do that?

The main event loop in a Gtk# program usually does very little except listen out for user interactions and requests for redraws from the windowing system. Applications can give it more to do by registering either a Glib.IdleHandler or a Glib.TimeoutHandler. The names of these handlers suggest their function. An IdleHandler is executed as soon as the main loop has nothing to do. A TimeoutHandler is executed as soon as possible after a specified time period has elapsed.

Both these handlers are parameterless methods that return a bool value. If one of them returns true then that handler remains in place, to be called again at the next idle moment or after the appropriate time interval. If one of them returns false, that handler is removed. Example 5-8 illustrates both concepts in an application that counts down ten seconds and then quits. The methods for manipulating the main loop come from the Glib namespace, which is included by the *gtk-sharp* package. Compile and run the example:

```
$ mcs Main.cs -pkg:gtk-sharp
$ mono Main.exe
```

Example 5-8. Timed events: 05-async/Main.cs

```
// 05-advdesktop/05-async
using System;
using Gtk;
using GLib;

class TimerDemo {
  Gtk.Label count;
  int i;

  public static void Main(string[ ] args)
  {
    Application.Init ();
    TimerDemo demo = new TimerDemo ();
    Application.Run ();
  }

  public TimerDemo ()
  {
    count = new Label ("Initializing.");
    Window w = new Window ("Timer demo");
    w.SetDefaultSize (200, 100);
    w.Add (count);
    w.ShowAll ();
    GLib.Idle.Add (new GLib.IdleHandler (this.Run_Once));
  }
```

Example 5-8. Timed events: 05-async/Main.cs (continued)

```
bool Run_Once ()
{
  i = 10;
  System.Console.WriteLine ("Initializing counter to {0}.", i);
  count.Text = String.Format ("Initializing counter to {0}.", i);
  GLib.Timeout.Add (1000, new GLib.TimeoutHandler (Time_Out));
  return false; // don't call me again
}

bool Time_Out ()
{
  i--;
  System.Console.WriteLine ("Count is {0}.", i);
  count.Text = String.Format ("Quitting in {0} seconds.", i);
  if (i == 0) {
    System.Console.WriteLine ("Exiting.");
    Application.Quit ();
  }
  return true; // call me again
}
}
```

The example needs very little explanation. As the program starts, it sets up the Run_Once method to run in the idle loop. When Run_Once is called, it sets up the Time_Out method to execute as soon as possible after 1000 milliseconds, i.e. one second, has elapsed. Run_Once returns false, so it is not invoked again. Time_Out checks the internal counter i, updates the GUI, and causes the program to quit when the counter reaches 0.

What is more interesting than the example itself is to outline some use cases for this technique.

When the main loop decides what to do next, IdleHandlers take lower priority than user interface redrawing or event processing.

Animation
> The timeout handler can be used to change frames in an animated image.

Polling
> Not all data sources will raise events to which handlers can be attached. A regular timeout could, for example, check an input stream to see if any more data is available, and then call an appropriate handler.

Timeouts
> There are many scenarios in which an operation may be terminated if it has not succeeded in a certain time, such as network connections or, more entertainingly, in quiz games.

Responsive interfaces
> If a computation performed as a result of a user interface event is deferred until the main loop is idle with an IdleHandler, it allows

Gtk# to finish drawing the interface before computation begins. Otherwise, irritating visual artifacts may occur such as a button not "coming up" as soon as the mouse button is released.

Background computation

If a computation is not time critical, an `IdleHandler` can be used to perform it in the background. An example might be indexing a store of email.

If for some reason an application cannot be written just using the main Gtk# loop, then you'll need to turn to threads. The next example demonstrates an application that uses threads to enable processing to continue while a long-running operation takes place. Threads are discussed in detail in "Multitask with Threads" in Chapter 3.

Figures 5-14 and 5-15 show an image viewing application that fetches an image from the web using HTTP and displays it in the main window. The button at the bottom is there to demonstrate that the interface remains responsive while the image is being fetched. The second screenshot shows what happens if the image could not be displayed for any reason.

Figure 5-14. Successfully loaded image

Example 5-9 shows the code necessary to set up the image fetching process in a separate thread from the main Gtk# event loop. A delegate is used to refer to the image-fetching method, and the `BeginInvoke` method of the delegate used to kick off the image fetch in another thread. The program can be compiled and run conventionally:

```
$ mcs Main.cs -pkg:gtk-sharp
$ mono Main.exe
```

Figure 5-15. Failed load

Run the program and verify that the cute image from the O'Reilly home page does indeed load, or change the URL in the source code to an image of your choice.

Example 5-9. Threading web fetch: 05-delegate/Main.cs

```
// 05-advdesktop/05-delegate
using System;
using System.Threading;
using System.Runtime.Remoting.Messaging;
using System.Net;
using System.IO;

using Gtk;
using Gdk;

delegate Gdk.Pixbuf PixbufFetcher (string url);

class ImageFetcher {
  public static void Main(string[] args)
  {
    Gdk.Threads.Init ();
    Application.Init ();
    ImageFetcher f = new ImageFetcher ();
    Application.Run ();
  }

  Gtk.Image img;
  static string tmpfile = "pixbuf.tmp";

  public ImageFetcher ()
  {
    Gtk.Window w = new Gtk.Window ("Image Fetcher");
    img = new Gtk.Image ();
    img.SetSizeRequest (200, 200);
```

Example 5-9. *Threading web fetch: 05-delegate/Main.cs (continued)*

```csharp
      Button b = new Button ("Click me");
      VBox v = new VBox ();
      w.Add (v);
      v.Add (img);
      v.PackEnd (b, false, false, 0);
      w.ShowAll ();
      w.DeleteEvent += Window_Delete;

      PixbufFetcher fetcher = new PixbufFetcher (FetchPixbuf);
      AsyncCallback ac = new AsyncCallback (DisplayImage);
      string url = "http://www.oreilly.com/images/oreilly/oreilly_header1.gif";
      IAsyncResult ar1 = fetcher.BeginInvoke (url, ac, url);
    }

    Gdk.Pixbuf FetchPixbuf (string url)
    {
      Gdk.Pixbuf ret = null;
      try {
        HttpWebRequest req = (HttpWebRequest) WebRequest.Create (url);
        WebResponse resp = req.GetResponse ();
        BinaryReader input = new BinaryReader (resp.GetResponseStream ());
        BinaryWriter output = new BinaryWriter (
          File.Open (tmpfile, FileMode.Create));

        System.Console.WriteLine ("Request made OK.");
        byte [] image = input.ReadBytes ((int) resp.ContentLength);
        output.Write (image);
        output.Close ();
        input.Close ();

        Gdk.Threads.Enter ();
        ret = new Gdk.Pixbuf (tmpfile);
        Gdk.Threads.Leave ();
      } catch (WebException e) {
        System.Console.WriteLine ("Failed\n{0}", e);
      }
      return ret;
    }

    void DisplayImage (IAsyncResult ar)
    {
      PixbufFetcher fetcher = (PixbufFetcher)
        ((AsyncResult) ar).AsyncDelegate;
      Gdk.Threads.Enter ();
      Gdk.Pixbuf buf = fetcher.EndInvoke (ar);
      if (buf != null) {
        img.Pixbuf = buf;
      } else {
        img.SetFromStock (Stock.DialogError, IconSize.Dialog);
      }
      Gdk.Threads.Leave ();
    }
```

Example 5-9. Threading web fetch: 05-delegate/Main.cs (continued)

```
  void Window_Delete (object o, DeleteEventArgs d)
  {
    Application.Quit ();
  }
}
```

How it works

The threaded example merits further explanation. The method to fetch the image, FetchPixbuf, is wrapped as a delegate. It is then invoked asynchronously in a new thread using the Delegate.BeginInvoke method, which, in this instance, takes three arguments. The first is the argument to FetchPixbuf itself, the URL to fetch. The second is an object of type AsyncCallback, which is required to deal with the return value of FetchPixbuf. The final argument is an arbitrary object used for purposes of storing state. It can be any object, just not null. When FetchPixbuf is finished, DisplayImage is executed.

BeginInvoke and EndInvoke are created by the compiler, so you won't find them in the API reference for the Delegate class.

Using EndInvoke, DisplayImage retrieves the return value of the image-fetching method FetchPixbuf and updates the user interface to display the picture. If an error has occurred and the image is null, a stock error image is displayed.

Aside from the rash of indirection and casting, there's nothing much new over and above what is shown in "Multitask with Threads" in Chapter 3. There is only one mysterious new addition, the calls to Gdk.Threads. Enter and Gdk.Threads.Leave. These are required because the functions from the Gdk part of the Gtk# toolkit are not threadsafe. Any method which uses the Gdk functionality from a thread other than the main event loop must wrap its access similarly. In practice this means all methods from Gtk# except for those in the Glib namespace. An alternative to locking up Gdk in this way is to use the thread to add a one-shot IdleHandler, which would be executed in the main loop when it became idle. This may be preferable to always having to remember to add the Enter/Leave code.

Try removing the Gdk.Threads. Enter and Leave from the example and run it a few times. Deadlock!

Where to learn more

Asynchronous programming, whether using threads or cooperative sharing of the main event loop thread, can be a complex topic. There's often no substitute for bitter experience! The .NET documentation on Microsoft's MSDN site does contain several useful articles on thread-based programming however. The easiest way to find these is to visit *http://msdn.microsoft.com/* and enter "Asynchronous Programming" into the MSDN library search box. For more information on the use of idle handlers and timeout loops, one of the most educational things to do is to download and study some of the many open source programs that use GTK+ from *http://ftp.gnome.org/pub/GNOME/desktop/*. Although these use C, the principles of using the main event loop can be seen clearly.

Render HTML

There are many reasons why an application might need to display an HTML document. An email client, for instance, might use it to display rich-text mails. A personal organizer program may use an embedded browser window to present server-driven functionality such as mapping.

Get rich text output by using a web browser component.

Within Mono, there is support for two different HTML display widgets, GtkHTML and Gecko. Gecko is the rendering component from the undisputed leader in open source web browsers, *Mozilla*. Its implementation of modern web standards is unmatched. GtkHTML is a less modern component, without support for technologies such as Cascading Style Sheets, but possessing the advantage of being small and lightweight.

This lab demonstrates how to use the Gecko browser component to provide web browsing functionality in a Gtk# application. (Having done the duty of mentioning GtkHTML's existence, it is better to consign it to the past!)

How do I do that?

The Gecko browser component is implemented in the *gecko-sharp* assembly. If MonoDevelop has been installed according to the instructions in Chapter 1, then this assembly will be available. If not, visit the MonoDevelop web site at *http://www.monodevelop.com/*, follow the "Installation" link, and use the instructions given there for installing *gtkmozembed* and *gecko-sharp*.

The Gecko.WebControl class implements the web browsing widget. Figure 5-16 shows a miniature web browsing application, with just a text entry widget for the URL, and the WebControl itself. Example 5-10 shows the code needed to implement the mini-browser. When compiling, the *gecko-sharp* package is needed for the Gecko namespace.

```
$ mcs Main.cs -pkg:gtk-sharp -pkg:gecko-sharp
$ mono Main.exe
```

Figure 5-16. Loaded web page

Example 5-10. Embedding the Gecko browser: 06-gecko/Main.cs

```
// 05-advdesktop/06-gecko
using System;
using Gtk;
using Gecko;

class Browser {
  public static void Main(string[ ] args)
  {
    Application.Init ();
    Browser b = new Browser ();
    Application.Run ();
  }

  Gecko.WebControl webctl;
  Gtk.Entry urlbox;

  static string greeting =
    "<html><head><title>My Browser</title></head>" +
    "<body><h1>Hello!</h1><p>Type a URL in the box " +
    "and press enter.</p></body></html>";

  public Browser ()
  {
    Window w = new Window ("Browser test");
    VBox v = new VBox ();
    w.Add (v);
```

Example 5-10. Embedding the Gecko browser: 06-gecko/Main.cs (continued)

```
        urlbox = new Entry ();
        urlbox.Activated += Load_Url;
        webctl = new WebControl ();
        webctl.SetSizeRequest (450, 350);
        v.PackStart (urlbox, false, false, 0);
        v.PackEnd (webctl, true, true, 0);
        w.ShowAll ();
        w.DeleteEvent += Window_Delete;
        webctl.RenderData (greeting, "file:///tmp", "text/html");
    }

    void Load_Url (object o, EventArgs args)
    {
        webctl.LoadUrl (urlbox.Text);
    }

    void Window_Delete (object o, DeleteEventArgs args)
    {
        Application.Quit ();
    }
}
```

Compile and run the example, and test it out by entering a URL into the box at the top. Notice that when the application starts up, it has the welcome message as shown in Figure 5-17. The message is generated by using the web control's ability to render data generated dynamically using WebControl.RenderData.

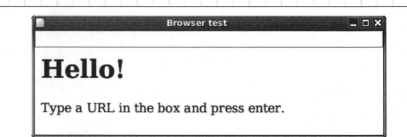

Figure 5-17. Browser startup message

What about ...

...The rest of the story? There's a lot more power to the WebControl widget than is shown in the example. The secret to customizing the behavior of the widget lies in handling the events it raises. Many of these events are used for conventional web browser purposes. For instance, the LinkMessage and JsStatus events are raised whenever the browser would normally want to write something into a status line.

One common requirement is to control the navigation process. The OpenUri event is raised when the user attempts to navigate to a new page. The containing application then performs some vetting on the potential destination, with a handler looking something like this:

```
webctl.OpenUri += Open_Uri;

...

void Open_Uri (object o, Gecko.OpenUriArgs args)
{
        if (SomeTestOrOther (args.AURI)) {
                // it's ok to visit
                args.RetVal = true;
        } else {
                // it's not ok to visit
                args.RetVal = false;
        }
}
```

Another common scenario is reporting the progress of loading a document:

```
webctl.Progress += Load_Progress;

...

void Load_Progress (object o, Gecko.ProgressArgs args)
{
        SetSomeIndicator (args.Curprogress, args.Maxprogress);
}
```

Where to learn more

API reference documentation for the Gecko namespace is available from Monodoc, under the section "Mozilla Libraries."

Provide Help Files

The GNOME desktop environment has a full-featured user help environment, delivered through the help browser *yelp*. Applications can activate the help browser through API calls from the Gnome.Help class. This lab demonstrates how to write user documentation for an application, and integrate it with the Help button and menu items in the user interface.

While a good interface guides the user, help is always needed.

This lab will not work on Windows. On other platforms it requires the GNOME desktop environment to be installed.

How do I do that?

Figure 5-18 shows a screenshot of the small application to be equipped with help documentation.

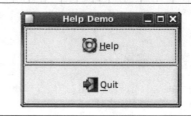

Figure 5-18. Help demo application window

The standard format for help documentation within GNOME is the Doc-Book XML DTD. DocBook is a well-established schema for technical documentation, supported by a wealth of tools and tutorial material. If the GNOME desktop, including the *yelp* help browser, is installed, then the DocBook DTDs will have been installed as a dependency. They can also be downloaded separately from *http://www.docbook.org/*.

Although DocBook can be written simply with a conventional text editor, it speeds up writing if XML-aware tools are used. Most popular text editors have XML editing modes or alternatively a dedicated XML editor such as *conglomerate*, available from *http://www.conglomerate.org/*. You can perform a syntax check on an XML document by using the *xmllint* tool from the *libxml2* toolkit, generally available as part of Linux systems and downloadable from *http://www.xmlsoft.org/*.

Example 5-11 shows a brief but meaningful DocBook file documenting the example application. Metadata such as the document's author and copyright information is placed in the `<articleinfo>` section at the top. A `<sect1>` is used to contain each main section of the documentation and will show up in the table of contents as depicted in Figure 5-19. Within each main section, `<sect2>` tags are used to contain the major subsections. If desired, `<sect3>` can be used within them. It is best to keep documentation as straightforward as possible, to make it easier for the user to read.

Think of the &app; and &appversion; shortcuts in the same way you would a #define in C.

Example 5-11. DocBook article: 07-help/gnome/help/monodn-help/C/monodn-help.xml

```
<?xml version="1.0"?>
<!DOCTYPE article PUBLIC "-//OASIS//DTD DocBook XML V4.1.2//EN"
  "http://www.oasis-open.org/docbook/xml/4.1.2/docbookx.dtd"
```

Example 5-11. DocBook article: 07-help/gnome/help/monodn-help/C/monodn-help.xml
(continued)

```
[
<!ENTITY app "Help Demo">
<!ENTITY appversion "0.1">
]>
<article id="index" lang="en">
  <articleinfo>
    <title>&app; Manual</title>
    <copyright>
      <year>2004</year>
      <holder>O'Reilly Media, Inc.</holder>
    </copyright>
    <publisher>
      <publishername>O'Reilly Media, Inc.</publishername>
    </publisher>
    <authorgroup>
      <author>
        <firstname>Edd</firstname>
        <surname>Dumbill</surname>
        <affiliation>
          <address>
            <email>edd@usefulinc.com</email>
          </address>
        </affiliation>
      </author>
    </authorgroup>
  </articleinfo>
  <sect1 id="intro">
    <title>Introduction</title>
    <sect2 id="about">
      <title>About &app;</title>
      <para>
          &app; demonstrates the use of context sensitive help
          in GNOME applications.
      </para>
    </sect2>
  </sect1>
  <sect1 id="using">
    <title>Using &app;</title>
    <para>
        Close the window or hit the "quit" button to quit
        &app;
    </para>
  </sect1>
</article>
```

It is often useful to preview the documentation independently of the target application. This can be done by running *yelp* from the command line, passing the filename as an argument:

```
$ yelp monodn-help.xml
```

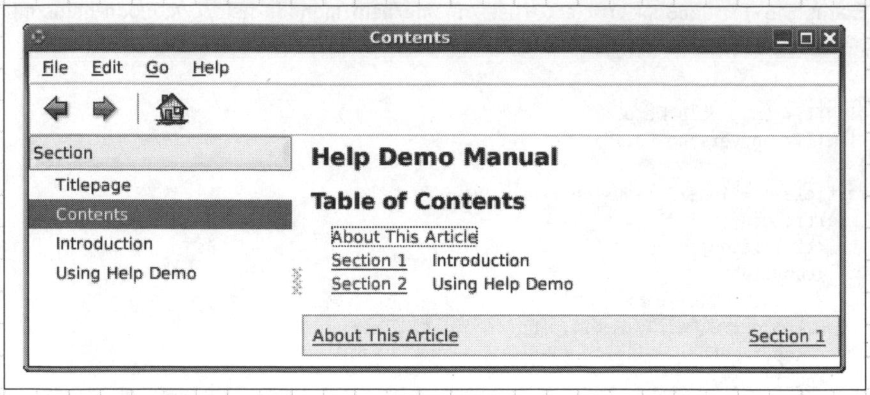

Figure 5-19. Reading the help file

If a document does not display as expected, more detailed error information can be obtained by using *xmllint*.

```
$ xmllint --valid --noout monodn-help.xml
```

Once the documentation is written, it can be activated by an application using the Gnome.Help.Display method. Two parameters must be passed: the name of the DocBook XML file to display, and an optional ID of a section to jump to. The API then figures out a pathname to pass to *yelp* using this scheme: *datadir*/gnome/help/*app-name*/*locale*/*xml-doc-filename*.

The *datadir* component of the path is the system-wide directory where application data is stored. On most Linux systems this is */usr/share*. An application can set it with the Gnome.Program.AppDatadir property. The *locale* component of the path is determined by the current system language settings. If the current language is not found, it will fall back to *C*, the default system locale.

For testing purposes it is adequate to set the AppDatadir to the current directory, and locate the help files relative to the directory the application is being run from. Example 5-12 shows the source code to create the application window and link in the help. Ensuring that the DocBook XML file is in a directory named *gnome/help/monodn-help/C* relative to where the binary is run from, compile and run the example. Click on the Help to display the documentation.

```
$ mcs Main.cs -pkg:gnome-sharp -pkg:gtk-sharp
$ mono Main.exe
```

Example 5-12. Help demo application: 07-help/Main.cs

```
// 05-advdesktop/07-help
using System;
using System.IO;
```

Example 5-12. Help demo application: 07-help/Main.cs (continued)

```csharp
using Gtk;
using Gnome;

public class MainClass
{
  public static void Main (string[ ] args)
  {
    new MyProgram (args);
  }
}

public class MyProgram
{
  public MyProgram (string [ ] args)
  {
    Program program = new Program ("monodn-help", "0.1",
      Modules.UI, args);
    // only use curdir for demo purposes
    program.AppDatadir = Directory.GetCurrentDirectory ();
    App app = new App ("monodn-help", "Help Demo");
    app.SetDefaultSize (200, 100);
    app.DeleteEvent += Window_Delete;
    VBox v = new VBox ();
    Button help = new Button (Gtk.Stock.Help);
    help.Clicked += Help_Clicked;
    v.Add (help);
    Button quit = new Button (Gtk.Stock.Quit);
    quit.Clicked += Quit_Clicked;
    v.Add (quit);
    app.Contents = v;
    app.ShowAll ();
    program.Run ();
  }

  void Help_Clicked (object o, EventArgs args)
  {
    Gnome.Help.Display ("monodn-help.xml", null);
  }

  void Window_Delete (object o, DeleteEventArgs args)
  {
    Application.Quit ();
  }

  void Quit_Clicked (object o, EventArgs args)
  {
    Application.Quit ();
  }
}
```

What about ...

...Distributing an application? Unlike the graphics and *Glade* files examined so far in this chapter, the DocBook files can't be bundled into a resource. While future revisions of the Gtk# toolkit may make this possible, a workaround is required.

One possible solution to the problem is to rely on the filesystem layout and the location of the installed program. By using the expression `System.IO.Path.GetDirectoryName (System.Reflection.Assembly. GetExecutingAssembly ().Location)` in the `Main` method, a program can determine where it is located in the filesystem. For instance, if the assembly was located in */usr/bin* and the data directory was */usr/share* then the program could determine the data directory using the following code:

```
using System.IO;
using System.Reflection;
using Gnome;

...

string mypath = Path.GetDirectoryName (
        Assembly.GetExecutingAssembly ().Location);

// == "/usr/bin"

program.Appdatadir = Path.Combine (
        Path.Combine (mypath, ".."), "share");

// == "/usr/bin/../share"
```

Where to learn more

The GNOME project has well-established tools and practices for managing documentation. The home page of the GNOME Documentation Project, *http://developer.gnome.org/projects/gdp/*, provides links to instructions on the construction and organization of documentation, as well as template DocBook files. When it comes to DocBook itself, the authoritative reference is Norman Walsh's book *DocBook: The Definitive Guide* (O'Reilly). Updates to Walsh's book are published at *http://www.docbook.org/*.

One tool of particular importance not mentioned so far in this lab is *scrollkeeper*, which keeps a system-wide catalog of documentation. This allows the user to see a categorized table of contents of all the manuals on their computer. More information on providing *scrollkeeper* support can be found at *http://scrollkeeper.sourceforge.net/* and examples in the source code of many GNOME programs.

Translate Your Programs

In the increasingly globalized world in which we live, software is distributed into many languages and cultures. This is true especially of open source software. The buzzword for the practice of making programs flexible enough to adapt to different languages and scripts is called *internationalization*. For reasons of brevity, this is often contracted to *I18N*. (I, 18 letters, N!). I18N is about more than just language. Different cultures have different ways of writing dates, decimal values, monetary amounts, and so on. This lab is restricted to considering issues of language and translation, although mention is made of associated issues in the closing discussion.

Mono is in an interesting position regarding translation technology. On the one hand it has available the common runtime `System.Globalization` functions, which work in an all-.NET world. On the other hand it is part of the Unix world, in which translation is usually provided by the *gettext* tool and API suite. The Gtk# toolkit is tied into the *gettext* way of doing things, and so that is the side of translation covered in this lab. Further information about `System.Globalization` can be found on Microsoft's MSDN web site at *http://msdn.microsoft.com/*.

Perhaps inevitably, there are two different approaches possible to using the *gettext* API with Mono, each with their advantages. One approach directly manipulates the functions built into the operating system's C library, while the other stays with an all-C# solution. Both however share the basic tools and technologies for creating translated programs. This lab demonstrates both approaches.

How do I do that?

The purpose of this lab is to create a simple program, the output of which can be presented in multiple languages, depending on the user's system locale setting. Before we describe the two available approaches to the API, we outline the business of creating translations, as it is common to either approach.

Ensure that the *gettext* tools are installed. Version 0.14 or better is required. These are usually available from the operating system's package manager (e.g., *apt-get* on Debian GNU/Linux, *fink* on Mac OS X, *cygwin* on Windows), but can also be downloaded from *http://www.gnu.org/software/gettext/*.

The first step in translating a program is to extract all the strings that require translation. To do this, they must be flagged in some way.

Bring an international feel to your programs by translating them into other languages.

Clearly, not every string in a program is intended as a message to the user. Similarly at runtime every translated string must be transformed in some way to the desired locale. Both of these birds can be killed with the same stone by consistently using the GetString and GetPluralString methods to wrap translated strings:

```
System.Console.WriteLine (Catalog.GetString ("Hello"));
System.Console.WriteLine (Catalog.GetPluralString (
        "I have {0} cake.",        "I have {0} cakes.", i),
        i);
```

To extract these strings from a source file, run *xgettext*. The *Main.cs* source file appears later in this lab. You can replace *monodn-intl.pot* with another name, so long as it matches what your program uses to initialize *gettext*:

```
$ xgettext -o monodn-intl.potMain.cs
```

The resulting *pot* file will be similar to that shown in Example 5-13. This is the master file for all translations and should be updated whenever strings in the source code change.

Example 5-13. POT file: 08-i18n/po/monodn-intl.pot

```
# SOME DESCRIPTIVE TITLE.
# Copyright (C) YEAR THE PACKAGE'S COPYRIGHT HOLDER
# This file is distributed under the same license as the PACKAGE package.
# FIRST AUTHOR <EMAIL@ADDRESS>, YEAR.
#
#, fuzzy
msgid ""
msgstr ""
"Project-Id-Version: PACKAGE VERSION\n"
"Report-Msgid-Bugs-To: \n"
"POT-Creation-Date: 2004-05-03 17:25+0100\n"
"PO-Revision-Date: YEAR-MO-DA HO:MI+ZONE\n"
"Last-Translator: FULL NAME <EMAIL@ADDRESS>\n"
"Language-Team: LANGUAGE <LL@li.org>\n"
"MIME-Version: 1.0\n"
"Content-Type: text/plain; charset=CHARSET\n"
"Content-Transfer-Encoding: 8bit\n"
"Plural-Forms: nplurals=INTEGER; plural=EXPRESSION;\n"

#: Main.cs:11
msgid "Hello"
msgstr ""

#: Main.cs:14
#, csharp-format
msgid "I have {0} cake."
msgid_plural "I have {0} cakes."
msgstr[0] ""
msgstr[1] ""
```

Once the master *pot* has been generated, translation *po* files for each target language must be created. This can be done with *msginit* program. For instance, to generate a template for a French translation, use:

```
$ msginit -l fr
```

This generates a *po* file for the French locale. When filled in with the translated strings, it will look similar to the file shown in Example 5-14. Be sure to match the charset option in the file to the character set being used on the translator's system.

Example 5-14. fr.po file: 08-i18n/po/fr.po

```
# French translations for  package.
# Copyright (C) 2004 THE 'S COPYRIGHT HOLDER
# This file is distributed under the same license as the  package.
# Edd Dumbill <edd@usefulinc.com>, 2004.
#
msgid ""
msgstr ""
"Project-Id-Version:  08-i18n\n"
"Report-Msgid-Bugs-To: \n"
"POT-Creation-Date: 2004-05-03 17:25+0100\n"
"PO-Revision-Date: 2004-05-03 17:29+0100\n"
"Last-Translator: Edd Dumbill <edd@usefulinc.com>\n"
"Language-Team: French <traduc@traduc.org>\n"
"MIME-Version: 1.0\n"
"Content-Type: text/plain; charset=UTF-8\n"
"Content-Transfer-Encoding: 8bit\n"
"Plural-Forms: nplurals=2; plural=(n > 1);\n"

#: Main.cs:11
msgid "Hello"
msgstr "Bonjour"

#: Main.cs:14
#, csharp-format
msgid "I have {0} cake."
msgid_plural "I have {0} cakes."
msgstr[0] "J'ai {0} gateau."
msgstr[1] "J'ai {0} gateaux."
```

The final step before the translations are ready to use is to compile the source *po* files into a binary form that can be used at runtime. The *msgfmt* program is used for this purpose. This is also the point at which the two techniques for using *gettext* start to differ. The first technique requires *mo* files to be generated and placed in a special directory structure. Relative to the application's locale directory, translations must be installed in: *lang-code*/LC_MESSAGES/*app-name*.mo.

For more about
distributing files
that can't be
added as
resources into an
assembly, see
"What about ..." in
"Provide Help Files."

Assuming that the example will use the current directory for the locale directory, the French translation is compiled like this:

```
$ mkdir -p ./locale/fr/LC_MESSAGES
$ msgfmt fr.po ./locale/fr/LC_MESSAGES/monodn-intl.mo
```

Finally, the translation can be tested. The example program is shown in Example 5-15. To work, it needs the interface to the C *gettext* functions, provided by *Catalog.cs* in Example 5-16. Additionally, to test an alternative language, that locale must be installed on the target machine. Unfortunately, the process for doing this tends to be highly specific to the operating system. (On Red Hat Linux, you must select the desired locales at install time. On Debian, it can be done any time by running dpkg-reconfigure locales as root.) Compile the program, then test with the default locale, and in the French translation:

```
$ mcs Main.cs Catalog.cs
$ LANG=C mono Main.exe
Hello
I have 0 cakes.
I have 1 cake.
I have 2 cakes.
$ LANG=fr_FR mono Main.exe
Bonjour
J'ai 0 gateau.
J'ai 1 gateau.
J'ai 2 gateaux.
```

Notice English
and French have
different plural
rules. Nifty, eh?

Example 5-15. I18N-aware example: 08-i18n/Main.cs

```
// 08-i18n/Main.cs
using System;

class MainClass {
  public static void Main(string[] args)
  {
    Catalog.Init ("monodn-intl", "./locale");
    System.Console.WriteLine ("{0}", Catalog.GetString ("Hello"));
    for (int i = 0; i < 3; i++) {
      System.Console.WriteLine (
        Catalog.GetPluralString ("I have {0} cake.",
          "I have {0} cakes.", i), i);
    }
  }
}
```

Example 5-16. Catalog implementation: 08-i18n/Catalog.cs

```
// 08-i18n/Catalog.cs
using System;
using System.Runtime.InteropServices;

class Catalog {
  [DllImport("libc")]
```

Example 5-16. Catalog implementation: 08-i18n/Catalog.cs (continued)

```
static extern IntPtr bindtextdomain (IntPtr domainname, IntPtr dirname);
[DllImport("libc")]
static extern IntPtr bind_textdomain_codeset (IntPtr domainname,
  String codeset);
[DllImport("libc")]
static extern IntPtr textdomain (IntPtr domainname);

public static void Init (String package, String localedir)
{
  IntPtr ipackage = Marshal.StringToHGlobalAuto (package);
  IntPtr ilocaledir = Marshal.StingToHGlobalAuto (localedir);
  IntPtr iutf8 = Marshal.StingToHGlobalAuto ("UTF-8")
  bindtextdomain (ipackage, ilocaledir);
  bind_textdomain_codeset (ipackage, iutf8);
  textdomain (ipackage);
  Marshal.FreeHGlobal (ipackage);
  Marshal.FreeHGlobal (ilocaledir);
  Marshal.FreeHGlobal (iutf8);
}


[DllImport("libc")]
static extern IntPtr gettext (IntPtr s);

public static String GetString (String s)
{
  IntPtr inptr = Marshal.StringToHGloablAuto (s);
  IntPtr sptr = gettext (inptr);
  Marshal.FreeHGlobal (inptr);
  if (inptr == sptr)
      return s;
  else
      return Marshal.PtrToStringAuto (sptr);
}


[DllImport("libc")]
static extern IntPtr ngettext (IntPtr s, IntPtr p, Int32 n);

public static String GetPluralString (String s, String p, Int32 n)
{
  IntPtr inptrs = Marshal.StringToHGlobalAuto (s);
  IntPtr inptrp = Marshal.StringToHGlobalAuto (p);
  IntPtr sptr = ngettext (inptrs, inptrp, n);
  Marshal.FreeHGlobal (inptrs);
  Marshal.FreeHGlobal (inptrp);
  if (sptr == inptrs)
      return s;
  else if (sptr == inptrp)
      return p;
  else
      return Marshal.PtrToStringAuto (sptr);
}
}
```

The second way to use *gettext* is to take advantage of the C# support in the 0.14 release. By linking with the assembly provided with *gettext*, GNU.Gettext, applications can use a more native approach to translated text. In this case, the *mo* files are not generated. Instead *msgfmt* directly generates an assembly *dll*.

Example 5-17 shows the program reworked to use GNU.Gettext. To generate translations for this program, follow the previous procedure as far as the *msgfmt* step. Then use the following to generate the translations and compile and run the program:

Adjust the /usr/ lib path if your GNU.Gettext.dll is installed elsewhere.

```
$ msgfmt -l fr -d . --csharp -r monodn-intl fr.po
$ mcs -r:/usr/lib/GNU.Gettext.dll Main.cs
$ LANG=fr_FR MONO_PATH=/usr/lib:$MONO_PATH mono Main.exe
```

Example 5-17. Translations using the GNU Gettext API: 08-i18n-gnu/Main.cs

The workaround for setting CurrentCulture should become unnecessary in future.

```
// 05-advdesktop/08-i18n-gnu
using System;
using GNU.Gettext;

class GettextDemo
{
  public static void Main (string[] args)
  {
    #if __MonoCS__
    // Some systems don't set CurrentCulture and CurrentUICulture
    // as specified by LC_ALL. So set it by hand.
    String locale = System.Environment.GetEnvironmentVariable("LC_ALL");
    if (locale == null || locale == "")
      locale = System.Environment.GetEnvironmentVariable("LANG");
    if (!(locale == null || locale == "")) {
      if (locale.IndexOf('.') >= 0)
        locale = locale.Substring(0,locale.IndexOf('.'));
      System.Threading.Thread.CurrentThread.CurrentCulture =
        System.Threading.Thread.CurrentThread.CurrentUICulture =
        new System.Globalization.CultureInfo(locale.Replace('_','-'));
    }
    #endif

    GettextResourceManager catalog =
      new GettextResourceManager ("monodn-intl");
    System.Console.WriteLine ("{0}", catalog.GetString ("Hello"));

    for (int i = 0; i < 3; i++) {
      System.Console.WriteLine (
        catalog.GetPluralString ("I have {0} cake.",
        "I have {0} cakes.", i), i);
    }
  }
}
```

How it works

The operation of gettext itself is simple. `GetString` returns the translated string appropriate for the current locale. `GetPluralString` selects between two strings, depending on an integer value, applying the correct rules for plural endings for the current locale.

The choice between the two techniques for using *gettext* comes down to how much an application is dependent on Gtk#. If an application uses a *Glade* user interface, then translations are done on that interface via the underlying C *gettext* library anyway. This means the *.mo*-style setup will be required, and therefore there's little point in duplicating work by using the *.dll* method. Additionally, very few Unix-like systems will have the *GNU.Gettext.dll* assembly installed, whereas all of them using the *glibc* C library will already have C *gettext* support. If an application wanted the *GNU.Gettext.dll* assembly, it would probably have to be included in the distribution. And as it's GNU software, the source of code would have to be included too as per the GNU licensing terms.

All of this seems to stack the odds against `GNU.Gettext`. However, the other side of the story is integration with the rest of the I18N or, to use the .NET word, globalization features of Mono. Manipulation and formatting of culture-sensitive data such as dates is influenced by the `System.Globalization` APIs, with which `GNU.Gettext` aims to work. An additional factor is that by generating the translations as resource *.dll* files, they only need to be placed in the directory of the running assembly, rather than requiring more elaborate distribution strategies.

As is perhaps evident, there's no straight and simple story to tell yet about internationalizing Mono applications. Over time, the situation will improve. In the meantime, both of the techniques described in this lab will work, and have been proven in the field.

Processing XML

Extensible Markup Language (XML) was introduced to the world with much hullabaloo by the World Wide Web Consortium (W3C) in 1996. Building on the popularity of its ancestor, SGML, and its sibling, HTML, XML has continued to provide employment for programmers, authors, and pundits ever since.

When the .NET Framework was introduced in 2000, XML formed an important building block in the Common Language Runtime. By supporting the core XML standards—Document Object Model, XPath, XSLT, and W3C XML Schema—as well as XML serialization, .NET provides almost everything a Mono hacker needs to hack XML. And what .NET itself does not provide, the Mono team and other open source contributors have provided with a managed implementation of Relax NG.

In this age, XML should be part of every programmer's repertoire. This chapter introduces you to Mono's XML support.

Read and Write XML

For those times when memory is limited and you just need to grab a chunk of data.

The simplest thing you can do with XML is to read and write it. The `System.Xml` namespace contains the `XmlReader` and `XmlWriter` classes, as well as a number of supporting classes, expressly for that purpose. This lab shows you the basics.

How do I do that?

Example 6-1 shows a program that writes XML to standard output.

Example 6-1. 01-basic/WriteXml.cs

```
// 06-xml/01-basic
using System;
using System.Collections;
using System.IO;
using System.Xml;

public class WriteXml {

  private const string RDF = "http://www.w3.org/1999/02/22-rdf-syntax-ns#";
  private static Hashtable resources;

  static WriteXml() {
    resources = new Hashtable();
    resources["About Mono"] = "http://www.mono-project.com/about";
    resources["Using Mono"] = "http://www.mono-project.com/using";
    resources["Contributing to Mono"] =
    "http://www.mono-project.com/contributing";
    resources["Contact Us"] =
    "http://www.mono-project.com/about/contactus.html";
    resources["Downloads"] = "http://www.mono-project.com/downloads";
    resources["Documentation"] = "http://www.go-mono.com:8080/";
  }

  public static void Main(string [] args) {

    XmlTextWriter writer = new XmlTextWriter(Console.Out);
    writer.Formatting = Formatting.Indented;
    writer.Indentation = 2;
    writer.IndentChar = ' ';

    writer.WriteStartDocument(true);

    writer.WriteStartElement("rdf", "RDF", RDF);
    writer.WriteAttributeString("xmlns", "http://purl.org/rss/1.0/");

    writer.WriteStartElement("channel");
    writer.WriteAttributeString("about", RDF, "http://www.mono-project.com/");

    writer.WriteElementString("title", "The Mono Project");
    writer.WriteElementString("link", "http://www.mono-project.com/");
    writer.WriteElementString("description",
      "Open Source .NET CLR Implementation");

    writer.WriteStartElement("items");

    writer.WriteStartElement("Seq", RDF);

    foreach (string url in resources.Values) {
      writer.WriteStartElement("li", RDF);
      writer.WriteAttributeString("resource", RDF, url);
      writer.WriteEndElement(); // li
    }
```

Example 6-1. 01-basic/WriteXml.cs (continued)

```
    writer.WriteEndElement(); //Seq

    writer.WriteEndElement(); // items

    writer.WriteEndElement(); // channel

    foreach (string title in resources.Keys) {
      string url = (string)resources[title];
      writer.WriteStartElement("item");
      writer.WriteAttributeString("about", RDF, url);
      writer.WriteElementString("link", url);
      writer.WriteElementString("title", title);
      writer.WriteEndElement(); // item
    }

    writer.WriteEndElement(); // rdf
  }
}
```

To compile and run *WriteXml.exe,* use the following command lines:

```
$ mcs WriteXml.cs
$ mono WriteXml.exe
```

Running *WriteXml.exe* produces the following output:

```
<?xml version="1.0" encoding="us-ascii" standalone="yes"?>
              <rdf:RDF xmlns="http://purl.org/rss/1.0/"
              xmlns:rdf="http://www.w3.org/1999/02/22-rdf-syntax-ns#">
    <channel rdf:about="http://www.mono-project.com/">
      <title>The Mono Project</title>
      <link>http://www.mono-project.com/</link>
      <description>Open Source .NET CLR Implementation</description>
      <items>
        <rdf:Seq>
          <rdf:li rdf:resource="http://www.go-mono.com:8080/" />
          <rdf:li rdf:resource="http://www.mono-project.com/downloads/" />
          <rdf:li rdf:resource="http://www.mono-project.com/about/" />
          <rdf:li rdf:resource="http://www.mono-project.com/using/" />
          <rdf:li rdf:resource="http://www.mono-project.com/contributing/" />
          <rdf:resource="http://www.mono-project.com/contactus.html" />
        </rdf:Seq>
      </items>
    </channel>
    <item rdf:about="http://www.go-mono.com:8080/">
      <link>http://www.go-mono.com:8080/</link>
      <title>Documentation</title>
    </item>
    <item rdf:about="http://www.mono-project.com/downloads/">
      <link>http://www.mono-project.com/downloads/</link>
      <title>Downloads</title>
    </item>
    <item rdf:about="http://www.mono-project.com/about/">
```

```
      <link>http://www.mono-project.com/about/</link>
      <title>About Mono</title>
    </item>
    <item rdf:about="http://www.mono-project.com/using/">
      <link>http://www.mono-project.com/using/</link>
      <title>Using Mono</title>
    </item>
    <item rdf:about="http://www.mono-project.com/contributing/">
      <link>http://www.mono-project.com/contributing/</link>
      <title>Contributing to Mono</title>
    </item>
    <item rdf:about="http://www.mono-project.com/contactus.html">
      <link>http://www.mono-project.com/contactus.html</link>
      <title>Contact Us</title>
    </item>
  </rdf:RDF>
```

You may recognize this file as a very rudimentary instance of the RSS 1.0 format. This document describes the links on the top of each page of the Mono web site, and can be read by any of the popular RSS readers on the market.

That's all well and good if you want to write XML, but you'll often want to consume XML as well. Example 6-2 shows a program that reads an XML file from disk and echoes some of its details to standard output.

We picked RSS 1.0 because it makes a good demonstration of writing XML with namespaces. We could go into the torrid history of the competing RSS standards, but let's not.

Example 6-2. 01-basic/ReadXml.cs

```csharp
// 06-xml/01-basic
using System;
using System.Xml;

public class ReadXml {
  public static void Main(string [] args) {
    string filename = args[0];
    XmlTextReader reader = new XmlTextReader(filename);

    while (reader.Read()) {
      Console.WriteLine("NodeType={0}, Name={1}, Value=\"{2}\"",
        reader.NodeType, reader.Name, reader.Value);
    }

    reader.Close();
  }
}
```

Here's a sample XML file called a CluePacket:

```xml
<CluePacket>
  <FrontEnd>Epiphany</FrontEnd>
  <Context>Tab 1</Context>
  <Focused>True</Focused>
  <Additive>False</Additive>
```

```
    <Clue Type="url" Relevance="10">
      http://www.mono-project.com/
    </Clue>
  </CluePacket>
```

You can compile *ReadXml.exe* and run it against *CluePacket.xml* with the these commands:

```
$ mcs ReadXml.cs
$ mono ReadXml.exe CluePacket.xml
```

CluePackets are used by the open source Dashboard project. Dashboard, which uses the Mono runtime, accepts socket connections and listens for CluePackets. When a CluePacket is received, Dashboard displays relevant information about the resource described in the CluePacket.

When run with the CluePacket above, *ReadXml.exe* will produce the following output:

```
NodeType=Element, Name=CluePacket, Value=""
NodeType=Whitespace, Name=, Value="
      "
NodeType=Element, Name=FrontEnd, Value=""
NodeType=Text, Name=, Value="Epiphany"
NodeType=EndElement, Name=FrontEnd, Value=""
NodeType=Whitespace, Name=, Value="
      "
NodeType=Element, Name=Context, Value=""
NodeType=Text, Name=, Value="Tab 1"
NodeType=EndElement, Name=Context, Value=""
NodeType=Whitespace, Name=, Value="
      "
NodeType=Element, Name=Focused, Value=""
NodeType=Text, Name=, Value="True"
NodeType=EndElement, Name=Focused, Value=""
NodeType=Whitespace, Name=, Value="
      "
NodeType=Element, Name=Additive, Value=""
NodeType=Text, Name=, Value="False"
NodeType=EndElement, Name=Additive, Value=""
NodeType=Whitespace, Name=, Value="

      "
NodeType=Element, Name=Clue, Value=""
NodeType=Text, Name=, Value="
               http://www.mono-project.com/
      "
NodeType=EndElement, Name=Clue, Value=""
NodeType=Whitespace, Name=, Value="
"
NodeType=EndElement, Name=CluePacket, Value=""
NodeType=Whitespace, Name=, Value="
"
```

As you can see, each time an XML node is read from the document, its type, name, and value are written to standard output. Some nodes have a name and a value, some simply have a name, and some simply have a value, but all have a type.

How it works

Writing XML, as in Example 6-1, uses the abstract XmlWriter class and its concrete subclass, XmlTextWriter. XmlTextWriter can be used to write XML to a Stream, TextWriter, or filename.

The XmlWriter declares a set of methods that can be used to write various data to XML. Most of their names are fairly obvious; WriteStartDocument(), for example, begins the document, and WriteEndDocument() ends it. Similarly, WriteStartElement() starts an XML element, and WriteEndElement() ends it. Many of XmlWriter's methods have overrides that are namespace aware.

XmlTextWriter adds a few features of its own. For example, the Formatting property, which can be set to *None* or *Indented*, and the Indentation property, which can be used to set the indentation level (if Formatting is *Indented*).

XmlWriter's evil twin is XmlReader. **Like** XmlWriter, XmlReader **is an abstract class, and it has three subclasses:** XmlTextReader, **which is used to read XML from a** Stream, TextReader, **or URL;** XmlNodeReader, **which is used to read XML from an** XmlNode; **and** XmlValidatingReader, **which can be used in conjunction with any other** XmlReader **to provide validation of the XML as it is read.**

The original Microsoft .NET implementation of XmlValidatingReader can only validate XML read from an XmlTextReader. Mono's XmlValidatingReader implementation, however, can accept any XmlReader.

Example 6-2 is a very simple demonstration of XmlReader and doesn't really show all the power of the *pull parser*.

In a pull parser, an event loop repeatedly calls the Read() method to retrieve the parsing events. The main program remains in control of the parser, leading to a *recursive descent parser* architecture, in which the structure of the parsing program reflects the structure of the XML document being parsed.

Contrast this with a *push parser*, such as Simple API for XML (SAX). In a push parser, the main program registers callback methods (delegates, in C#) with a parser, and calls a Parse() method. In this model, program

XmlWriter is fairly smart. It knows that if you call WriteStartElement("foo") followed by WriteEndElement() without writing any sub-elements or content, it should be written as <foo />, rather than <foo></foo>. You can force it to write the full end element with WriteFullEndElement().

The SAX API was originally developed in 1997 for use in Java. SAX2 has been ported to C# as an open source project. SAXdotNET may be downloaded from http://saxdotnet.sourceforge.net/.

execution is handed over to the parser until the end of the document is reached or an error occurs. Events are returned to the main program as they occur, by means of the callbacks.

Where to learn more

Chris Lovett of Microsoft has written an XmlCsvReader, which extends XmlReader to read CSV files, available at *http://msdn.microsoft.com/library/en-us/dnxmlnet/html/xmlcsvreader.asp*. There is a PowerPoint presentation on the more general topic of extending System.Xml, by Ted Neward of DevelopMentor, available at *http://www.neward.net/ted/DT03-ExtXML.ppt*. The true power of this becomes more obvious when you realize that you can pass an XmlReader instance to some of the other XML classes discussed in the next few labs.

You can learn more about the original SAX API at the project's home page, *http://www.saxproject.org/*.

Manipulate XML in Memory

When it comes to working with a document in memory, the DOM dominates.

The Document Object Model (DOM) was developed by the Worldwide Web Consortium to provide a standard API for manipulating XML in memory. Unlike XmlReader and XmlWriter, DOM allows you to access an XML document nonsequentially, and it allows you to change any part of the document at any time. The tradeoff for this flexibility is memory; the entire document has to be loaded into memory.

In this lab, we'll talk about another important weapon in the Mono XML arsenal, the DOM.

How do I do that?

Example 6-3 shows a program that uses the DOM to read in an XML document and display information about it.

Example 6-3. 02-dom/ReadDocument.cs

```
// 06-xml/02-dom
using System;
using System.Xml;

public class ReadDocument {

  public static void Main(string [] args) {
    string filename = args[0];
    XmlDocument document = new XmlDocument();
```

Example 6-3. 02-dom/ReadDocument.cs (continued)

```
  document.Load(filename);

  PrintNode(document.DocumentElement, 0);
}

private static void PrintNode(XmlNode parent, int depth) {
  string indent = new string (' ', (depth++) * 2);
  Console.WriteLine("{0}NodeType={1}, Name={2}, Value=\"{3}\"",
    indent, parent.NodeType, parent.Name, parent.Value);

  foreach (XmlNode node in parent.ChildNodes) {
    PrintNode(node, depth);
  }
}
}
```

The program in Example 6-3 loads an XML document into an XmlDocument instance, and then prints out information about its structure. You can compile it and run it against the CluePacket XML from "Read and Write XML" with the following commands:

```
$ mcs ReadDocument.cs
$ mono ReadDocument.exe CluePacket.xml
```

When you run it, you'll see the following output:

```
NodeType=Element, Name=CluePacket, Value=""
  NodeType=Element, Name=FrontEnd, Value=""
    NodeType=Text, Name=#text, Value="Epiphany"
  NodeType=Element, Name=Context, Value=""
    NodeType=Text, Name=#text, Value="Tab 1"
  NodeType=Element, Name=Focused, Value=""
    NodeType=Text, Name=#text, Value="True"
  NodeType=Element, Name=Additive, Value=""
    NodeType=Text, Name=#text, Value="False"
  NodeType=Element, Name=Clue, Value=""
    NodeType=Text, Name=#text, Value="
                  http://www.mono-project.com/
      "
```

How it works

The DOM is an object-oriented model for XML documents. The base class for all the .NET DOM classes is XmlNode. XmlNode is an abstract base class which represents any type of XML node, whether it be XmlElement, XmlAttribute, XmlText, or any of the dozens of others.

Example 6-3 creates a new XmlDocument instance and then loads it from an XML document on disk. An XmlDocument can also be loaded from a

Stream, TextReader, or XmlReader, or, with the LoadXml( ) method, from a string containing XML.

The example program then recursively crawls through the XML tree, printing information about each node it encounters. It starts with the document's document element, which is accessed through the XmlDocument's DocumentElement property. Then the document element is passed to the local static method PrintNode( ).

PrintNode( ) examines the passed-in node and prints its type, name, and value. Each XmlNode has a NodeType property which returns a member of the *XmlNodeType* enum; the members include *Element*, *Attribute*, *Whitespace*, etc.

After printing this information, PrintNode( ) calls itself recursively for every child node (obtained from the ChildNodes property).

What about ...

...Modifying an XML document in memory? In the introduction to this lab, we promised you that you can do this, and so you can. Take a look at Example 6-4.

Example 6-4. 02-dom/AddElement.cs

```
// 06-xml/02-dom
using System;
using System.Xml;

public class ReadDocument {

  public static void Main(string [ ] args) {
    string filename = args[0];
    XmlDocument document = new XmlDocument( );
    document.Load(filename);

    XmlElement element = document.CreateElement("item",
      "http://purl.org/rss/1.0/");
    XmlAttribute attribute = document.CreateAttribute("about",
      "http://www.w3.org/1999/02/22-rdf-syntax-ns#");

    element.Attributes.Append(attribute);
    document.DocumentElement.AppendChild(element);

    XmlTextWriter writer = new XmlTextWriter(Console.Out);
    writer.Formatting = Formatting.Indented;
    document.WriteTo(writer);
  }
}
```

This example will add a new `item` element at the end of the input document, which we're assuming will be one of those RSS documents from "Read and Write XML." You can create one now with these commands:

```
$ cd 01-basic
$ mono WriteXml.exe > rss.xml
```

You can compile and run *AddElement.exe* with these commands:

```
$ mcs AddElement.cs
$ mono AddElement.exe rss.xml
```

`XmlDocument` includes a `CreateElement()` method which creates a new instance of `XmlElement`. Each `XmlElement` is tied to a specific instance of `XmlDocument`; you must use the factory method to create one, because there is no public constructor.

Once you've created an element, you can also add attributes to it. Again, the `XmlDocument` has a `CreateAttribute()` method to do this. Both `CreateElement()` and `CreateAttribute()` are namespace-aware, as you can see in this example.

Just because you've created an element and an attribute, and they are connected to the document, doesn't mean they are included in the document. You must append the `XmlAttribute` to the `XmlElement`'s `XmlAttributeCollection`, and you must add the `XmlElement` to the document element's list of child nodes.

Finally, having modified the XML document, you'll want to save it somewhere. In this case, we've constructed a new `XmlTextWriter` around the standard output stream, set its formatting to *Indented*, and then called `XmlDocument`'s `WriteTo()` method.

Where to learn more

The DOM is language- and platform-neutral, so it looks pretty much the same anywhere you run it. The definitive guide to all things DOM is the W3C's web site at *http://www.w3.org/DOM/*.

Navigate XML Documents

XPath is another one of those W3C standards that everyone should know about. XPath allows you to find a specific node or set of nodes within an XML document using a query that looks something like a Unix path.

XPath is deeply integrated into another XML technology, XSLT, which we'll talk about in "Transform XML," but it can also be used as a standal-

Don't use XmlReader to pluck a single element out of an XML file!

one XML feature, or in conjunction with XmlDocument. In this lab, you'll see how you can use XPath to navigate XML documents.

How do I do that?

Example 6-5 shows a program that loads an XmlDocument from a file on disk, and then queries the document for an XPath expression passed on the command line.

Example 6-5. 03-xpath/UseXPath.cs

```
// 06-xml/03-xpath
using System;
using System.Xml;

public class UseXPath {
  public static void Main(string [] args) {
    string filename = args[0];
    string query = args[1];

    XmlDocument document = new XmlDocument();
    document.Load(filename);
    XmlNodeList nodes = document.SelectNodes(query);
    Console.WriteLine("{0} nodes match the query {1}",
      nodes.Count, query);
    foreach (XmlNode node in nodes) {
      Console.WriteLine(node.Name);
    }
  }
}
```

The compilation and usage commands are simple:

```
$ mcs UseXPath.cs
$ mono UseXPath.exe filename.xml xpathquery
```

You may find that you need to enclose the *xpathquery* parameter in quotes and escape any shell special characters to make sure they get passed to the program verbatim.

That's C:\Program Files\Mono-1.0\ etc\mono\ machine.config to you Windows users.

For an example of using XPath, start with the Mono machine configuration file, located at *etc/mono/machine.config* (relative to the Mono installation directory). A section of the file is reproduced here:

```
<?xml version="1.0" encoding="utf-8"?>
<configuration>
  ...
  <appSettings>
    <!--<add key="yourkey" value="your value" /> -->
    <!--<remove key="a key defined higher in the hierarchy" /> -->
    <!--<clear/> Removes all defined settings -->
  </appSettings>
```

```
    ...
  </configuration>
```

To find all the `<appSettings>` elements in *machine.config*, you would use the following query to see these results:

```
$ mono UseXPath.exe /etc/mono/config/machine.config //appSettings
1 nodes match the query //appSettings
appSettings
```

`XmlDocument`, as a subclass of `XmlNode`, inherits a couple of methods that allow you to query the document with XPath. You can select a single node with the `SelectSingleNode()` method, or you can select multiple nodes with the `SelectNodes()` method. `SelectSingleNode()` returns a `XmlNode`, and `SelectNodes()` returns an `XmlNodeList`.

What about ...

...Performance? Example 6-5 uses `XmlDocument` and its `SelectNodes()` method to navigate the XML document. This method requires you to load the XML document into an `XmlDocument` instance in memory. Of course, for a large document, this means a lot of overhead, and even for a small-ish document, there's overhead involved in creating a DOM instance.

One way around this memory usage problem is to use `XPathDocument`, from the `System.Xml.XPath` namespace. Example 6-6 shows a program that produces the same results using the more efficient `XPathDocument`.

Example 6-6. 03-xpath/UseXPathDocument.cs

```
// 06-xml/03-xpath
using System;
using System.Xml.XPath;

public class UseXPathDocument {
  public static void Main(string [] args) {
    string filename = args[0];
    string query = args[1];

    XPathDocument document = new XPathDocument(filename);
    XPathNavigator navigator = document.CreateNavigator();
    XPathNodeIterator iterator = navigator.Select(query);
    Console.WriteLine("{0} nodes match the query {1}",
      iterator.Count, query);
    while (iterator.MoveNext()) {
      Console.WriteLine(iterator.Current.Name);
    }
  }
}
```

Working with XPath the XPathDocument way is a little different from XmlDocument. All XPathDocument does is to implement IXPathNavigable. This interface declares a single method, CreateNavigator, which returns a new XPathNavigator. XmlNode also implements IXPathNavigable, which means that it also defines the CreateNavigator method. You still have to create an XmlNode, however, with all its DOM overhead, so if all you're doing is using the XPathNavigator, you're better off with XPathDocument.

One small difference: an XPathNavigator retrieved from an XmlNode also implements IHasXmlNode, which is an interface that declares the GetNode( ) method. This method allows you to access an XmlNode from an XPathNavigator, which you can't do when it comes from an XPathDocument. The following snippet shows one usage for the IHasXmlNode interface:

```
XmlDocument document = new XmlDocument( );
document.Load(filename);
XPathNavigator navigator = document.CreateNavigator( );
XPathNodeIterator iterator = navigator.Select(query);
Console.WriteLine("{0} nodes match the query {1}",
    iterator.Count, query);
while (iterator.MoveNext( )) {
    XmlNode node = ((IHasXmlNode)iterator.Current).GetNode( );
    Console.WriteLine(node.NodeType);
}
```

NodeType is a property of XmlNode, so the only way to get to it is to get the underlying XmlNode. XPathNodeIterator.Current returns an XPathNavigator, which you can only cast to IHasXmlNode if everything originally came from a XmlNode.

Where to learn more

The official W3C technical recommendation for XPath 1.0. is available online at *http://www.w3.org/TR/xpath*.

Zvon has an excellent XPath tutorial at *http://www.zvon.org/xxl/XPathTutorial/General/examples.html*.

Transform XML

Despite the introduction of XML, web browsers still work best with HTML, and text editors still like text.

Sometimes you need to take data in some arbitrary XML format and transform it into something else. Whether the target is HTML, XML, plain text, or some binary format, XML Stylesheet Language Transformation, (XSLT) is your buddy.

In this lab, you'll learn how to transform any arbitrary XML document into any other format with the right XSLT stylesheet.

How do I do that?

Example 6-7 shows a program that takes an XML source file, a stylesheet file, and a destination file as parameters and executes the XSLT transformation.

Example 6-7. 04-xslt/Transform.cs

```
// 06-xml/04-xslt
using System;
using System.Xml.Xsl;

public class Transform {
  public static void Main(string [] args) {
    string source = args[0];
    string stylesheet = args[1];
    string target = args[2];

    try {
      XslTransform transform = new XslTransform();
      transform.Load(stylesheet);
      transform.Transform(source, target, null);
    } catch (Exception e) {
      Console.Error.WriteLine(e);
    }
  }
}
```

XslTransform had a lot of changes between versions 1.0 and 1.1 of the .NET Framework. Mono version 1.0 implements all of the obsolete .NET version 1.0 overloads of the Transform method, as well as the .NET version 1.1 overloads, even though there's no installed base to worry about.

It doesn't get much simpler than that. The XslTransform class is created and then loaded. The Load( ) method has several overloads, which allow it to be loaded from a variety of sources, including a URL, XPathNavigator, IXPathNavigable, and XmlReader. The final parameter to Load( ) is an optional XmlResolver, which is used to resolve references to external stylesheets through an XSLT include or import element. If the parameter is null, these external resources are not resolved.

By default, Mono will use a managed implementation of XLST. If you want to use the unmanaged implementation from *libxslt*, define the shell variable MONO_UNMANAGED_XSLT (any value will do). You might use the managed implementation if you need to use the <msxsl:script> element to embed scripts in the stylesheet. In general, some operations are more efficient using the managed version, and some are more efficient using the unmanaged version.

Example 6-8 shows an XML document for this lab.

Example 6-8. 04-xslt/StockQuote.xml

```
<?xml version="1.0"?>
<!-- 06-xml/04-xslt -->
<StockQuote Symbol="NOVL" Name="Novell, Inc">
  <LastTrade>9.78</LastTrade>
  <TradeTime>2004-05-04T10:56-0400</TradeTime>
  <Change>
    <Amount>0.00</Amount>
    <Percent>0.00</Percent>
  </Change>
  <PrevClose>9.78</PrevClose>
  <Open>9.77</Open>
  <OneDayRange>
    <Low>9.72</Low>
    <High>10.02</High>
  </OneDayRange>
  <OneYearRange>
    <Low>2.70</Low>
    <High>14.24</High>
  </OneYearRange>
  <Volume>1,203,227</Volume>
</StockQuote>
```

Unlike its cousin the Cascading Style Sheet, which has its own syntax, an XSLT stylesheet is itself an XML document. Example 6-9 shows an XSLT stylesheet that can be used to transform the XML in Example 6-8 into text.

Example 6-9. 04-xslt/StockQuote.xsl

```
<?xml version="1.0"?>
<!-- 06-xml/04-xslt -->
<xsl:stylesheet version="1.0"
  xmlns:xsl="http://www.w3.org/1999/XSL/Transform">

  <xsl:output method="text" />

  <xsl:template match="/">
    <xsl:apply-templates select="StockQuote" />
  </xsl:template>

  <xsl:template match="StockQuote">
Ticker Symbol: <xsl:value-of select="@Symbol" />
Name: <xsl:value-of select="@Name" />
    <xsl:apply-templates select="LastTrade" />
  </xsl:template>

  <xsl:template match="LastTrade">
Last Trade: US$<xsl:value-of select="." />
  </xsl:template>

</xsl:stylesheet>
```

Compile and run the program with the following commands:

```
$ mcs Transform.cs
$ mono Transform.exe StockQuote.xml StockQuote.xsl StockQuote.txt
```

This will create the file *StockQuote.txt* with the following content:

```
Ticker Symbol: NOVL
Name: Novell, Inc
Last Trade: US$9.78
```

What about ...

...Editing XSLT stylesheets programmatically? There's nothing to stop you from doing anything you want to a stylesheet with any of the Mono XML tools. You can create one using XmlWriter, read in an existing one with XmlReader, even create one or load one in an XmlDocument instance and have at it.

Where to learn more

The source of all XSLT knowledge is, once again, the W3C. See the page at *http://www.w3.org/Style/XSL/* for everything about XSLT.

Zvon also has an XSLT tutorial and reference, at *http://www.zvon.org/xxl/ XSLTutorial/Books/Book1/* and *http://www.zvon.org/xxl/XSLTreference/Output/*, respectively.

To learn about the <msxsl:script> element, see the article "XSLT Stylesheet Scripting using <msxsl:script>" in the *.NET Framework Developer's Guide* at *http://msdn.microsoft.com/library/en-us/cpguide/html/ cpconXSLTStylesheetScriptingUsingMsxslscript.asp*.

Constrain XML Documents

In the early days of XML, the language inherited the concept of a Document Type Declaration (DTD) from SGML. DTDs helped you define valid content for an XML document, but they didn't go far enough to precisely constrain XML document content. A bunch of bright folks at the W3C got together and came up with the W3C XML Schema.

Meanwhile, another set of bright people were coming up with other standards to do the same thing. The next lab will cover the results of that effort, but first, this lab will show you how to validate an XML document with a W3C XML Schema.

Imagine a world where anyone could add anything they wanted to any XML document. That's what W3C XML Schema is here to prevent.

We keep calling it
W3C XML
Schema, which is
very annoying, but
we have a good
reason. We call it
that to differen-
tiate it from
other schema
languages, all of
which are collec-
tively called XML
schema languages.

How do I do that?

In "Read and Write XML," we alluded to the XmlValidatingReader, a class that allows you to validate an XML document read by any other XmlReader. Example 6-10 shows you how to validate an XML document with a W3C XML Schema.

Example 6-10. 05-schema/ValidateXml.cs

```
// 06-xml/05-schema
using System;
using System.Xml;
using System.Xml.Schema;

public class ValidateXml {

  private static int errors = 0;

  public static void Main(string [] args) {
    string xmlfile = args[0];
    string schemafile = args[1];

    XmlTextReader reader = new XmlTextReader(xmlfile);

    XmlValidatingReader validator = new XmlValidatingReader(reader);

    validator.ValidationType = ValidationType.Schema;
    validator.Schemas.Add(string.Empty, schemafile);

    validator.ValidationEventHandler +=
      new ValidationEventHandler(OnValidationEvent);

    while (validator.Read()) {
      // do nothing, errors will be reported through the event
    }

    Console.WriteLine("{0} validation errors found.", errors);
  }

  private static void OnValidationEvent(object sender,
      ValidationEventArgs e) {
    Console.Error.WriteLine(e.Message);
    errors++;
  }
}
```

This program creates an XmlTextReader to read the XML document whose filename is passed in on the command line, much the same as we did in "Read and Write XML." But then it creates an XmlValidatingReader to wrap the XmlTextReader; XmlValidatingReader has a number of extra members that control the validation process.

The first of these, ValidationType, is an enum whose value may be one of *Auto*, to determine the validation type automatically from the XML document's contents; *DTD*, to validate by DTD; *None*, to skip the validation; *Schema*, to use a W3C XML Schema; or *XDR*, to validate by XML Data Reduced. In this case, we're using *Schema*.

XML Data Reduced is used mostly by Microsoft's BizTalk Server. It is not supported by Mono.

Next, the XmlValidatingReader has to be told which schema to use to do the actual validation. Its property Schemas returns an XmlSchemaCollection, to which you can add a new XmlSchema using the Add() method. You can have more than one XmlSchema in the collection, of course; this allows you to validate the XML document against a different schema for each namespace in it.

The next trick is adding a ValidationEventHandler delegate instance to the XmlValidatingReader's ValidationEventHandler event. The private static method OnValidationEvent() will be used to handle each validation error that comes up during parsing. If we did not assign a ValidationEventHandler, the first validation error would cause an exception to be thrown, and no further errors would be reported.

In our OnValidationEvent() event handler, we'll just print the error information to standard error and increment an error counter.

Finally, we call the XmlValidatingReader's Read() method to parse the document, just as you would without validation. In this case, we're not going to do anything but read the document and wait for errors. When that's done, we print the number of errors to standard output.

Example 6-11 shows an XML document that represents an address book.

Example 6-11. 05-schema/AddressBook.xml

```
<?xml version="1.0"?>
<!-- 06-xml/05-schema -->
<AddressBook>
  <AddressBookEntry>
    <Name>
      <First>Niel</First>
      <Middle>M</Middle>
      <Last>Bornstein</Last>
    </Name>
    <Telephone Type="mobile">
      <CountryCode>1</CountryCode>
      <AreaCode>404</AreaCode>
      <Exchange>784</Exchange>
      <Number>0696</Number>
    </Telephone>
    <EmailAddress>niel@bornstein.atlanta.ga.us</EmailAddress>
  </AddressBookEntry>
  <AddressBookEntry>
```

Example 6-11. 05-schema/AddressBook.xml (continued)

```
    <Name>
      <First>Edd</First>
      <Last>Dumbill</Last>
    </Name>
    <EmailAddress>edd@usefulinc.com</EmailAddress>
  </AddressBookEntry>
</AddressBook>
```

Example 6-12 shows an XSD for the address book in Example 6-11.

Example 6-12. 05-schema/AddressBook.xsd

```xml
<?xml version="1.0"?>
<!-- 06-xml/05-schema -->
<xs:schema xmlns:xs="http://www.w3.org/2001/XMLSchema">

  <xs:element name="Name">
    <xs:complexType>
      <xs:all>
        <xs:element name="First" type="xs:string" minOccurs="0" />
        <xs:element name="Middle" type="xs:string" minOccurs="0" />
        <xs:element name="Last" type="xs:string" minOccurs="0" />
      </xs:all>
    </xs:complexType>
  </xs:element>

  <xs:element name="Telephone">
    <xs:complexType>
      <xs:sequence>
        <xs:element name="CountryCode" type="xs:string" />
        <xs:element name="AreaCode" type="xs:string" minOccurs="0" />
        <xs:element name="Exchange" type="xs:string" minOccurs="0" />
        <xs:element name="Number" type="xs:string" minOccurs="1"/>
      </xs:sequence>
      <xs:attribute name="Type" type="xs:string" use="required" />
    </xs:complexType>
  </xs:element>

  <xs:element name="Email" type="xs:string" />

  <xs:element name="AddressBookEntry">
    <xs:complexType>
      <xs:sequence>
        <xs:element ref="Name" />
        <xs:element ref="Telephone" minOccurs="0" maxOccurs="unbounded" />
        <xs:element ref="Email" minOccurs="0" maxOccurs="unbounded" />
      </xs:sequence>
    </xs:complexType>
  </xs:element>

  <xs:element name="AddressBook">
    <xs:complexType>
```

You can worry about what the XSD means later if you want to. For now, just trust us that it defines what an address book should look like.

Example 6-12. 05-schema/AddressBook.xsd (continued)

```
      <xs:sequence>
        <xs:element ref="AddressBookEntry" minOccurs="0" maxOccurs="unbounded" />
      </xs:sequence>
    </xs:complexType>
  </xs:element>

</xs:schema>
```

Surprise! We actually introduced a subtle error into the XML document in Example 6-11. You'll see the error if you compile and run *ValidateXml. exe* as below:

```
$ mcs ValidateXml.xs
$ mono ValidateXml.exe AddressBook.xml AddressBook.xsd
XmlSchema error: Invalid start element: :EmailAddress XML  Line 15, Position
3.
XmlSchema error: Element declaration for EmailAddress is missing. XML  Line
15, Position 3.
XmlSchema error: Invalid end element: AddressBookEntry XML  Line 16,
Position 2.
XmlSchema error: Invalid start element: :EmailAddress XML  Line 22, Position
3.
XmlSchema error: Element declaration for EmailAddress is missing. XML  Line
22, Position 3.
XmlSchema error: Invalid end element: AddressBookEntry XML  Line 23,
Position 2.
6 validation errors found
```

As you can see, the XML document uses `EmailAddress` as the element for email addresses, while the XSD expects `Email`. You can change it in either place and see that no more errors are found.

What about ...

...Working with a W3C XML Schema programmatically? Like XSLT stylesheets, XML Schema Documents (XSDs) are XML documents, so you can work with them just like any other XML document. But in addition to the standard XML stuff, there's something called the Schema Object Model (SOM).

The SOM allows you to work with an XSD as first-class objects. Example 6-13 shows a way to load a XSD document into memory and deal with it either as an `XmlDocument` or as an instance of `XmlSchema`.

Example 6-13. 05-schema/LoadSchema.cs

```
// 06-xml/05-schema
using System;
using System.IO;
```

Example 6-13. 05-schema/LoadSchema.cs (continued)

```
using System.Xml;
using System.Xml.Schema;

public class LoadSchema {

  private static int errors = 0;

  public static void Main(string [] args) {
    string filename = args[0];

    // load it into a DOM
    XmlDocument document = new XmlDocument( );
    document.Load(filename);

    // now load it into a SOM
    XmlSchema schema;
    using (TextReader reader = File.OpenText(filename)) {
      schema = XmlSchema.Read(reader, null);
    }
    schema.Compile(new ValidationEventHandler(OnValidationEvent));

    Console.WriteLine("{0} errors found during schema compilation.",
      errors);
  }

  private static void OnValidationEvent(object sender,
      ValidationEventArgs e) {
    Console.Error.WriteLine(e.Message);
    errors++;
  }
}
```

Compile and run this with the following commands:

```
$ mcs LoadSchema.cs
$ mono LoadSchema.exe AddressBook.xsd
```

As you can see from Example 6-13, you can load an XSD into a DOM just like any XML document, and use any of XmlDocument's properties and methods. The problem is that unless you really know what you're doing, you may end up with a perfectly valid and well-formed XML document whose content is not valid as an XSD. That's where the XmlSchema class comes in.

XmlSchema has a factory method, CreateSchema( ), which creates an instance of XmlSchema for a given Stream, TextReader, or XmlReader. It also has a Write( ) method to save the XSD after any modifications.

But more importantly, it has a Compile( ) method. Compile( ) takes a ValidationEventHandler as a parameter, and it will report any problems with the XSD as they are encountered. This event handler has the same signature as the one in Example 6-10, so you can use the same delegate instance as in that case.

If you don't call Compile( ), you can still save the XSD to a file. But if you try to validate an XML document against an XSD with errors, the errors will be reported to you by the XmlValidatingReader, either through an exception or through the ValidationEventHandler you register with XmlValidatingReader.

Constrain XML Another Way

Around the same time that the W3C was developing their W3C XML Schema standard, James Clark and Murata Makoto were working on their own schema languages, TREX and RELAX, respectively. These two languages were combined into RELAX NG, and the standard was sponsored by OASIS.

The great thing about standards is that there are so many to choose from.

RELAX NG's main claim is that it is simple and easy to learn. Like W3C XML Schema, RELAX NG has an XML syntax, but it also has a compact, non-XML syntax.

In this lab, you'll learn how to validate an XML document with the RELAX NG schema language.

How do I do that?

Example 6-14 shows a program that validates an XML document against a RELAX NG document, called a *pattern*.

Example 6-14. 06-relaxng/ValidateRelaxNG.cs

```
// 06-xml/06-relaxng
using System;
using System.Xml;

using Commons.Xml.Relaxng;

public class ValidateRelaxNG {

  public static void Main(string [] args) {
    try {
      string xmlfile = args[0];
      string patternfile = args[1];

      XmlTextReader xmlReader = new XmlTextReader(xmlfile);
      XmlTextReader patternReader = new XmlTextReader(patternfile);

      RelaxngValidatingReader validator =
```

Example 6-14. 06-relaxng/ValidateRelaxNG.cs (continued)

```
        new RelaxngValidatingReader(xmlReader, patternReader);

    while (validator.Read()) {
        // do nothing, errors will be reported through exceptions
    }
    } catch (Exception e) {
        Console.Error.WriteLine(e);
    }
  }
}
```

Unlike the `XmlValidatingReader` class introduced in "Constrain XML Documents," which supports validation by DTD, W3C XML Schema, and (theoretically) XDR, RELAX NG has a dedicated validating parser. Validating an XML document against a RELAX NG pattern is as simple as instantiating a `RelaxngValidatingReader` with the appropriate `XmlReader` instances for the XML document and the pattern. Example 6-14 demonstrates how to use the `RelaxngValidatingReader`.

`RelaxngValidatingReader` lives in the `Commons.Xml.Relaxng` namespace, so you'll need to reference the *Commons.Xml.Relaxng.dll* assembly on the command line when you compile *ValidateRelaxNG.exe*:

```
$ mcs -r:Commons.Xml.Relaxng ValidateRelaxNG.cs
```

Again, you'll just have to trust us when we say that this grammar defines a valid address book. You can at least see that it seems to match the W3C XML Schema in Example 6-12.

You can use the following command to validate the same XML document from Example 6-11 using the RELAX NG pattern in Example 6-15:

```
$ mono ValidateRelaxNG.exe AddressBook.xml AddressBook.rng
```

Example 6-15. 06-relaxng/AddressBook.rng

```xml
<?xml version="1.0"?>
<!-- 06-xml/06-relaxng -->
<grammar xmlns="http://relaxng.org/ns/structure/1.0">

  <define name="NameContent">
    <element name="Name">
      <element name="First">
        <text/>
      </element>
      <optional>
        <element name="Middle">
          <text/>
        </element>
      </optional>
      <element name="Last">
        <text/>
      </element>
    </element>
  </define>
```

Example 6-15. 06-relaxng/AddressBook.rng (continued)

```xml
<define name="TelephoneContent">
  <element name="Telephone">
    <element name="CountryCode">
      <text/>
    </element>
    <optional>
      <element name="AreaCode">
        <text/>
      </element>
    </optional>
    <optional>
      <element name="Exchange">
        <text/>
      </element>
    </optional>
    <element name="Number">
      <text/>
    </element>
    <attribute name="Type">
      <text/>
    </attribute>
  </element>
</define>

<define name="EmailContent">
  <element name="Email">
    <text/>
  </element>
</define>

<define name="AddressBookEntryContent">
  <zeroOrMore>
    <element name="AddressBookEntry">
      <ref name="NameContent" />
      <zeroOrMore>
        <ref name="TelephoneContent" />
      </zeroOrMore>
      <ref name="EmailContent" />
    </element>
  </zeroOrMore>
</define>

<start>
  <element name="AddressBook">
    <ref name="AddressBookEntryContent" />
  </element>
</start>

</grammar>
```

Without changing *AddressBook.xml* as we did to correct the error in "Constrain XML Documents," you'll see the following output during validation:

```
$ mono ValidateRelaxNG.exe AddressBook.xml AddressBook.rng
Commons.Xml.Relaxng.RelaxngException: Invalid start tag found. LocalName =
EmailAddress, NS = . file:///Mono%20Developers%20Notebook/06-xml/
AddressBook.xml line 15, column 3
in <0x002b8> Commons.Xml.Relaxng.RelaxngValidatingReader:Read ()
in <0x002b8> Commons.Xml.Relaxng.RelaxngValidatingReader:Read ()
in <0x00128> ValidateRelaxNG:Main (string[])
```

You receive only one error, because the errors are reported by an exception. The first exception you receive will be caught and the program will exit. Fix the error in *AddressBook.xml* and the document will validate correctly.

What about...

...Using RELAX NG compact syntax (RNC)? RELAX NG supports a compact syntax, which is less verbose than the standard XML syntax. For example, the RELAX NG compact syntax pattern in Example 6-16 is identical in meaning to the one in Example 6-15.

Example 6-16. 06-relaxng/AddressBook.rnc

```
# 06-xml/06-relaxng
NameDef =
  element Name {
    element First { text },
    element Middle { text }?,
    element Last { text }
  }

TelephoneDef =
  element Telephone {
    element CountryCode { text },
    element AreaCode { text }?,
    element Exchange { text }?,
    element Number { text },
    attribute Type { text }
  }

EmailDef =
  element Email { text }

AddressBookEntryDef =
  element AddressBookEntry {
    NameDef,
    TelephoneDef*,
    EmailDef*
  }*

start =
  element AddressBook { AddressBookEntryDef }
```

As you can see, the RNC version provides exactly the same information without the need for the overhead of end tags and angle brackets. To validate an XML document with an RNC pattern in RelaxngValidatingReader, you would use the code in Example 6-17 instead.

Example 6-17. 06-relaxng/ValidateRelaxNGCompact.cs

```
// 06-xml/06-relaxng
using System;
using System.IO;
using System.Text;
using System.Xml;

using Commons.Xml.Relaxng;
using Commons.Xml.Relaxng.Rnc;

public class ValidateRelaxNG {

  public static void Main(string [] args) {
    try {
      string xmlfile = args[0];
      string patternfile = args[1];

      XmlTextReader xmlReader = new XmlTextReader(xmlfile);

      RelaxngValidatingReader validator;

      using (TextReader source = File.OpenText(patternfile)) {
        RncParser parser = new RncParser(new NameTable());
        RelaxngPattern pattern = parser.Parse(source);
        validator = new RelaxngValidatingReader(xmlReader,
          pattern);
      }

      while (validator.Read()) {
        // do nothing, errors will be reported through exceptions
      }
    } catch (Exception e) {
      Console.Error.WriteLine(e);
    }
  }
}
```

This usage of the using keyword was introduced in "Work with Files" in Chapter 3.

You can compile and run *ValidateRelaxNGCompact.exe* with the following commands:

```
$ mcs -r:Commons.Xml.Relaxng ValidateRelaxNGCompact.cs
$ mono ValidateRelaxNGCompact.exe AddressBook.xml AddressBook.rnc
```

The main difference between Examples 6-14 and 6-17 is the fact that the RELAX NG compact syntax file is not XML, so it can't be accessed with a simple `XmlTextReader`. Instead, you have to open the file using a `TextReader` and instantiate an `RncParser` to parse it into a `RelaxngPattern`. Then you can instantiate a `RelaxngValidatingReader` for the `XmlReader` and `RelaxngPattern`.

Where to learn more

The main RELAX NG web page is located at *http://www.relaxng.org/*. That site also contains a tutorial, at *http://www.relaxng.org/tutorial-20011203.html*, and a compact syntax tutorial, at *http://www.relaxng.org/compact-tutorial-20030326.html*.

Serialize Objects to XML

The .NET framework includes two general categories of object serialization, and their names don't do a very good job of explaining the difference. *Runtime serialization* refers to the ability to serialize an object to arbitrary XML syntax, or to a binary format, as defined in the object itself. *XML serialization*, on the other hand, refers to the serialization of an object to SOAP or arbitrary XML syntax.

Tired of writing ToXml() methods? Any CLR class can write itself as XML.

In this lab, we show you how to use runtime serialization to serialize and object instance to XML, and to deserialize XML back into an object instance.

How do I do that?

Example 6-18 shows a program that will serialize an instance of a class to XML.

Example 6-18. 07-serialization/SerializeObject.cs

```
// 06-xml/07-serialization
using System;
using System.Xml;
using System.Xml.Serialization;

public class SerializeObject {
  public static void Main(string [] args) {
    SerializableObject obj = new SerializableObject();

    XmlSerializer serializer = new XmlSerializer(obj.GetType());
    serializer.Serialize(Console.Out, obj);
  }
```

Example 6-18. 07-serialization/SerializeObject.cs (continued)

```csharp
}

[Serializable]
public class SerializableObject {

  public string MyString = "some string value";

  [XmlElement("MyInt")]
  public int MyInt32 = new Random( ).Next( );

  [XmlAttribute]
  public DateTime MyDateTime = DateTime.Now;

  public AnotherSerializableObject [ ] MyOtherSerializableObjects =
    new AnotherSerializableObject [ ] {
      new AnotherSerializableObject( ),
      new AnotherSerializableObject( )
    };
}

[Serializable]
public class AnotherSerializableObject {

  [XmlAttribute]
  public double MyDouble = new Random( ).NextDouble( );
}
```

Compiling and running Example 6-18 will produce the following output:

```
$ mcs SerializeObject.cs
$ mono SerializeObject.exe
<?xml version="1.0" encoding="us-ascii"?>
<SerializableObject xmlns:xsi="http://www.w3.org/2001/XMLSchema-instance"
  xmlns:xsd="http://www.w3.org/2001/XMLSchema"
  MyDateTime="2004-05-04T10:01:48.2486730-04:00">
  <MyString>some string value</MyString>
  <MyInt>1326585172</MyInt>
  <MyOtherSerializableObjects>
    <AnotherSerializableObject MyDouble="0.694154440282916" />
    <AnotherSerializableObject MyDouble="0.216579754472049" />
  </MyOtherSerializableObjects>
</SerializableObject>
```

Of course, you would have randomly different values for the MyInt element and MyDouble attributes when you run it.

How it works

XmlSerializer, in the System.Xml.Serialization namespace, is the class responsible for serializing objects to XML. When you create an XmlSerializer instance, you pass in the Type of class that this particular instance will know how to convert to and from XML. There are other overloads that provide additional information, such as the default namespace. The `XmlSerializer` instance uses reflection to generate code on the fly to serialize and deserialize objects of the specified type. The `Serialize()` method will write the object to either a `Stream`, a `TextWriter`, or an `XmlWriter`.

The object being serialized, and any objects it references that will also be serialized, must bear the `Serializable` attribute. Certain other attributes can be applied to the members of the class to customize how it will be serialized. For example, the `XmlElement` attribute on the field `MyInt32` tells the serializer to write the element name as `MyInt`; without this attribute, the serializer would use the field's name.

Similarly, the `XmlAttribute` attribute tells the serializer to write the field as an XML attribute rather than the default XML element. You can also pass in a name to `XmlAttribute`.

Collection types, including arrays, are handled automatically. By default, the serializer will create a single collection element with the name of the field (in this case, `MyOtherSerializableObject`). The collection's elements will be serialized with the name of the internal object (in this case `AnotherSerializableObject`).

Deserialization is the reverse of serialization. The `XmlSerializer` class has a `Deserialize()` method that takes either a `Stream`, a `TextReader`, or an `XmlReader` instance as a parameter and returns an `object` that you can cast to the correct type. There's also a `CanDeserialize()` method that will look into an `XmlReader` to determine whether this instance is able to deserialize the given XML stream.

## CHAPTER 7

Networking, Remoting, and Web Services

Computing in the 21st century is all about networking. While a disconnected computer can still be useful for word processing, spreadsheets, and single-player games, a connected computer opens up the world of email, the World Wide Web, and multiplayer games.

Mono gives you access to all the common networking technologies from the hackneyed TCP/IP sockets to higher-level protocols such as HTTP and SOAP, and de facto standards like XML-RPC, as well as database access.

In this chapter, you'll see how Mono lets you use networking technologies to connect to remote computers, call remote procedures, and access databases.

Set Up ASP.NET

It used to be that running ASP.NET required a large investment in software. The Microsoft web application framework requires the Internet Information Services (IIS) that comes with Windows. The Windows End User License Agreement limits how many users may be served from a Windows workstation install, so that means you might need to install Microsoft Windows Server.

Along with the software license cost, there is the cost of administering IIS and Windows Server. If you've got a shop full of experienced Linux administrators, it may be difficult to add Windows administration to their repertoire.

Now you can run ASP.NET on Linux and on other Unix versions, and on Mac OS X. Thanks to Mono's *mod_mono*, your familiar Apache web servers will dish up all the ASP.NET you care to eat.

Mono brings the popular ASP.NET web application environment to non-Windows machines.

In this lab, you'll learn how to download, install, and run *mod_mono* with an Apache web server on Linux and Mac OS X. If you're on Windows, or can't install *mod_mono* for other reasons, you'll learn how to use Apache as a frontend to the standalone ASP.NET server, *xsp*.

How do I do that?

To serve ASP.NET pages, you need two components installed. The first of these, *xsp*, provides the server pages functionality. The second, *mod_mono*, provides integration with the Apache 1.3 and 2.0 web servers. Both of these packages are available from the Mono download page, linked from Mono's home page at *http://www.go-mono.com/*. The packages can be downloaded as RPMs or as source.

First, install *xsp*. If compiling from source, use these commands:

```
$ tar xfz xsp-0.13.tar.gz
$ cd xsp-0.13
Replace /opt/mono with the root of your Mono installation.
This will be /usr if you installed from packages.
$ ./configure --prefix=/opt/mono
$ make
$ sudo make install
```

As *xsp* offers a standalone ASP.NET web server, you can test it now before going further. Part of *xsp* is a handy set of test pages that will have been copied to the *share/doc/xsp/test* subdirectory of your Mono installation. You can use these to verify everything's working. Run the server like this:

```
$ cd /opt/mono/share/doc/xsp/test
$ mono /opt/mono/bin/xsp.exe
Listening on port: 8080
Listening on address: 0.0.0.0
Root directory: /opt/mono/share/doc/xsp/test
Hit Return to stop the server.
```

The first access of a page seems slow, because it's being compiled into bytecode by xsp. On the next access it will load quickly.

By default, xsp.exe will start a server listening on your computer at port 8080. Fire up a web browser and point it to *http://localhost:8080/*. If all went well, you'll see a list of ASP.NET demonstration pages you can run.

The next step is to configure your Apache web server to serve ASP.NET pages. First, ensure that the development files for your Apache server are available. These will already be available if you compiled Apache from source, otherwise they will need to be installed as packages. Next, either install the *mod_mono* RPM on your system or compile it from source like this:

```
$ tar xfz mod_mono-0.8.tar.gz
Replace /opt/mono with the root of your Mono installation.
```

```
$ ./configure --prefix=/opt/mono
$ make
$ sudo make install
```

If your Apache 1.3 or 2.0 server is installed in a nonstandard location, you can tell the configure script about this. For Apache 1.3, provide the location of the apxs program with the option --with-apxs=/path/to/apxs. For Apache 2, give the location of the apr-config program with --with-apr-config=/path/to/apr-config.

In order to get Apache to serve ASP.NET pages, you must configure Apache. Edit your Apache's *httpd.conf* file (usually in */etc/apache*, */etc/httpd*, or */etc/apache2*) and add in the following configuration, adjusting the paths for your Mono installation:

```
Alias /mono "/opt/mono/share/doc/xsp/test"
MonoApplications "/mono:/opt/mono/share/doc/xsp/test"

<Directory /opt/mono/share/doc/xsp/test>
    SetHandler mono
    <IfModule mod_dir.c>
        DirectoryIndex index.aspx
    </IfModule>
</Directory>
```

Reload your Apache's configuration with `apachectl graceful` or `apache2ctl graceful`. Point a web browser at *http://localhost/mono*, and you should see the same list of demonstration pages viewed earlier. If at this point you do not see what you expect, check the Apache error logs, and go over the installation steps again checking that all the paths specified are correct.

mod_mono spawns a helper program, *mod-mono-server.exe*, which is expected to be found at the Mono installation prefix given at configure time. If for any reason your Mono installation changes, this could cause problems. The *INSTALL* file from the *mod_mono* source contains a comprehensive list of Apache configuration directives supported by *mod_mono*. You can use these to adjust the path to Mono after installation.

What about ...

...If you can't install *mod_mono*? There may be various reasons from administrative to technical why you can't install *mod_mono*. Happily, an alternative strategy is available. You've already seen that the *xsp* program can function as a standalone server. This is fine for testing purposes, but may not fit happily into a more formal web serving context where things like server logs or virtual hosts are required.

Installation adds the LoadModule mono_module directive into your Apache configuration automatically. If you change your configuration, don't forget to keep this line in!

Use the --nonstop option to xsp to prevent it from terminating when you press Enter.

The solution is to run *xsp* listening on the local interface and use Apache to proxy it. Invoke *xsp* like this, replacing */var/www/mono* with the location of your content:

```
$ mono /opt/mono/bin/xsp.exe --nonstop --root \
  /var/www/mono --port 8080 --address 127.0.0.1
```

If you have administrative privileges (or can convince the administrator to do this), you can add configuration to your Apache to make it proxy the URL-space */mono/* to *xsp*:

```
LoadModule proxy_module /usr/lib/apache/1.3/libproxy.so

<IfModule mod_proxy.c>
        ProxyRequests Off
</IfModule>
```
The preceding lines will probably already be in your
Apache config, in which case you should not change them.
```
ProxyPass          /mono  http://localhost:8080/
ProxyPassReverse   /mono  http://localhost:8080/
```

Test again by pointing a web browser at *http://localhost:8080/mono/*. Be careful with proxy configuration: you don't want to inadvertently create an "open proxy" that can be misused by malicious remote users. Read the Apache documentation carefully.

Where to learn more

Rather than passing configuration on the command line, it is possible to provide configuration files for *xsp*. Further information is in the manual page, which you can read by typing man xsp. You can also learn a lot from the example files installed by *xsp*. Be sure to check out the *aspx* files, covered further in "Run Web Applications," as well as the *xsp.exe.config* and *sample.webapp* files.

The documentation for the Apache web server is essential reading when it comes to configuring Apache. It should be available as part of your system's Apache installation, and is also online at *http://httpd.apache.org/*.

Run Web Applications

Hordes of
developers around
the world have
already discov-
ered ASP.NET.

Once you have XSP running on your server, whether through Apache or *xsp*, you're ready to start serving up dynamic content. XSP, like its brethren JSP and PHP, provides a server-side scripting environment for web development. But where it excels is in its integration with the CLR. You have full access to the .NET FCL, and you can write code in your choice of .NET languages.

In this lab, you'll see how to run XSP web applications using Mono.

How do I do that?

Example 7-1 shows an XSP page, referred to as an *ASPX*, called *hello.aspx*. It's a simple "Hello, world" sort of page, and it demonstrates several features of XSP.

Example 7-1. 02-webapps/hello.aspx

```
<!-- 07-network/02-webapps -->

<script runat="server" language="C#">
  void SayHello() {
    string name = Request["name"];
    if (name == null || name.Length == 0) {
      name = Request["REMOTE_HOST"];
    }
    Response.Write(string.Format("Hello, {0}!", name));
  }
</script>

<%
string lastVisit = string.Empty;
HttpCookie lastVisitCookie = Request.Cookies["LastVisit"];
if (lastVisitCookie != null) {
  lastVisit = lastVisitCookie.Value;
}

DateTime dateTime = DateTime.Now;
lastVisitCookie = new HttpCookie("LastVisit");
lastVisitCookie.Value = dateTime.ToString();
lastVisitCookie.Expires = dateTime.AddHours(1);
Response.Cookies.Add(lastVisitCookie);
%>

<html>
  <head>
    <title>Hello from ASP.NET</title>
  </head>
  <body>
    <p><% SayHello(); %></p>
    <p>Last visited at <%= lastVisit %></p>
  </body>
</html>
```

The issue of where to put the ASPX files is dependent on your Apache or *xsp.exe* configuration, or your operating system or distribution. On Debian Linux, it might be a subdirectory of */var/www*. You can specify the XSP root directory with the `--root` command-line argument.

With *hello.aspx* in the directory */var/www/monodn*, for example, you can start up *xsp* with the following command line:

```
$ mono /opt/mono/bin/xsp.exe --root /var/www/monodn
Listening on port: 8080
Listening on address: 0.0.0.0
Root directory: /var/www/monodn
Hit Return to stop the server.
```

Point your web browser at *http://localhost:8080/hello.aspx?name=Niel* to see the XSP page in action, as in Figure 7-1.

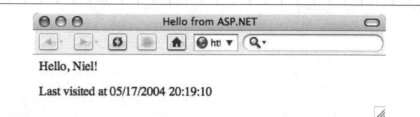

Figure 7-1. hello.aspx in a web browser

How it works

In Example 7-1, you can see that an XSP page, or ASPX, contains two types of content. First, the static content consists of static HTML, including <script> elements, which contain scripts used to process data and generate dynamic content. In this case, one script is a C# method called SayHello( ) that interrogates the HTTP request for certain variables, then writes a string to the HTTP response.

The second type of content, enclosed in <% %> blocks, contains code that is executed when the page is requested. A special form of this block is the <%= %> block, which contains a variable whose ToString( ) method is called and written to the HTTP response.

You can declare variables and methods within a <script> element, but code is only executed within a <% %> block.

In a <script> in *hello.aspx*, we define a server-side method called SayHello( ) that reads a variable from the web request. Each XSP page has access to the System.Web.UI.Page class; in fact, the generated code for an ASPX file is a subclass of Page, so you can access its properties and methods without specifying the class name at all.

One of Page's properties is Request, which returns an instance of System.Web.HttpRequest, which gives you access to all sorts of properties of the HTTP request.

The HttpRequest has an indexer that returns any variables defined in either a cookie, a form field, the query string, in POST parameters, or in server variables. In this example, we're using name, if it is passed in, or REMOTE_HOST, a server variable, if the name is not passed in. The method writes a message to the HttpWebResponse, which comes from the Response property of Page.

Next, in a <% %> block, we declare a string variable called lastVisit. Then we retrieve any existing cookie called "LastVisit". If the cookie has been set by the client, we set the value of lastVisit to the cookie's value.

Now, still within the same <% %> block, we declare a DateTime variable called dateTime, and set its value to the current date and time. We create a new HttpCookie to store this value on the client, and add it to the HttpWebResponse.

Within the static HTML, we invoke the SayHello( ) method within a <% %> block, which writes its message into the HTTP response interleaved with the static HTML. And then we output the value of the LastVisit cookie within a <%= %> block, which also inserts itself into the response. We also set the cookie to expire in one hour.

What about ...

...Separating the code from the presentation? Using a technique called *code-behind*, you can keep .NET code, written by developers, separate from the HTML code, written by designers.

The first step is to write your C# code. Example 7-2 shows the C# code from the SayHello( ) method in Example 7-1 extracted into its own class.

Example 7-2. 02-webapps/Hello.cs

```
// 07-network/02-webapps

using System;
using System.Web.UI;

public class Hello : Page {
  protected void SayHello() {
    string name = Request["name"];
    if (name == null || name.Length == 0) {
      name = Request["REMOTE_HOST"];
    }
    Response.Write(string.Format("Hello, {0}!", name));
  }
}
```

The Hello class extends System.Web.UI.Page, because we need to use the Request and Response properties, and because the compiled ASPX page must inherit from `Hello`. Otherwise, the code is identical to that from the original code in *hello.aspx*.

To access this code–behind assembly, you need to insert the appropriate commands in the ASPX file. Example 7-3 shows the modified *hello.aspx* file.

Example 7-3. 02-webapps/hello2.aspx

```
<!-- 07-network/02-webapps -->

<%@ Assembly Src="Hello.cs" %>
<%@ Page Inherits="Hello" %>

<%
string lastVisit = string.Empty;
HttpCookie lastVisitCookie = Request.Cookies["LastVisit"];
if (lastVisitCookie != null) {
  lastVisit = lastVisitCookie.Value;
}

DateTime dateTime = DateTime.Now;
lastVisitCookie = new HttpCookie("LastVisit");
lastVisitCookie.Value = dateTime.ToString();
lastVisitCookie.Expires = dateTime.AddHours(1);
Response.Cookies.Add(lastVisitCookie);
%>

<html>
  <head>
    <title>Hello from ASP.NET</title>
  </head>
  <body>
    <p><% SayHello(); %></p>
    <p>Last visited at <%= lastVisit %></p>
  </body>
</html>
```

The main change is the removal of the `<% %>` where `SayHello()` was defined, and the addition of two `<%@ %>` blocks. These blocks contain directives that control how XSP processes the ASPX page. In this case, the `<%@ Assembly Src="Hello.cs" %>` directive tells XSP to compile the file named *Hello.cs*, located in the same directory as the ASPX file, and import the assembly at runtime. The `<%@ Page Inherits="Hello" %>` directive instructs XSP to compile the page as a subclass of `Hello`.

The protected `SayHello()` method is now available for use by the generated ASPX page class.

Deploy Web Services

Besides handling web applications, XSP is also responsible for web services in Mono. In fact, web services are really just a special type of XSP page.

Ensure buzzword-compliance with minimal configuration hassles.

In this lab, you'll see how you can deploy web services using Mono and XSP.

How do I do that?

First of all, the server side. Web services are defined with an ASMX file. Example 7-4 shows a web service that takes a pathname and returns an array of strings containing all the files and directories in that path.

Example 7-4. 03-webservices/DirectoryLister.asmx

```
<%@ WebService Language="C#" Class="DirectoryLister" %>

// 07-network/03-webservices

using System.IO;
using System.Web.Services;

[WebService(Namespace="http://www.example.org/",
  Description="Provides a listing of directory contents.")]
public class DirectoryLister {

  [WebMethod(Description="Lists the contents of the given directory.")]
  public string [] ListDirectory(string path) {
    return Directory.GetFileSystemEntries(path);
  }
}
```

Don't forget that you can specify the XSP root directory with the --root command-line argument.

Put *DirectoryLister.asmx* in your XSP root directory, and visit it with a web browser. You'll see the page in Figure 7-2, generated automatically by the XSP host.

You can click around the links to see what's available from the web services host. For example, you can click on the "Client proxy" link to be taken to the automatically generated client proxy code, shown in Figure 7-3. You can choose to have code generated in either C# or Visual Basic.

Click the "Download" link to save the code to a file named *DirectoryListerProxy.cs*. You can also generate the code on the command line with the *wsdl.exe* program. Use this command:

Like a lot of Mono tools, wsdl.exe has a wrapper called wsdl that spares you from the slightly more complex "mono wsdl.exe" invocation.

```
$ wsdl -o:DirectoryListerProxy.cs http://localhost:8080/DirectoryLister.asmx
Mono Web Services Description Language Utility
Writing file 'DirectoryListerProxy.cs'
```

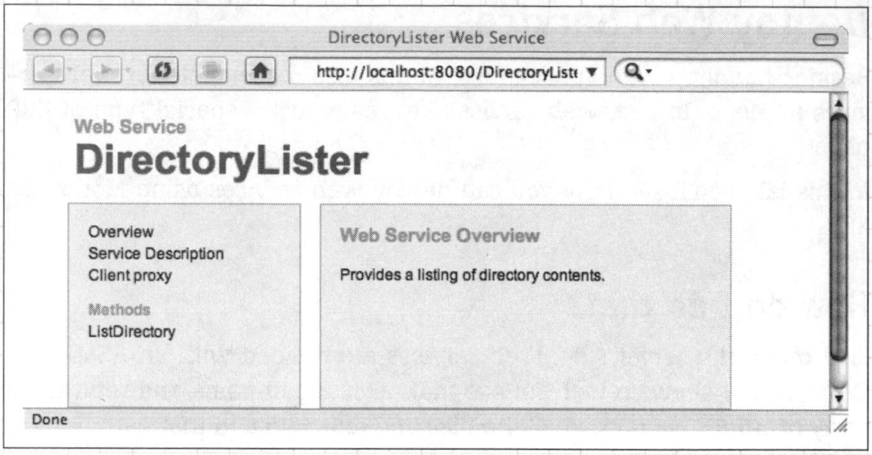

Figure 7-2. DirectoryLister.asmx in a web browser

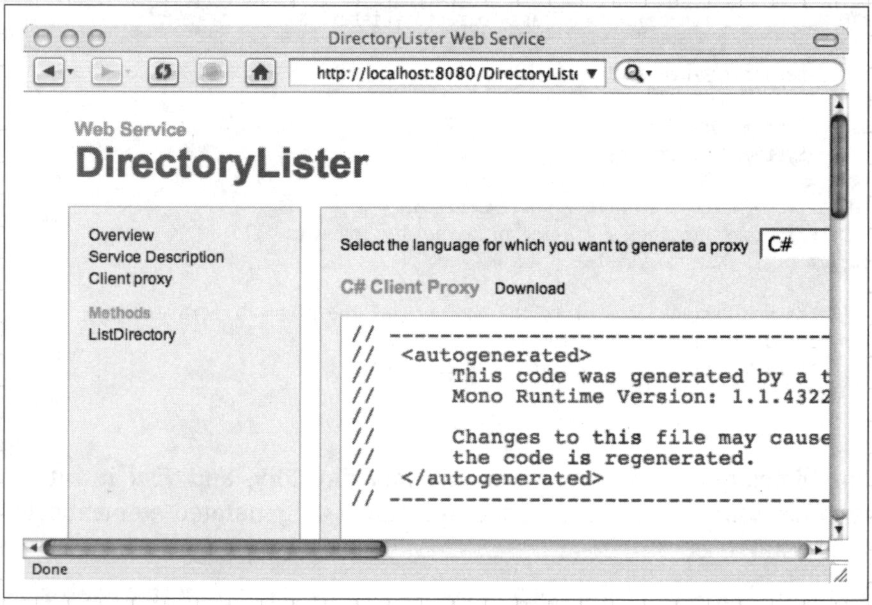

Figure 7-3. Generated client proxy code for DirectoryLister.asmx in a web browser

Either way you can use the generated client proxy class to build a client application. A program that makes use of this generated proxy class is shown in Example 7-5.

Example 7-5. 03-webservices/DirectoryListerClient.cs

```
// 07-network/03-webservices

using System;
```

Example 7-5. 03-webservices/DirectoryListerClient.cs (continued)

```
public class DirectoryListerClient {

  public static void Main(string [] args) {
    string path = args[0];

    DirectoryLister lister = new DirectoryLister();
    foreach (string fileSystemEntry in lister.ListDirectory(path)) {
      Console.WriteLine(fileSystemEntry);
    }
  }
}
```

Build and execute the client with the following commands:

```
$ mcs -r:System.Web.Services DirectoryListerClient.cs \
    DirectoryListerProxy.cs -out:DirectoryListerClient.exe
$ mono DirectoryListerClient.exe /usr
/usr/X11R6
/usr/bin
/usr/dict
/usr/doc
/usr/games
/usr/include
/usr/info
/usr/lib
/usr/local
/usr/man
/usr/sbin
/usr/share
/usr/src
```

What about ...

...Exposing a class from a different assembly as a web service? This is
another form of code-behind, as first seen in "Run Web Applications."

The changes to *DirectoryLister.asmx* make it nearly negligible. All it has
to contain is the `<%@ WebService %>` directive, as shown in Example 7-6.

Example 7-6. 03-webservices/DirectoryLister2.asmx

```
<%@ WebService Language="C#" Class="DirectoryLister,DirectoryLister" %>

// 07-network/03-webservices
```

The `<%@ WebService %>` directive has an attribute named `<Class>` which,
in code-behind, indicates the full assembly and class name. You move
the code itself into a separate file, called *DirectoryLister.cs*, as shown in
Example 7-7.

Example 7-7. 03-webservices/DirectoryLister.cs

```
// 07-network/03-webservices

using System.IO;
using System.Web.Services;

[WebService(Namespace="http://www.example.org/",
  Description="Provides a listing of directory contents.")]
public class DirectoryLister {

  [WebMethod(Description="Lists the contents of the given directory.")]
  public string [] ListDirectory(string path) {
    return Directory.GetFileSystemEntries(path);
  }
}
```

In order to locate the DLL at runtime, the ASMX will look in a subdirectory called *bin* that you need to create. Compile *DirectoryLister.cs* into a library with the following command:

```
$ mcs -t:library -r:System.Web.Services \
-out:bin/ DirectoryLister.dll DirectoryLister.cs
```

The web services interface is the same as before, so you can use the same *DirectoryListerClient.exe* as before to access it.

Communicate with Other Networked Systems

Modern computers are all about networking. Whether something as simple as a telnet session or email, or as complex as SOAP web services, computer network protocols all require a set of lower-level abstractions over the networking stack.

Reach out and touch someone's sockets.

In this lab, you'll see how to communicate over TCP/IP, using both raw sockets and HTTP.

How do I do that?

Example 7-8 shows a program that connects to an HTTP server on the Internet using a TCP/IP socket.

Example 7-8. 04-tcp/TelnetReader.cs

```
// 07-network/04-tcp
using System;
using System.IO;
using System.Net;
```

Example 7-8. 04-tcp/TelnetReader.cs (continued)

```csharp
using System.Net.Sockets;
using System.Text;
using System.Threading;

public class TelnetReader {

  public static void Main(string [] args) {

    Uri uri = new Uri(args[0]);

    TcpClient client = new TcpClient( );

    client.Connect(uri.Host, uri.Port);

    NetworkStream stream = client.GetStream( );
    StreamWriter writer = new StreamWriter(stream);
    StreamReader reader = new StreamReader(stream);

    try {
      WriteLine(writer, "GET {0} HTTP/1.0", uri.ToString( ));
      WriteLine(writer, "Accept: text/html");
      WriteLine(writer, "\r\n");
      Read(reader);

    } catch (ApplicationException e) {
      Console.Error.WriteLine("Got unexpected data: {0}", e.Message);

    } finally {
      stream.Close( );
    }
  }

  private static string Read(StreamReader reader) {
    StringBuilder buffer = new StringBuilder( );
    while (reader.Peek( ) != -1) {
      buffer.Append(reader.ReadLine( ));
      buffer.Append(Environment.NewLine);
    }
    Console.WriteLine(buffer.ToString( ));
    return buffer.ToString( );

  }

  private static void WriteLine(TextWriter writer, string line,
      params object [] args) {
    writer.WriteLine(line, args);
    writer.Flush( );
    Console.WriteLine(line, args);
  }
}
```

Example 7-8 can be run and compiled with the following commands:

```
$ mcs TelnetReader.cs
$ mono TelnetReader.exe http://www.oreilly.com/catalog/0596007922/
```

The result will be something similar to the following, depending on the URL you use:

```
HTTP/1.1 200 OK
Date: Thu, 27 May 2004 14:28:41 GMT
Server: Apache/1.3.29 (Unix) PHP/4.3.4 mod_perl/1.29
P3P: policyref="http://www.oreillynet.com/w3c/p3p.xml",CP="CAO DSP COR CURa
ADMa DEVa TAIa PSAa PSDa IVAa IVDa CONo OUR
DELa PUBi OTRa IND PHY ONL UNI PUR COM NAV INT DEM CNT STA PRE"
Last-Modified: Thu, 27 May 2004 10:45:59 GMT
ETag: "b4d18-7256-40b5c6e7"
Accept-Ranges: bytes
Content-Length: 29270
Content-Type: text/html
X-Cache: MISS from www.oreilly.com
Connection: close

<html>
<head>
...
```

How it works

The TcpClient class represents a TCP/IP client. There's a corresponding TcpServer class for TCP/IP servers. You can create a TcpClient instance and then call its Connect( ) method to connect to a specific hostname and port.

Once the connection is established, you can call the TcpClient's GetStream( ) method to get a Stream instance. Given a Stream, you can create StreamReader and StreamWriter instances to read from and write to the Stream.

After the setup, communication with the HTTP server can take place. Here, we've created private methods to write to and read from the socket, and also echo the communication to standard output. Notice that after writing to the socket, you must call Flush( ) to ensure that the data is actually transmitted to the network.

What about ...

...Connecting to and reading data from a web server without having to deal with sockets? This is simple, thanks to the WebRequest class and its subclasses. Example 7-9 shows a program that connects to a web page and prints its contents to standard output.

Example 7-9. *04-tcp/WebReader.cs*

```
// 07-network/04-tcp
using System;
using System.IO;
using System.Net;

public class WebReader {

    public static void Main(string [] args) {
        Uri uri = new Uri(args[0]);

        WebRequest request = WebRequest.Create(uri);
        WebResponse response = request.GetResponse();

        using (StreamReader reader =
            new StreamReader(response.GetResponseStream())) {
            Console.WriteLine(reader.ReadToEnd());
        }
    }
}
```

Compile and run *WebReader.exe* with the following commands:

```
$ mcs WebReader.cs
$ mono WebReader.exe http://www.oreilly.com/catalog/0596007922/
<html>
<head>

<title>oreilly.com -- Online Catalog: Mono: A Developer's Notebook</title>
<meta name="target" content="Mono: A Developer's Notebook, 0-596-00792-2" />
<meta name="upcoming" content="New" />
<meta name="reference" content="0596007922" />
<meta name="isbn" content="0596007922" />
...
```

Notice that the results don't include the HTTP headers this time. They're all still available, however, as properties of the WebResponse class.

The WebRequest class has a factory method, Create(), which returns an appropriate WebRequest subclass for a given Uri. Specifically, for a URI with the http scheme, an HttpWebRequest will be returned.

WebRequest and its subclasses have a GetResponse() method, which returns an appropriate subclass of WebResponse. For an HttpWebRequest, that's an HttpWebResponse.

The WebResponse class has a GetResponseStream() method, which returns a Stream, which can then be accessed using the other classes in the System.IO namespace.

WebRequest and HttpWebRequest have a few other properties of interest. Some of WebRequest's properties include:

ContentLength
    The size of the web request's content

ContentType
: The MIME type of the web request's content

Credentials
: An ICredentials instance used for authentication

Headers
: A WebHeaderCollection containing the web request's headers

Method
: The protocol method to be used in the web request (for example, POST or GET for an HTTP request)

Proxy
: An IWebProxy used as a proxy for the web request

RequestUri
: The Uri the web request will attempt to access

Timeout
: The number of milliseconds until the request times out

To these, HttpWebRequest adds many others, including several that provide direct access to HTTP headers.

Access Remote Objects

Mono opens the source of truly network-native applications.

When Microsoft announced the .NET Framework in 2000, one of the main selling points was the introduction of a truly network-native application environment. Applications would be able to run anywhere, and would *just know* how to communicate with any other components needed to do the task at hand. Mono makes good on this promise by adding the missing cross-platform piece to the puzzle.

We've introduced a lot of the other framework components through the course of this book, but now it's time for the pièce de résistance. In this lab, we discuss .NET remoting, and show you how to build your own cross-platform networked application.

How do I do that?

Ah, our old friend DirectoryLister again. Be sure to pay attention to how it's changed for Remoting.

There are three pieces to an application that uses remoting. First, the type to be remoted itself. Example 7-10 shows an example of a type which can be remoted, because it extends MarshalByRefObject.

Example 7-10. 05-remoting/DirectoryLister.cs

```
// 07-network/05-remoting
```

Example 7-10. 05-remoting/DirectoryLister.cs (continued)

```
using System;
using System.IO;

public class DirectoryLister : MarshalByRefObject {
    public string [] ListDirectory(string path) {
        return Directory.GetFileSystemEntries(path);
    }
}
```

In addition to the type being remoted, you need a *remoting host*, an executable program to serve the remoted type. Example 7-11 shows a class that can serve DirectoryLister to remote clients.

Example 7-11. 05-remoting/RemotingHost.cs

```
// 07-network/05-remoting

using System;
using System.Runtime.Remoting;
using System.Runtime.Remoting.Channels;
using System.Runtime.Remoting.Channels.Http;

public class RemotingHost {

    public static void Main(string [] args) {
        ChannelServices.RegisterChannel(new HttpChannel(8080));
        RemotingConfiguration.RegisterWellKnownServiceType(
            typeof(DirectoryLister), "dir",
            WellKnownObjectMode.Singleton);

        Console.WriteLine("Press Enter to exit...");
        Console.ReadLine();
    }
}
```

Now you need a client to access the remoted type. Example 7-12 shows a class that can access DirectoryLister remotely.

Example 7-12. 05-remoting/RemotingClient.cs

```
// 07-network/05-remoting

using System;
using System.Runtime.Remoting;
using System.Runtime.Remoting.Channels;
using System.Runtime.Remoting.Channels.Http;

public class RemotingClient {

    public static void Main(string [] args){
        string path = args[0];
```

Example 7-12. 05-remoting/RemotingClient.cs (continued)

```
            ChannelServices.RegisterChannel(new HttpChannel());
            RemotingConfiguration.RegisterWellKnownClientType(
                typeof(DirectoryLister), "http://localhost:8080/dir");

            DirectoryLister remoteObject = new DirectoryLister();
            foreach (string fileSystemEntry in remoteObject.ListDirectory(path)) {
                Console.WriteLine(fileSystemEntry);
            }
        }
    }
}
```

This example is a huge security hole. RemotingHost.exe runs with all of the permissions of the user who started it. Some other user can connect to it and see all of those files, even if her permissions would not normally allow her to. You can beef up the security a bit by limiting the directories that DirectoryLister can access.

To compile all the pieces of this application, enter the following commands:

```
$ mcs -t:library DirectoryLister.cs
$ mcs -r:DirectoryLister.dll -r:System.Runtime.Remoting RemotingHost.cs
$ mcs -r:DirectoryLister.dll -r:System.Runtime.Remoting RemotingClient.cs
```

To run the server, type the following command:

```
$ mono RemotingHost.exe
Press Enter to exit...
```

Now, to run the client, start another shell and type this command:

```
$ mono RemotingClient.exe /usr
/usr/.DS_Store
/usr/bin
/usr/include
/usr/lib
/usr/libexec
/usr/local
/usr/sbin
/usr/share
/usr/standalone
/usr/X11R6
```

For extra credit, change the URL in *RemotingClient.cs* to point to another machine and recompile it. Now copy *RemotingHost.exe* and *DirectoryLister.dll* to that other machine and run *RemotingHost.exe* from there. Now that's remoting!

How it works

Remoting is a special type of web service that uses binary serialization to access objects remotely over a network. Any type that extends MarshalByRefObject may be remoted. Example 7-10 shows such a class, DirectoryLister. Its only method, ListDirectory() takes a string containing the path to a directory and returns an array of strings containing the names of the files and directories within that directory.

A remotable class does not, by itself, do anything special. You need another class to register a remoting channel, and register the type being remoted. In Example 7-11, RemotingHost is that class. The ChannelServices class is used to register the HTTP channel. The RemotingConfiguration class is used to register the well-known service DirectoryLister, with the URL query string "DirectoryLister," as a singleton.

After configuring the remoting infrastructure, the server starts up and listens for incoming connections on the configured port. By calling Console.ReadLine(), the main thread will wait until the user hits the **enter** key, while the remoting server runs in another thread.

On the client side, Example 7-12 shows again how you configure the remoting infrastructure with the ChannelServices and RemotingConfiguration classes. Based on this configuration, the remoting system knows that the DirectoryLister type lives on a "remote" server with the address *http://localhost:8080/DirectoryLister*, and any time that class is instantiated, it will actually create a local proxy to a remote object. You can then use the proxy as though it were a normal, local object instance.

What about ...

...Configuring remoting at runtime? If you're contemplating moving your application tiers from one machine to another, or you want to experiment with different ports and protocols, you don't want to have to recompile every time you change something. The configuration file format is used throughout the .NET framework for application and system configuration, and it can be used for remoting configuration.

The RemotingConfiguration class can be configured from a configuration file, using the method Configure(). Example 7-13 shows the configuration file for the server, which should be named *RemotingHost2.exe.config*. This configuration file includes all of the same information that was defined programmatically in Example 7-11 but allows it to be changed at runtime.

Example 7-13. 05-remoting/RemotingHost2.exe.config

```
<?xml version="1.0" ?>
<!-- 07-network/05-remoting -->
<configuration>
  <system.runtime.remoting>
    <application>
      <service>
        <wellknown mode="Singleton"
          type="DirectoryLister, DirectoryLister"
```

Because remoting uses binary serialization, it's only recommended for use on an intranet, where you have full control of all of the network topology between client and server. For Internet applications, where data may have to pass through gateways that may not like binary data, you should use web services.

You can serve multiple types remotely by including an additional <service> elements in the configuration file for each type to be remoted.

Example 7-13. 05-remoting/RemotingHost2.exe.config (continued)

```
         objectUri="dir" />
      </service>
      <channels>
        <channel ref="http" port="8080"/>
      </channels>
    </application>
  </system.runtime.remoting>
</configuration>
```

To use the configuration file instead of configuring remoting program-matically, use the RemotingHost2 class in Example 7-14.

Example 7-14. 05-remoting/RemotingHost2.cs

```
// 07-network/05-remoting

using System;
using System.Runtime.Remoting;

public class RemotingHost2 {

  public static void Main(string [] args) {
    RemotingConfiguration.Configure("RemotingHost2.exe.config");

    Console.WriteLine("Press Enter to exit...");
    Console.ReadLine();
  }
}
```

The client also requires a configuration file, named *RemotingClient2.exe. config.* Example 7-15 shows that configuration file, which indicates which types are accessed remotely and where the remoted objects will be found.

Example 7-15. 05-remoting/RemotingClient2.exe.config

```
<?xml version="1.0" ?>
<!-- 07-network/05-remoting -->
<configuration>
  <system.runtime.remoting>
    <application>
      <client>
        <wellknown type="DirectoryLister, DirectoryLister"
        url="http://localhost:8080/dir" />
      </client>
    </application>
  </system.runtime.remoting>
</configuration>
```

Again, to use the configuration file instead of configuring remoting programmatically, use the `RemotingClient2` class in Example 7-16.

Example 7-16. 05-remoting/RemotingClient2.cs

```
// 07-network/05-remoting

using System;
using System.Runtime.Remoting;

public class RemotingClient2 {

  public static void Main(string [] args){
    string path = args[0];

    RemotingConfiguration.Configure("RemotingClient2.exe.config");

    DirectoryLister remoteObject = new DirectoryLister();
    foreach (string fileSystemEntry in remoteObject.ListDirectory(path)) {
      Console.WriteLine(fileSystemEntry);
    }
  }
}
```

Another benefit of this runtime configuration technique is that the server doesn't even need to know which classes are being remoted at compile time. It also doesn't need a reference to *System.Runtime.Remoting.dll*. The compilation line becomes much simpler:

```
$ mcs RemotingHost2.cs
```

The client side still needs to know about the `DirectoryLister` class at compile time, because it needs a proxy to the class. But, like the server, it doesn't need to know about *System.Runtime.Remoting.dll*. Its compile line is also simpler:

```
$ mcs -r:DirectoryLister.dll RemotingClient2.cs
```

Now you can run *RemotingServer2.exe* and *RemotingClient2.exe* just as before. But if you want to change the hostname on which `DirectoryLister` is located, you can simply change *RemotingClient2.exe.config* on the client machine to point to the correct server. Or if you need to change the protocol or port number of the service, you can change it in both configuration files without having to recompile the classes themselves.

Invoke Remote Procedures with XML

Have another XML remote procedure call format, they're free.

SOAP web services are great for accessing remote objects, but sometimes they're overkill. .NET remoting is wonderful, too, but it only works when both endpoints are Mono or .NET. XML-RPC, which predates SOAP and .NET remoting, is a simpler, platform- and language-neutral remote procedure call language.

In this lab, you'll see how you can use XML-RPC to invoke procedures on remote machines.

How do I do that?

As of this writing, XML-RPC.NET is at version 0.8.1. Make sure you get the latest version when you install it.

The implementation of XML-RPC for .NET and Mono is called XML-RPC. NET. It's a third-party product from Cook Computing, available under the MIT X11 license. To install, download the latest zip file from *http:// www.xml-rpc.net/* and unzip it onto your system:

```
$ wget http://www.xml-rpc.net/release/xml-rpc.net.0.8.1.zip
$ unzip xml-rpc.net.0.8.1.zip
Archive:  xml-rpc.net.0.8.1.zip
   creating: bin/
   inflating: bin/asyncbettyapp.exe
   inflating: bin/bettyapp.exe
   inflating: bin/CookComputing.XmlRpc.dll
   inflating: bin/mathapp.exe
   inflating: bin/mathservice.dll
  ...
```

XML-RPC.NET also installs with source, although the build system depends on the availability of Microsoft's NMake program maintenance utility. Unless you're building on a Windows machine, you may need to hack some makefiles if you want to rebuild it from source.

After installing, you will find the assembly *CookComputing.XmlRpc.dll* in the *bin* directory. You can copy this assembly into your working directory for local access, or you may wish to install *CookComputing.XmlRpc. dll* in the GAC (see "Package Related Classes with Assemblies" in Chapter 2 for more information on using *gacutil.exe*).

Example 7-17 shows a class that serves an object using XML-RPC. It's similar to those in Examples 7-7 and 7-10 that use web services and .NET remoting, respectively.

Example 7-17. 06-xmlrpc/DirectoryLister.cs

```
// 07-network/06-xmlrpc

using System;
using System.IO;

using CookComputing.XmlRpc;

public class DirectoryLister : MarshalByRefObject {

  [XmlRpcMethod("ListDirectory")]
  public string [] ListDirectory(string path) {
    return Directory.GetFileSystemEntries(path);
  }
}
```

Compile *DirectoryLister.cs* into a library with this command:

```
$ mcs -t:library -r:CookComputing.XmlRpc.dll DirectoryLister.cs
```

Like the SOAP remoting example, DirectoryLister requires a program to host it. You can use the RemotingHost class from Example 7-11 to host DirectoryLister, just like any MarshalByRefObject class. We'll call it *RemotingHost3.exe*, just to keep it clear. Example 7-18 shows the file's contents.

Example 7-18. 06-xmlrpc/RemotingHost3.cs

```
// 07-network/06-xmlrpc

using System;
using System.Runtime.Remoting;

public class XmlRpcServer {

  public static void Main(string [] args) {
    RemotingConfiguration.Configure("XmlRpcHost.exe.config");

    Console.WriteLine("Press Enter to exit...");
    Console.ReadLine();
  }
}
```

To serve objects with XML-RPC, use the config file *XmlRpcHost.exe. config*. It will have to have slightly different contents than those in "Access Remote Objects." Example 7-19 shows the modified configuration file.

Example 7-19. 06-xmlrpc/XmlRpcHost.exe.config

```
<?xml version="1.0" ?>
<!-- 07-network/06-xmlrpc -->
<configuration>
  <system.runtime.remoting>
    <application>
      <service>
        <wellknown mode="Singleton"
          type="DirectoryLister, DirectoryLister"
          objectUri="dir" />
      </service>
      <channels>
        <channel ref="http" port="8080">
          <serverProviders>
            <formatter type="CookComputing.XmlRpc.
XmlRpcServerFormatterSinkProvider, CookComputing.XmlRpc" />
          </serverProviders>
        </channel>
      </channels>
```

Example 7-19. 06-xmlrpc/XmlRpcHost.exe.config (continued)

```
    </application>
  </system.runtime.remoting>
</configuration>
```

Compile *RemotingHost3.cs* with this command:

```
$ mcs RemotingHost3.cs
```

The client program differs from the remoting client in "Access Remote Objects." It's using XML-RPC instead of remoting, so none of the classes in System.Runtime.Remoting are used. Instead, it uses the CookComputing.XmlRpc namespace, and a proxy to the remote object.

XmlRpcClient.cs is shown in Example 7-20.

Example 7-20. 06-xmlrpc/XmlRpcClient.cs

```
// 07-network/06-xmlrpc

using System;

using CookComputing.XmlRpc;

public class XmlRpcClient {

  public static void Main(string [] args){
    string path = args[0];

    DirectoryListerProxy proxy = new DirectoryListerProxy( );

    try {
      foreach (string fileSystemEntry in proxy.ListDirectory(path)) {
        Console.WriteLine(fileSystemEntry);
      }
    } catch (XmlRpcFaultException fex) {
      Console.Error.WriteLine("Fault Response: {0} {1}",
        fex.FaultCode, fex.FaultString);
    }
  }
}
```

Finally, Example 7-21 shows *DirectoryListerProxy.cs*, which is served as a proxy to the remote DirectoryLister object.

Example 7-21. 06-xmlrpc/DirectoryListerProxy.cs

```
// 07-network/06-xmlrpc

using CookComputing.XmlRpc;

[XmlRpcUrl("http://localhost:8080/dir")]
public class DirectoryListerProxy : XmlRpcClientProtocol {
```

Example 7-21. 06-xmlrpc/DirectoryListerProxy.cs (continued)

```
[XmlRpcMethod("ListDirectory")]
public string [] ListDirectory(string path) {
  return (string [])Invoke("ListDirectory",
    new object [] { path });
  }
}
```

Compile *XmlRpcClient.exe* with this command:

```
$ mcs -r:CookComputing.XmlRpc.dll XmlRpcClient.cs DirectoryListerProxy.cs
```

Now, like in "Invoke Remote Procedures with XML," you can run the server from one command shell:

```
$ mono RemotingHost3.exe
Press Enter to exit...
```

and run the client from another:

```
$ mono XmlRpcClient.exe /usr
/usr/.DS_Store
/usr/bin
/usr/include
/usr/lib
/usr/libexec
/usr/local
/usr/sbin
/usr/share
/usr/standalone
/usr/X11R6
```

How it works

The simplest way for XML-RPC.NET to serve objects is to use .NET remoting, as we've done here. Just like regular .NET remoting, you use the RemotingConfiguration class and a configuration file to configure remoting. However, to enable XML-RPC, you must change the <channel> element in the configuration file (as we did in Example 7-18):

```
<channel ref="http" port="8080">
  <serverProviders>
    <formatter type="CookComputing.XmlRpc.XmlRpcServerFormatterSinkProvider,
CookComputing.XmlRpc" />
  </serverProviders>
</channel>
```

The <channel> element now gets a child element called <serverProviders> and its <formatter> child element. These elements indicate the name of the class that will provide the format of the remoted object. By default, the format is SOAP, but in this case, we're using XML-RPC.

On Windows, XML-RPC.NET can also use IIS to serve objects. Because this is a cross-platform book, we'll leave Windows users to investigate that using the XML-RPC.NET documentation.

On the client side, we've used a proxy class, `DirectoryLister`. Although the remoting infrastructure takes care of generating a proxy at runtime in .NET remoting, we have to define the proxy ourselves in XML-RPC. All access to the remote object in `XmlRpcClient` will use the proxy.

If there are any errors in the remote procedure call, the XML-RPC server returns a fault response. On the client side, XML-RPC.NET detects this fault response and throws a `XmlRpcFaultException`, which your client code can catch and handle as needed.

Where to learn more

The official web site for the XML-RPC specification is *http://www.xml-rpc.com/*. There you will find the specification, mailing lists, samples, and much more.

The home page for XML-RPC.NET, maintained by Cook Computing, is *http://www.xml-rpc.net/*. The latest release can always be found there, as well as an FAQ and sample code.

Secure Data from Prying Eyes

The `System.Security.Cryptography` namespace contains numerous classes that allow you encrypt, verify, and secure data with a variety of symmetric and asymmetric algorithms, digital signatures, and hashes, including DES, triple DES, DSA, MD5, RC2, RSA, SHA1, and others.

In this lab, we introduce the Mono cryptographic model and show you how to work with the encryption classes.

How do I do that?

Symmetric, or private key, encryption uses a single, secret key to encrypt and decrypt data. It's called private key encryption because it is only useful if the key is kept secret. The first step in private-key encryption is to create the key. Example 7-22 shows a program that creates a random private key and initialization vector for use in the Triple-DES algorithm, and saves them to disk.

Example 7-22. 07-encryption/Create3DESKeys.cs

```
// 07-network/07-encryption

using System;
using System.IO;
using System.Security.Cryptography;
```

Example 7-22. 07-encryption/Create3DESKeys.cs (continued)

```
public class Create3DESKeys {

  public static void Main(string [] args) {

    TripleDESCryptoServiceProvider des =
      new TripleDESCryptoServiceProvider( );

    des.GenerateKey( );
    Write("private.key", des.Key);

    des.GenerateIV( );
    Write("private.iv", des.IV);
  }

  private static void Write(string filename, byte [] data) {
    using (Stream stream = File.Create(filename)) {
      stream.Write(data, 0, data.Length);
    }
  }
 }
}
```

Compile and run *Create3DESKeys.exe* with the following commands:

```
$ mcs Create3DESKeys.cs
$ mono Create3DESKeys.exe
```

Your generated key will be different, of course, and you probably shouldn't publish it in a book.

You will now have two files, called *private.key* and *private.iv*, that can be used as a private key and initialization vector, respectively, for Triple-DES encryption.

You can view the contents of these files with a tool like od:

```
$ od -x private.key
0000000     f944    7918    0c67    e282    c3a5    6099    040a    bc5f
0000020     b56a    d8a3    9f5e    6b5d
0000030
$ od -x private.iv
0000000     baa1    6300    04a3    51d9
0000010
```

The next step is to use the private key and initialization vector to encrypt data. Example 7-23 shows a program that reads a credit card number from standard input, encrypts it using the Triple-DES algorithm, and saves the encrypted data to a file.

Example 7-23. 07-encryption/CreditCardEncryptor.cs

```
// 07-network/07-encryption

using System;
using System.IO;
using System.Security.Cryptography;
```

Example 7-23. 07-encryption/CreditCardEncryptor.cs (continued)

```
using System.Text;

public class CreditCardEncryptor {

  public static void Main(string [] args) {
    string creditCardNumber = args[0];
    string outFilename = args[1];

    string keyFilename = "private.key";
    string ivFilename = "private.iv";

    byte [] encrypted = Encrypt(creditCardNumber,
      keyFilename, ivFilename);

    using (FileStream stream =
        File.Open(outFilename, FileMode.Create)) {
      stream.Write(encrypted, 0, encrypted.Length);
    }
  }

  // read a file's contents into an array of bytes
  private static byte [] FileContents(string filename) {
    FileInfo file = new FileInfo(filename);
    byte [] contents = new byte [file.Length];
    using (Stream stream = file.Open(FileMode.Open)) {
      stream.Read(contents, 0, contents.Length);
    }
    return contents;
  }

  private static byte [] Encrypt(string clearText,
    string keyFilename, string ivFilename) {

    byte [] key = FileContents(keyFilename);
    byte [] iv = FileContents(ivFilename);

    TripleDESCryptoServiceProvider des =
      new TripleDESCryptoServiceProvider();
    des.Key = key;
    des.IV = iv;

    MemoryStream stream = new MemoryStream();
    CryptoStream cs = new CryptoStream(stream,
      des.CreateEncryptor(), CryptoStreamMode.Write);
    cs.Write(Encoding.ASCII.GetBytes(clearText), 0,
      clearText.Length);
    cs.FlushFinalBlock();

    byte [] encrypted = stream.ToArray();

    return encrypted;
```

Example 7-23. 07-encryption/CreditCardEncryptor.cs (continued)

```
  }
}
```

You can compile and run *CreditCardEncryptor.exe* with the following commands:

```
$ mcs CreditCardEncryptor.cs
$ mono CreditCardEncryptor.exe 4444333322221111 encrypted.dat
```

That's not a real credit card number, of course, but it has the advantage of being memorable and passing the Luhn algorithm.

The resulting file will contain the encrypted credit card number. You can use od again to view its contents:

```
$ od -x encrypted.dat
0000000    9dcb    ae0d    415b    fd45    1a8b    398e    f639    c0e2
0000020    49e9    2c13    38c0    3bd8
0000030
```

Encryption is only useful if you can decrypt the data. Example 7-24 shows a program that reads the encrypted credit card number from the file created in Example 7-23 and prints the decrypted number to standard output.

Example 7-24. 07-encryption/CreditCardDecryptor.cs

```csharp
// 07-network/07-encryption

using System;
using System.IO;
using System.Security.Cryptography;
using System.Text;

public class CreditCardDecryptor {

  public static void Main(string [] args) {
    string inFilename = args[0];

    string keyFilename = "private.key";
    string ivFilename = "private.iv";

    byte [] encrypted = FileContents(inFilename);

    string decrypted = Decrypt(inFilename,
      keyFilename, ivFilename);

    Console.WriteLine(decrypted);
  }

  // read a file's contents into an array of bytes
  private static byte [] FileContents(string filename) {
    FileInfo file = new FileInfo(filename);
    byte [] contents = new byte [file.Length];
    using (Stream stream = file.Open(FileMode.Open)) {
```

Example 7-24. 07-encryption/CreditCardDecryptor.cs (continued)

```
        stream.Read(contents, 0, contents.Length);
    }
    return contents;
}

private static string Decrypt(string inFilename,
    string keyFilename, string ivFilename) {

    byte [ ] key = FileContents(keyFilename);
    byte [ ] iv = FileContents(ivFilename);
    byte [ ] encrypted = FileContents(inFilename);

    TripleDESCryptoServiceProvider des =
        new TripleDESCryptoServiceProvider( );
    des.Key = key;
    des.IV = iv;

    MemoryStream stream = new MemoryStream( );
    CryptoStream cs = new CryptoStream(stream,
        des.CreateDecryptor( ), CryptoStreamMode.Write);
    cs.Write(encrypted, 0, encrypted.Length);
    cs.FlushFinalBlock( );

    stream.Seek(0, SeekOrigin.Begin);
    StreamReader reader = new StreamReader(stream);
    string decrypted = reader.ReadToEnd( );

    return decrypted;
  }
}
```

To compile and run *CreditCardDecryptor.exe* use these commands:

```
$ mcs CreditCardDecryptor.cs
$ mono CreditCardDecryptor.exe encrypted.dat
4444333322221111
```

How it works

The Mono System.Security.Cryptography namespace contains 100% managed code, unlike the Microsoft .NET implementation, which merely wraps the Win32 Cryptography API. There is a level of abstract base classes representing each type of algorithm: AsymmetricAlgorithm, HashAlgorithm, and SymmetricAlgorithm. There are additional abstract subclasses of these, such as RSA and TripleDES, that provide virtual methods that concrete cryptographic providers must implement. We've chosen TripleDESCryptoServiceProvider for this example because it is one of the most commonly used encryption algorithms, although not the strongest.

The basic routine for symmetric encryption begins with the creation of a key, as in Example 7-22. You can either assign a key directly to the `TripleDESCryptoServiceProvider`, or do as we've done and have the provider generate a random one for you the first time you need one.

You can generate an initialization vector at the same time. The initialization vector is an array of bytes that can be used by all the symmetric encryption classes to add additional security to the data. You should store both the key and the initialization vector somewhere safe, of course, because you'll need them to decrypt the data later.

Now that you have a key and an initialization vector, you can begin to encrypt data. All the cryptography algorithms deal with arrays of `bytes`, because the data being encrypted is not necessarily text. Rather than requiring you to deal with reading and writing `byte` arrays, however, the `CryptoStream` class is provided.

`CryptoStream` allows you to chain streams together. All you need to do is instantiate a `CryptoStream`, write data to it, and then read the encrypted data out of it. This is what we've done in the `Encrypt()` method of `CreditCardEncryptor`.

First, we create a `MemoryStream` to hold the encrypted data. Then we create a `CryptoStream` to wrap the `MemoryStream`. The data being encrypted is initially a `string`, so we use the `Encoding` class to convert it into a `byte` array. Then we write the array to the `CryptoStream`, and read the encrypted data from the `MemoryStream`.

In `CreditCardDecryptor`, the same is done in reverse. This time, however, we know that the data coming out will be a `string`, so we can use a `StreamReader` to get the decryptedstring.

In many cases, substituting a different encryption algorithm is as simple as instantiating a difference cryptographic provider at runtime; for example, try replacing `TripleDESCryptoServiceProvider` with `RijndaelManaged` in the examples from this lab and see what happens.

RijndaelManaged happens to be one cryptographic service provider that Microsoft has implemented in managed code.

Where to learn more

Applied Cryptography by Bruce Schneier (Wiley) is widely held to be the definitive text on the subject.

Talk to Databases

It's all about the data.

Everyone knows that when you have a lot of data to store, a database is what you need. There are many, many relational database management systems out there to choose from, and Mono has the ability to communicate with nearly all of them.

Out of the box, Mono has data providers for IBM DB2, MySQL, ODBC, Oracle, OLE DB, PostgreSQL, Microsoft SQL Server, SQLite, and Sybase. These data providers all use the appropriate unmanaged drivers for access. In addition, other projects have provided 100% managed code data providers for Firebird Interbase, PostgreSQL, and MySQL.

This lab will introduce ADO.NET and some of the database drivers provided for Mono.

How do I do that?

Example 7-25 shows a program that connects to a MySQL database, creates a table, inserts some data, and selects the data. The assumptions here are that you have MySQL installed on your local machine, with a database called "monodn" and a username and password with all rights on it.

Example 7-25. 08-database/CreateTable.cs

This program will create a table in your database. If you run it twice, it will fail because the table already exists. Before running it again, you should log in to MySQL with the mysql command-line tool and drop the book table manually.

```
// 07-network/08-database

using System;
using System.Data;

using ByteFX.Data.MySqlClient;

public class CreateTable {

  public static void Main(string [] args) {

      string username = args[0];
      string password = args[1];

      string connectionString = string.Format("Server=localhost;" +
            "Database=monodn;User ID={0};Password={1};", username, password);

      MySqlConnection conn = null;

      try {
        conn = new MySqlConnection(connectionString);

        MySqlCommand command1 = new MySqlCommand("create table book " +
          "( id int auto_increment primary key, title varchar(128), " +
          "pubdate datetime )", conn);

        MySqlCommand command2 = new MySqlCommand("insert into book " +
          "( title, pubdate ) values " +
```

Example 7-25. 08-database/CreateTable.cs (continued)

```
    "( @title, @pubdate )", conn);

  MySqlCommand command3 = new MySqlCommand(
    "select count(*) from book", conn);

  MySqlCommand command4 = new MySqlCommand(
    "select * from book order by pubdate", conn);

  conn.Open( );

  command1.ExecuteNonQuery( );

  command2.Parameters.Add("@title", "Linux Unwired");
  command2.Parameters.Add("@pubdate", new DateTime(2004, 4, 1));
  command2.ExecuteNonQuery( );

  command2.Parameters["@title"].Value =
    "Programming Web Services with XML-RPC";
  command2.Parameters["@pubdate"].Value = new DateTime(2001, 6, 1);
  command2.ExecuteNonQuery( );

  command2.Parameters["@title"].Value = ".NET and XML";
  command2.Parameters["@pubdate"].Value = new DateTime(2003, 11, 1);
  command2.ExecuteNonQuery( );

  int numRows = (int)command3.ExecuteScalar( );
  Console.WriteLine("{0} rows in table book", numRows);

  MySqlDataReader reader = command4.ExecuteReader( );
  while (reader.Read( )) {
    Console.WriteLine("id = {0}, title='{1}', pubdate={2}",
      reader["id"], reader["title"], reader["pubdate"]);
  }
  reader.Close( );

} catch (Exception e) {
  Console.Error.WriteLine(e);
} finally {
  if (conn != null && conn.State == ConnectionState.Open) {
    conn.Close( );
  }
}
  }
}
```

To compile and run *CreateTable.exe*, use these commands:

```
$ mcs -debug -r:ByteFX.Data -r:System.Data CreateTable.cs
$ mono CreateTable.exe username password
```

Of course, passing a password on the command line in cleartext is a bad idea. You should never, never do that in a real application.

You will see the following results:

```
id = 2, title='Programming Web Services with XML-RPC', pubdate=Friday, 01
June 2001 00:00:00
id = 3, title='.NET and XML', pubdate=Saturday, 01 November 2003 00:00:00
id = 1, title='Linux Unwired', pubdate=Thursday, 01 April 2004 00:00:00
```

How it works

The FCL includes an abstract layer of database access APIs, called *ADO. NET*, which is implemented or extended for each particular database server. In Example 7-25, the MySqlConnection represents a MySQL database connection. MySqlConnection implements the IDbConnection interface. Similarly, MySqlCommand implements IDbCommand, and MySqlDataReader implements IDataReader.

To create a database connection, you create an instance of MySqlConnection, passing in the necessary connection string. The format of the string varies according to the specific type of database connection; usually that includes a hostname, database name, username, and password, but it can also include other parameters, such as a connection timeout and the maximum number of connections in the pool.

After creating the connection, you can create MySqlCommand instances against it. Because the connection does not need to be opened yet, you can efficiently create any number of commands in advance and minimize the amount of time that the connection needs to be open.

A MySqlCommand can be any SQL command. In Example 7-25, four commands are shown: a create table, an insert, and two selects.

It's important to note that the connection is not actually opened until its Open( ) method is called. That method can fail if some part of the connection string is incorrect, or if the database server cannot be contacted for some reason.

Each command is executed with one of three methods: ExecuteNonQuery( ), which executes the command and returns the number of rows affected; ExecuteScalar( ), which executes the command and returns the first numeric result value; and ExecuteReader, which executes the command and returns a MySqlDataReader that can be used to iterate over the query result set. More about the MySqlDataReader in a moment.

The insert command in Example 7-25, command2, is particularly interesting. In the values clause, there are placeholders for the column values. The actual values are not assigned until after the connection is actually opened with the Open( ) method.

At that time, the values are added to the MySqlCommand through its Parameters property. This property returns a MySqlParameterCollection, and individual MySqlParameter instances can be added to the collection with its Add( ) method.

The same MySqlCommand instance is used three times, each time with a different set of parameters. The second and third times, the existing MySqlParameter instances are reused. The MySqlParameter has a Value property that can be used to set the parameter's value.

As previously mentioned, the fourth MySqlCommand is executed with the ExecuteReader() method. The MySqlDataReader advances to the next query result each time Read() is called. The MySqlDataReader indexer returns the value of the result set columns. After the result set is exhausted, the MySqlDataReader's Close() method must be called to release its resources.

The entire sequence is wrapped in a try...catch...finally to report any errors and make sure that all the database resources are released by calling the connection's Close() method.

What about ...

...These *disconnected data sets* I keep hearing about? The DataSet class represents an offline view of a database, complete with tables, rows, constraints, and indexes. The DataSet contains collections of DataTable and DataColumn instances, and the DataTable contains a collection of DataRow instances. Each of these types also has numerous other properties to access primary keys, relations, and other relational database features.

You can create a DataSet, fill it with data from a database, and then close the connection. Then you can modify the data in the DataSet offline, re-connect, and update the database with the modified data.

Example 7-26 shows a program that does that.

Example 7-26. 08-database/OfflineDatabase.cs

```
// 07-network/08-database

using System;
using System.Data;

using ByteFX.Data.MySqlClient;

public class ConnectToDatabase {

  public static void Main(string [] args) {

    string username = args[0];
    string password = args[1];

    string connectionString = string.Format("Server=localhost;" +
        "Database=monodn;User ID={0};Password={1};", username, password);
```

Example 7-26. 08-database/OfflineDatabase.cs (continued)

```
          MySqlConnection conn = null;
          DataSet monodn = new DataSet("monodn");

          try {
            conn = new MySqlConnection(connectionString);
            conn.Open();

            MySqlDataAdapter adapter = new MySqlDataAdapter(
              "select * from book", conn);
            MySqlCommandBuilder cmdBuilder =
              new MySqlCommandBuilder(adapter);

            adapter.Fill(monodn);
            conn.Close();

            DataRow [] rows = monodn.Tables[0].Select("id = 1");
            DataRow row = rows[0];

            DateTime pubDate = (DateTime)row["pubdate"];
            Console.WriteLine("original pubdate: {0}", pubDate);
            row["pubdate"] = pubDate.AddDays(15);
            Console.WriteLine("new pubdate:      {0}",
              monodn.Tables[0].Rows[0]["pubdate"]);

            conn.Open();
            adapter.Update(monodn);
            conn.Close();

          } catch (Exception e) {
            Console.Error.WriteLine(e);
          } finally {
            if (conn != null && conn.State == ConnectionState.Open) {
              conn.Close();
            }
          }
        }
      }
```

In addition to DataSet, Example 7-26 also introduces two other new classes. MySqlDataAdapter works as a go-between between a DataTable in a DataSet and a data provider-specific IDbConnection, in this case MySqlConnection. The adapter knows how to fill a DataSet with data from the IDbConnection; in fact, the method that does this is called Fill().

After calling Fill(), you're free to close the database connection and work with the data in the DataSet offline. The DataTable has a Select() method that returns an array of DataRows based on column values. You can then edit the row, and the DataSet will keep track of the changes you make.

The second new class is `MySqlCommandBuilder`. This class can take a `MySqlDataAdapter` for a particular table and create the appropriate insert, update, and delete statements for that table. When the `MySqlDataAdapter`'s `Update()` method is called to update the database with changed data from the `DataSet`, the `MySqlCommandBuilder` generates the appropriate SQL statement to do the update.

Compile and run *OfflineDatabase.exe* with these commands:

```
$ mcs -r:ByteFX.Data -r:System.Data OfflineDatabase.cs
$ mono OfflineDatabase.exe username password
original pubdate: Thursday, 01 April 2004 00:00:00
new pubdate:      Friday, 16 April 2004 00:00:00
```

Now if you examine the database with one of the MySQL tools, you'll see that the `pubdate` field has been changed for the row in `book` whose `id` value is 1.

Where to learn more

Each of the database managements systems supported by Mono has a variety of resources available on the Internet. MySQL, for example, provides corporate support as well as an active user community. The web site is *http://www.mysql.com/*

ADO.NET in a Nutshell by Bill Hamilton and Matthew MacDonald (O'Reilly) provides a reference to the `System.Data` namespace as well as miniature tutorials on using ADO.NET. The *ADO.NET Cookbook*, also by Bill Hamilton (O'Reilly), also provides practical recipes for using ADO.NET in real-world situations.

Cutting Edge Mono

This chapter is all about the really cool things you can do with Mono: how to create finished source code distributions, how to use the latest development features, and how to integrate Mono with other computing environments.

If you intend to use Mono seriously, you'll need to know how to give a professional finish to your application code. The labs on cross-platform compatibility and creating source code distributions with *autoconf* and *automake* programs will help. If you're following Mono's development, or plan to get involved, you'll find the labs on using CVS Mono and new features like generics useful. Lastly, you'll likely want to integrate Mono into the rest of your computing world. This chapter covers how to use BASIC in Mono, and how to get Java and Mono interoperating smoothly.

Maintain Your Sources with the Autotools

Love 'em or hate 'em, GNU autoconf and automake bring predictability and portability to your projects.

If you've ever downloaded source code to an open source project, it's likely you've used GNU *autoconf* and *automake*. These tools are responsible for generating the familiar `configure` script, run before building the software to gather information about your system, and the makefiles that control the software build. These "autotools" have been developed over time to enable trouble-free building of programs on practically any Unix-like system. This includes of course, Mac OS X and Windows-Cygwin (see "Fit Mono into Your World" in Chapter 1) as well as Linux.

Distributing the source code for Mono projects, even within an organization where configurations are relatively predictable, brings with it quite a few of the same problems solved by the autotools, especially if cross-platform deployment is required. Despite a reputation for being a little difficult to understand, packaging source code with autotools brings a developer the advantages of a reliable build system. Indeed, use of autotools is these days practically obligatory for any Linux open source project.

This lab demonstrates setting up *autoconf* and *automake* to create a source package for a Mono executable and assembly. It may prove useful to you to download the full source from the book's web site and refer to it as you read the lab. This lab assumes that you have installed the *autoconf* and *automake* packages from your operating system's package manager. They can also be obtained in source form from the GNU project at *http://www.gnu.org/*.

How do I do that?

To explain the full workings of *autoconf* and *automake* requires more space than is available within these pages. Instead, the aspects of their use most relevant to deploying Mono projects will be noted.

Figure 8-1 shows the layout of files and directories within the example project. After you run *autoconf* and *automake*, there will be many more files, but Figure 8-1 shows the ones that a developer actually needs to create themselves. The directory *src* contains the source code for a simple Gtk# application. The directory *monodn* contains the source for a library assembly that, on installation, will be made available for other programs to use. Typically, these might be distributed in independent packages, but for the convenience of the example here, they are combined in one source package.

The configure stage of the project build gathers information about the users system, and checks that the required programs to build the source code are installed. The configure script then transforms template files given to it, typically with the file suffix *.in*, filling in the right values for the user's system. To create the configure script, you need to create a *configure.in* file, which includes configuration directives that are then compiled into the final script by the `autoconf` command. Example 8-1 shows the source for this lab's example project.

```
helloworld/
        AUTHORS
        ChangeLog
        Makefile.am
        NEWS
        README
        autogen.sh
        configure.in
        src/
                AssemblyInfo.cs.in
                HelloWorld.cs
                HelloWorld.in
                Makefile.am
        monodn/
                AssemblyInfo.cs.in
                Makefile.am
                MonkeyImage.cs
                MonoDN.Demo.pub
        resources/
                Makefile.am
                monkey.png
```

Figure 8-1. Project directory layout

Example 8-1. Configure source file: 01-autotools/helloworld/configure.in

The string dnl introduces a comment in configure.in files. Really.

```
dnl 08-advanced/01-autotools/helloworld
AC_INIT(HelloWorld, 0.1, bugs@example.org)
AC_CANONICAL_SYSTEM
AC_PREREQ(2.13)
AM_INIT_AUTOMAKE
AM_MAINTAINER_MODE

AC_PROG_INSTALL

dnl pkg-config
AC_PATH_PROG(PKG_CONFIG, pkg-config, no)
if test "x$PKG_CONFIG" = "xno"; then
  AC_MSG_ERROR([You need to install pkg-config])
fi

MONO_REQUIRED_VERSION=0.91
PKG_CHECK_MODULES(MONO, mono >= $MONO_REQUIRED_VERSION)

MONODIR=`$PKG_CONFIG --variable=exec_prefix mono`
MONOBIN="$MONODIR/bin"
MONO="$MONOBIN/mono"
MINT="$MONOBIN/mint"
MCS="$MONOBIN/mcs"
GACUTIL="$MONOBIN/gacutil"

if test ! -x "$MONO" -a ! -x "$MINT"; then
  AC_MSG_ERROR([No Mono runtime found])
fi
```

Example 8-1. Configure source file: 01-autotools/helloworld/configure.in (continued)

```
if test ! -x "$MONO"; then
    MONO = $MINT
fi

CS="C#"
if test ! -x "$MCS"; then
  AC_MSG_ERROR([No $CS compiler found])
fi

if test ! -x "$GACUTIL"; then
  AC_MSG_ERROR([No Mono gacutil found])
fi

AC_SUBST(MCS)
AC_SUBST(MONO)
AC_SUBST(GACUTIL)

dnl gtk-sharp
GTKSHARP_REQUIRED_VERSION=0.91.99
PKG_CHECK_MODULES(GTKSHARP, gtk-sharp >= $GTKSHARP_REQUIRED_VERSION)
AC_SUBST(GTKSHARP_LIBS)

AC_OUTPUT([
Makefile
src/Makefile
src/AssemblyInfo.cs
src/HelloWorld
monodn/Makefile
monodn/AssemblyInfo.cs
resources/Makefile
])
```

There are a few things to note from Example 8-1. A program called *pkg-config* determines version and configuration details of Mono and Gtk#. The configurations themselves can be found in the *lib/pkgconfig* directory of your Mono installation. Be sure to have set PKG_CONFIG_PATH as shown in "Install Mono" in Chapter 1 so that *pkg-config* can find the configuration files. Configuration data, specifically Mono's installation prefix, is then used to determine the location of the rest of the Mono tools needed for the compilation: the runtime, the compiler, and the GAC utility. As a somewhat belt-and-braces precaution, these tools are all checked individually to see whether they exist and whether the current user has permissions to execute them. The AC_SUBST directives ensure that the location of these tools are then available for substitution in the template makefiles. Gtk# is checked in a similar way. The PKG_CHECK_MODULES directive automatically fills GTKSHARP_LIBS with the right options to pass to *mcs* to compile Gtk# programs

You should find pkg-config available within your operating system. If not, download it from http:// freedesktop.org/ Software/ pkgconfig.

The final directive in Example 8-1 determines which templates should be filled in by the configure script. For each file in the AC_OUTPUT list, a corresponding file with a *.in* suffix is used as the template. At-signs (@) are used to surround variables in the templates. For instance, the string @MONO@ will be replaced with the path of the Mono runtime determined earlier in the configuration.

Notice that in Figure 8-1 there are no *Makefile.in* files listed. It is the role of *automake* to generate these from the *Makefile.am* files. Example 8-2 shows the automake source for compiling the standalone executable.

You could skip automake if you wanted and roll your own Makefile.in, but automake contains a lot of useful machinery for generating source distributions.

Example 8-2. Executable makefile source: 01-autotools/helloworld/src/Makefile.am

```
# 08-advanced/01-autotools/helloworld/src
hellowrapdir = $(bindir)
hellowrap_SCRIPTS = HelloWorld

helloworlddir = $(pkglibdir)
helloworld_SCRIPTS = HelloWorld.exe

EXTRA_DIST = $(helloworld_sources) $(helloworld_sources_in) \
        HelloWorld.in

CLEANFILES = HelloWorld.exe
DISTCLEANFILES = HelloWorld $(helloworld_generated_sources)

helloworld_sources_in = AssemblyInfo.cs.in
helloworld_generated_sources = $(helloworld_sources_in:.in=)
helloworld_sources = HelloWorld.cs

helloworld_build_sources = $(addprefix $(srcdir)/, $(helloworld_sources))
helloworld_build_sources += $(helloworld_generated_sources)

helloworld_resources = $(srcdir)/../resources/monkey.png
helloworld_embedded = $(foreach res,$(helloworld_resources),\
  $(addprefix -resource:,$(res)),$(notdir $(res)))

HelloWorld.exe: $(helloworld_build_sources) $(helloworld_resources)
  $(MCS) $(GTKSHARP_LIBS) $(helloworld_embedded) -out:$@ \
  $(helloworld_build_sources)
```

Example 8-2 actually deals with two distinct targets, *hellowrap* and *helloworld*. As automake does not have a native understanding of what a Mono program is, it is most convenient to treat them as if they were simple scripts. Looking at the simplest target first, *hellowrap* controls the installation of a small shell script that executes the Mono executable. This script, *HelloWorld*, is created by the configure script, from a *HelloWorld.in* file that looks like this:

```
#!/bin/sh
```

```
# wrapper script to run the HelloWorld mono program
exec @MONO@ @prefix@/lib/@PACKAGE@/HelloWorld.exe "$@"
```

The actual Mono executable itself is installed not in the main executable path, *bin*, but in a subdirectory of *lib* specific to this software package. This path is provided by the variable $(pkglibdir). This way, only natively executable programs get installed in a system's *bin* directories, keeping things neat and tidy.

The other target in the makefile, *helloworld*, is the Mono executable assembly itself. Although the number of variable definitions look complex, it is in fact some flexible *make* magic to ensure a clean compile. With *automake*, there tends to be a big up-front investment in configuration. Further development of the application would probably only require changes to helloworld_sources and helloworld_resources.

The final bit of housekeeping required for distributing a Mono assembly is the creation and inclusion of the *AssemblyInfo.cs*, introduced in "Package Related Classes with Assemblies" in Chapter 2. Example 8-3 shows the template that the configure script uses to generate *AssemblyInfo.cs*.

Go through the effort to ensure that the .cs files have the source directory $(srcdir) prefixed to them so that the program can be compiled in a different directory from the source code.

Example 8-3. Executable AssemblyInfo template: 01-autotools/helloworld/src/ AssemblyInfo.cs.in

```
// 08-advanced/01-autotools/helloworld/src
//
// AssemblyInfo.cs.in for project 'hello world'
//
// Authors:
//   Edd Dumbill <edd@usefulinc.com>
//
using System.Reflection;
using System.Runtime.CompilerServices;

[assembly: AssemblyVersion("@VERSION@.*.*")]
[assembly: AssemblyTitle ("Gtk# Hello World")]
[assembly: AssemblyDescription ("Simple Gtk# Demo Application")]
[assembly: AssemblyCopyright ("Copyright (C) O'Reilly Media, Inc.")]
[assembly: AssemblyCompany ("O'Reilly Media, Inc.")]
```

The AssemblyVersion given in Example 8-3 contains four-numbered components: *major.minor.build.revision*. The major and minor numbers are derived directly from those specified in AC_INIT in *configure.in*. The build number should be a monotonically increasing number representing a checkpoint of the source code. Imagine, for instance, distributing your code to an internal QA team before making a release. The build number can be used to identify these "internal releases." The revision number should be increased each time a change is made within a current build.

The complexity of the version number scheme is likely to prove burdensome in situations where such control is not needed, especially where there are only one or two developers working on a project. This is where writing *.* for build and revision number comes in handy, as in Example 8-3. The compiler interprets this wildcard, and substitutes an arbitrary number that increases daily for the build and the number of seconds since midnight for the revision. This way the properties of the two version components are satisfied without any developer intervention being required. For example, after you build the example from this lab, try:

```
$ monodis --assembly src/HelloWorld.exe | grep Version
Version:        0.1.1597.39133
```

How you use version numbers will depend a lot on whether you intend to distribute the source code of your application, rather than binary-only builds. In the open source world, it is traditionally the job of distributors to take care of the binary builds. With commercial software, the vendors distributes the binary builds. In both these scenarios the build and revision numbers are vital for bug-tracking purposes. If you just intend to distribute the source, you don't need to pay much attention to build and revision, as you will increase the main version number with each release.

The *automake* source for compiling the library assembly is shown in Example 8-4. It follows the same basic pattern as that for the standalone executable.

The indents in Example 8-4 are tabs, not spaces, as with all makefiles.

Example 8-4. Library makefile source:01-autotools/helloworld/monodn/Makefile.am

```
# 08-advanced/01-autotools/helloworld/monodn
monodndll = MonoDN.Demo.dll

EXTRA_DIST = $(monodndll_sources) $(monodndll_sources_in) \
        MonoDN.Demo.pub

ASSEMBLY = $(monodndll)
ASSEMBLY_NAME = $(subst .dll,,$(ASSEMBLY))

noinst_SCRIPTS = $(monodndll)
CLEANFILES = $(monodndll)
DISTCLEANFILES = $(monodndll_generated_sources)

monodndll_sources_in = AssemblyInfo.cs.in
monodndll_generated_sources = $(monodndll_sources_in:.in=)
monodndll_sources = MonkeyImage.cs

monodndll_build_sources = $(addprefix $(srcdir)/, $(monodndll_sources))
monodndll_build_sources += $(monodndll_generated_sources)
```

Example 8-4. Library makefile source:01-autotools/helloworld/monodn/Makefile.am

```
monodndll_resources = $(srcdir)/../resources/monkey.png
monodndll_embedded = $(foreach res,$(monodndll_resources),\
    $(addprefix -resource:,$(res)),$(notdir $(res)))

$(monodndll): $(monodndll_build_sources) $(monodndll_resources)
  $(MCS) $(GTKSHARP_LIBS) $(monodndll_embedded) \
    -target:library -out:$@ $(monodndll_build_sources)

# GAC installation of DLL
install-data-local:
  $(GACUTIL) /i $(ASSEMBLY) /f /package $(PACKAGE) \
    /root $(DESTDIR)$(libdir)

uninstall-local:
  $(GACUTIL) /u $(ASSEMBLY_NAME) /package $(PACKAGE) \
    /root $(DESTDIR)$(libdir)
```

The difference between the executable and the library lies primarily in
what happens when the software is installed by the user running make
install. Whereas the executable and its wrapper script can be copied
into the proper place in the filesystem, the library must be installed in
the GAC using the gacutil program. The custom install-data-local
rule in Example 8-4 achieves this. The specification at the top of the file
of the library assembly as a noinst_SCRIPT prevents *automake* from generating any installation rules itself.

The structure of the *AssemblyInfo.cs* file for the assembly is a little more
involved, as the installation destination is the GAC. "Package Related
Classes with Assemblies" in Chapter 2 introduced the concept of signing
assemblies. However, if you intend to distribute the source code to the
assembly you do not want to distribute your private signing key, or anybody could pass off a build as being created by you. For this reason, you
can use the public part of the signing key pair to give the assembly the
strong name it needs for the GAC, and indicate that you will delay signing the assembly until later. Example 8-5 shows the *AssemblyInfo.cs*
template for the *MonoDN.Demo.dll* library assembly.

Example 8-5. Library AssemblyInfo template: 01-autotools/helloworld/monodn/
AssemblyInfo.cs.in

```
// 08-advanced/01-autotools/helloworld/monodn
//
// AssemblyInfo.cs.in for project 'hello world'
//
// Authors:
//   Edd Dumbill <edd@usefulinc.com>
```

Example 8-5. *Library AssemblyInfo template: 01-autotools/helloworld/monodn/ AssemblyInfo.cs.in (continued)*

```
//
using System.Reflection;
using System.Runtime.CompilerServices;

[assembly: AssemblyVersion("@VERSION@.*.*")]
[assembly: AssemblyTitle ("MonoDN Demo Library")]
[assembly: AssemblyDescription ("Simple Demo Assembly")]
[assembly: AssemblyCopyright ("Copyright (C) O'Reilly Media, Inc.")]
[assembly: AssemblyCompany ("O'Reilly Media, Inc.")]

[assembly: AssemblyDelaySign(true)]
[assembly: AssemblyKeyFile("@srcdir@/MonoDN.Demo.pub")]

// generate the pubkey from your private .snk file
// like this: sn -p key.snk key.pub
```

Unlike Microsoft's .NET GAC, Mono 1.0 permits the execution of unsigned assemblies by default, so signing the assembly before installation is not required. Nevertheless, distributors of binary packages may still want to sign their assemblies. This can be done by inserting the following just after the $(MCS) compilation step:

```
sn -R MonoDN.Demo.dll keypair.snk
```

Running *monodis* on the compiled assembly yields the following results:

```
$ monodis --assembly monodn/MonoDN.Demo.dll
Assembly Table
Name:          MonoDN.Demo
Hash Algoritm: 0x00008004
Version:       0.1.1597.39134
Flags:         0x00000000
PublicKey:     BlobPtr (0x00000032)
       Dump:
0x00000000: 00 24 00 00 04 80 00 00 94 00 00 00 06 02 00 00
0x00000010: 00 24 00 00 52 53 41 31 00 04 00 00 11 00 00 00
0x00000020: 79 B2 79 D1 38 F3 43 05 7F 96 44 0E CD F7 2E 2E
0x00000030: 61 5B 8B 13 B2 83 E6 D4 C1 E3 15 5B 64 EE 0F A1
0x00000040: 08 16 B4 82 9E A4 59 59 60 69 0B B5 9F FB 81 A9
0x00000050: B7 B9 1E 41 20 67 86 98 91 29 EE 14 E8 E0 EE 68
0x00000060: F1 6B E5 CE FE 19 A3 58 8B 87 D4 DB F7 4F EF 38
0x00000070: FF E7 7C FC B4 B1 6B 21 D7 90 DA C7 39 30 C8 76
0x00000080: 5A CF D1 81 E1 BA 6D CC 1C 36 DD C6 37 DF 79 1F
0x00000090: AB 50 94 45 DB 0F 44 8D 8A 04 F4 54 0F 49 81 9B
Culture:
```

Having explained the component pieces, it's time to make the whole thing work. Using the source from the book's web site, invoke the *autogen.sh* script to run the automake and autoconf commands in the right order. *autogen.sh* then runs the generated `configure` script. The demo program and assembly can then be compiled with `make`:

```
$ ./autogen.sh --prefix=/opt/demo
$ make
```

Running the `make install` command as the root user will install the software, and you are ready to try it out by running `HelloWorld`. Verify that the demonstration assembly has been installed in the GAC:

```
$ gacutil -l | grep MonoDN
MonoDN.Demo, Version=0.1.1597.39134, Culture=neutral,
PublicKeyToken=f3f93bddb91a82f4
```

Finally, you can generate a source archive, which can be distributed to other people so they can compile and install the software themselves.

```
$ make distcheck
...
=====================================================
HelloWorld-0.1.tar.gz is ready for distribution
=====================================================
```

If an error occurs with make distcheck you've probably made an assumption in your makefiles about the location of a file. Go back and prefix it with the appropriate path, relative to $(srcdir).

Write Cross-Platform Compatible Programs

Mono programs will run on all of today's major computing platforms, thanks to the porting efforts of the Mono team. However, not everything is under the control of the Mono team, and decisions that developers make will dictate how well their programs run on all platforms. Assumptions about the filesystem, graphic user interface environment, and other resources can limit the number of platforms on which a program will run properly.

Not all operating systems are created equal. Learn the limits, and your programs will run fine everywhere.

Not all programs will be targeted at running everywhere of course, but if there is no reason to restrict the portability of your application, why do so? This lab contains a variety of questions you should ask yourself when designing and developing Mono programs in order to obtain the greatest portability. It also has hints for Windows .NET programmers wanting to ensure their code can run on Mono too.

How do I do that?

Here are the most common cross-platform issues that programmers will encounter:

Manipulating files
> Differences between filesystems are one of the biggest causes of cross-platform incompatibility. And among such errors, the most

frequent assumption is that of the character used as a filename path separator. On Windows, this is \, and on Unix systems it is /. These should never ever appear hardcoded in programs. Use `System.IO.Path.DirectorySeparatorChar`. Even better, use the `System.IO.Path.Combine` method:

```
string directory = "tmp";
string filename = "myfile";
// WRONG
string wrongpath = directory + "/" + filename;
// RIGHT!
string rightpath = System.IO.Path.Combine (directory, filename);
```

Other methods in `System.IO.Path` provide convenience functions for manipulating paths, to avoid tiresome string manipulation. Use `IsPathRooted` to determine if a file lies in a certain path, and `GetPathRoot` and `GetFileName` to get the directory name and filename respectively from a path.

Programs should also never rely on filesystem layout. For example, on Unix-like operating systems, such as Linux and Mac OS X, the path */tmp* is generally available for writing temporary files. Windows prefers the *TEMP* subdirectory of the OS install directory. You can always reliably get a temporary filename using `GetTempFileName`.

While Unix-like systems assume a unified filesystem layout, in which there is one and only one logical root /, Windows systems have multiple logical roots. Programs offering operations on arbitrary files should consider this when presenting a choice of path to the user. Example 8-6 shows how to discover the possible logical roots.

Example 8-6. Discovering logical roots: 02-compat/ListVolumes.cs

```
// 08-advanced/02-compat
using System;
using System.IO;

public class Demo {
  public static void Main (string [] args)
  {
    foreach (string dir in Directory.GetLogicalDrives ()) {
      Console.WriteLine ("{0}", dir);
    }
  }
}
```

On Windows, you can't give a file a reserved name like CON, PRN, AUX, COM1 etc. or LPT1 etc.

Another thing to watch out for when manipulating files is the case-sensitivity of the filesystem. By default, Unix-like platforms excepting Mac OS X have case-sensitive filesystems, Windows and OS X do not. So on Linux, *ReadMe* and *README* are two separate files, on

Windows they are the same file. If you've done most of your programming on Windows, this is an easy trap to fall into. Perhaps the best strategy is to decide to make all your filenames lower case, and leave it that way.

Graphical user interfaces

The accepted wisdom among designers of user interfaces is that interfaces ought to integrate with the platform on which they are run. So, using `System.Windows.Forms` provides the best-looking interface on Windows, while using Gtk# gives the best results on GNOME-using platforms such as Linux or Solaris. It's not just the toolkit choice that's at stake, other conventions such as menu titles, dialog button order, drag and drop and so on all come into play.

However, there are many scenarios in which you can't justify the effort of coding a separate UI layer for Windows, Linux, and OS X. Instead you have to make a choice between `System.Windows.Forms` (SWF) and Gtk#. The advantage of SWF is that it's part of Microsoft's .NET framework, and a good conversion route for bringing software from Windows onto Linux. The disadvantage is that Mono's SWF will only run on x86 Linux. It's not terribly cross platform, and it also exists as a free product only at Microsoft's discretion. The only real choice for cross-platform interfaces is to use Gtk#.

Even with Gtk#, there are things to watch out for. Some parts of Gtk# are not available on Windows platforms. The namespaces that are implemented everywhere include `GLib`, `Pango`, `Atk`, `Gdk`, `Gtk`, and `Glade`. Cross-platform GUIs are unfortunately a compromise at the best of times.

Configuration

Many Windows programs written in the .NET framework use the Windows registry to store their configuration. This prevents such programs running on Mono. Unfortunately GConf is not available on Windows, so is not a one-size-fits-all solution either. One solution to this problem is to create an abstract configuration class to use the Windows registry when compiled on Microsoft's .NET Framework on Windows, and to use GConf on other platforms when compiled with Mono. A less complex, and more reliable, method is to just use files to store configuration.

P/Invoke

Invoking functions from platform libraries is always going to be a large opportunity for cross-platform inconsistencies. One of the major issues is the difference in naming schemes between Unix-like systems and Windows for native dynamic libraries. Fortunately, Mono has a mechanism for coping with this. When an assembly is installed into the GAC, any *.config* file for it is installed too. The *.config* file for *gtk-sharp.dll* on a Linux machine looks something like Example 8-7, and provides a mapping between DLLs imported with the `DllImport` attribute and the libraries existing on the target system.

Example 8-7. gtk-sharp config file

```
<configuration>
  <dllmap dll="libglib-2.0-0.dll" target="libglib-2.0.so.0"/>
  <dllmap dll="libgobject-2.0-0.dll" target="libgobject-2.0.so.0"/>
  <dllmap dll="libatk-1.0-0.dll" target="libatk-1.0.so.0"/>
  <dllmap dll="libgtk-win32-2.0-0.dll" target="libgtk-x11-2.0.so.0"/>
</configuration>
```

Using a mapping similar to that shown in Example 8-7 the code need not reference different DLL names depending on where it is deployed, as this code snippet from the *gtk-sharp* source shows:

```
[DllImport("libgtk-win32-2.0-0.dll")]
static extern IntPtr gtk_window_list_toplevels();
```

As long as the same compiled library with the same API is installed on all target platforms, it can be used with P/Invoke.

What about ...

...Coding workarounds? Sooner or later in a cross-platform application there'll come a time when platform-specific code is needed. To do that, a program needs to discover at runtime on what sort of system it is running. Example 8-8 shows code that detects the runtime platform.

Yes, this is a hack! Hopefully things will get better as Mono evolves.

Example 8-8. Platform-specific execution: 02-compat/PrintOS.cs

```
// 08-advanced/02-compat
using System;
using System.Diagnostics;
using System.IO;

class PrintOS {
  public static void Main (string [] args)
  {
    OperatingSystem os = Environment.OSVersion;

    switch ((int) os.Platform) {
      case 128:
        // Unix-specific code
        string kernel = DiscoverUnixKernel ();
        switch (kernel) {
```

Example 8-8. Platform-specific execution: 02-compat/PrintOS.cs (continued)

```
          case "Linux":
            Console.WriteLine ("On Linux");
            break;
          case "Darwin":
            Console.WriteLine ("On Mac OS X");
            break;
        }
        break;
      case (int) PlatformID.WinCE:
        // Win-CE specific code, etc.
        break;
      default:
        break;
    }
}

public static string DiscoverUnixKernel ()
{
  ProcessStartInfo startInfo = new ProcessStartInfo();
  startInfo.Arguments = "-s";
  startInfo.RedirectStandardOutput = true;
  startInfo.RedirectStandardError = true;
  startInfo.UseShellExecute = false;
  foreach (string unameprog in new string [] {
      "/usr/bin/uname", "/bin/uname" }) {
    try {
      startInfo.FileName = unameprog;
      Process uname = Process.Start (startInfo);
      StreamReader stdout = uname.StandardOutput;
      return stdout.ReadLine (). Trim ();
    } catch (System.ComponentModel.Win32Exception e) {
      // no uname. no idea what to do next
    }
  }
  return null;
}
}
```

Run Java in Mono

There has been much made in the computer press of the rivalry between the common runtime used by Mono and Microsoft's .NET, and Sun's Java technology. In fact, the two can actually work together, thanks to a remarkable tool called IKVM. IKVM is a runtime for Java that works by translating Java bytecode into Common Intermediate Language bytecode. By incorporating bridging technology, IKVM enables Java programs to make calls to Mono assemblies, and Mono code to use Java class libraries.

Java versus Mono need not be an exclusive choice. IKVM brings the two worlds together.

The aim of the IKVM project is to be a full implementation of Java 1.4, but its creators acknowledge there are some areas of incomplete implementation. The Java APIs themselves are provided by GNU Classpath, a project to implement completely free runtime libraries for Java.

This lab demonstrates how to use IKVM. You'll need a Java Development Kit, Version 1.4, installed.

How do I do that?

To use IKVM, Mono must first be compiled with IKVM Java Native Interface (JNI) enabled. If you installed Mono from packages (see "Install Mono" in Chapter 1), install the *mono-ikvm* package. If your Mono was compiled from source, re-rerun the configure step, passing the --with-ikvm-jni=yes option and specifying the path to your Java JDK with the --with-jdk=*/path/to/jdk* option.

Next, IKVM must be installed. IKVM can be installed either from the Mono *ikvm* package or directly from the IKVM web site at *http://www.ikvm.net*. The advantage of installing from the IKVM web site is that you may find improvements over the version of IKVM shipped with Mono. Both source and binary distributions are available. To build from source, you'll need the *NAnt* build tool, described in "Fit Mono into Your World" in Chapter 1. For the purposes of this lab, the IKVM binary distribution will suffice. You can install the contents of the IKVM *bin* directory wherever you please. This lab assumes that you've set the environmental variable IKVMDIR to the path of the *bin* directory. If you installed from packages, this will be */usr/bin*.

To demonstrate calling Mono assemblies from Java, a suitable assembly is needed. Example 8-9 shows a C# class that can add two integers together. This is compiled into an assembly and then invoked from Java code.

Example 8-9. C# Adder class: 03-ikvm/Adder.cs

```
// 08-advanced/03-ikvm
using System;

public class Adder
{
  public int Add (int a, int b)
  {
    return a + b;
  }

  // example usage from C#
  public static void Main (string[ ] args)
  {
```

Example 8-9. C# Adder class: 03-ikvm/Adder.cs (continued)

```
    Adder a = new Adder ();
    Console.WriteLine ("1 + 2 = {0}",
        a.Add (1, 2));
  }
}
```

Normal Mono assemblies are placed into *.dll* files. However, the Java compiler and runtime require libraries to be available as *jar* files. IKVM provides a tool to do the conversion, called *ikvmstub* (older IKVM versions called this program *netexp*). This generates the necessary code to expose the classes in the assemblies in a way Java can use. Compile the Mono assembly and generate the *jar* file using the following commands:

```
$ mcs -target:library Adder.cs
$ mono $IKVMDIR/ikvmstub.exe Adder.dll
```

Example 8-10 shows a small Java program to test the Adder class. Note that all classes exposed to Java by the *ikvmstub* tool start with cli. So, the class Foo.Bar.Baz in Mono becomes called cli.Foo.Bar.Baz in Java.

Example 8-10. Java Adder client class: 03-ikvm/AddClient.java

```
// 08-advanced/03-ikvm
import cli.Adder;

public class AddClient {
  public static void main (String[ ] args) {
    Adder adder = new Adder ();
    System.out.println ("1 + 2 = " +
            Integer.toString (adder.Add (1, 2)));
  }
}
```

Compile and run Example 8-11 using the following commands. You should see the result of the calculation written to the console.

```
$ javac -classpath Adder.jar AddClient.java
$ MONO_PATH=$MONO_PATH:. mono $IKVMDIR/ikvm.exe \
    -classpath .:Adder.jar AddClient
1 + 2 = 3
```

The setting of MONO_PATH instructs Mono to look in the current directory for assemblies, as well as in the existing path and the global assembly cache. Without that the runtime would not be able to find the implementation of Adder from *Adder.dll*.

It's worth remarking on the fact that the Java *AddClient* program is executing inside the Mono runtime, thanks to being translated at start-up time by *ikvm.exe*. IKVM also ships a tool called *ikvmc.exe*, which performs the bytecode translation and creates a Mono *exe* or *dll* assembly. This enables faster startup times.

These simple examples are just part of the story. IKVM can be used successfully to run the Eclipse IDE, a truly massive Java application!

Another, more significant, use of *ikvmc.exe* is to make Java class libraries available to Mono applications. Examples 8-11 and 8-12 show an implementation of the first example in reverse. The JAdder adding service is implemented in Java, and the client in C#.

Compile and run 8-11 and 8-12 using the following commands. Note the reference to *IKVM.GNU.Classpath.dll*, which makes the Java runtime APIs available to Mono.

```
$ javac JAdder.java
$ mono $IKVMDIR/ikvmc.exe -reference:$IKVMDIR/IKVM.GNU.Classpath.dll \
        -target:library JAdder.class
$ MONO_PATH=$MONO_PATH:.:$IKVMDIR mcs -r:JAdder.dll JAddClient.cs
$ MONO_PATH=$MONO_PATH:.:$IKVMDIR mono JAddClient.exe
1 + 2 = 3
```

Example 8-11. Java Adder class: 03-ikvm/JAdder.java

```
// 08-advanced/03-ikvm
public class JAdder
{
  public int Add (int a, int b)
  {
    return a + b;
  }
}
```

Example 8-12. C# JAdder client: 03-ikvm/JAddClient.cs

```
// 08-advanced/03-ikvm
using System;

public class JAddClient
{
  public static void Main (string[ ] args)
  {
    JAdder j = new JAdder ();
    Console.WriteLine ("1 + 2 = {0}",
        j.Add (1, 2));
  }
}
```

What about ...

...Accessing delegates and properties from Java? The Java language has no syntax for these things, but they can still be used. Example 8-13 shows a complex Java example, using some Gtk# classes to create a user interface, and accessing properties and events. Events from C# are translated into two methods, add_*EventName* and remove_*EventName*. Similarly, properties become the familiar method pair set_*PropertyName* and get_*PropertyMame*.

To compile and run the example, Java needs *jar* versions of all the assemblies used, not just the ones mentioned explicitly in the source code. Finding this out can be involve some trial and error, but the diagnostic messages from the compiler are usually helpful.

Example 8-13. Gtk# Java demo: 03-ikvm/GtkDemo.java

```
// 08-advanced/03-ikvm
import cli.Gtk.*;

public class GtkDemo {
  public static void main (String[ ] args) {
    Application.Init ();
    Window w = new Window ("IKVM Demo");
    Button b = new Button ();
    b.set_Label ("Click me!");
    w.SetDefaultSize (200, 200);
    w.Add (b);
    w.ShowAll ();

    // add window delete event handler
    w.add_DeleteEvent (
        new DeleteEventHandler (
          new DeleteEventHandler.Method () {
            public void Invoke (java.lang.Object obj, DeleteEventArgs args) {
              Application.Quit ();
            }
          }
        )
      );

    Application.Run ();
  }
}
```

Try compiling and running Example 8-13 with the following commands, amending the paths of the assemblies to suit your Mono installation (depending on how you installed mono, some of the Mono assemblies may be in a location other than */usr/lib/mono*):

```
$ mono $IKVMDIR/ikvmstub.exe /usr/lib/mono/mscorlib.dll
$ mono $IKVMDIR/ikvmstub.exe /usr/lib/mono/gtk-sharp/glib-sharp.dll
$ mono $IKVMDIR/ikvmstub.exe /usr/lib/mono/gtk-sharp/gtk-sharp.dll
$ mono $IKVMDIR/ikvmstub.exe /usr/lib/mono/gtk-sharp/atk-sharp.dll
$ javac -classpath \
  .:mscorlib.jar:gtk-sharp.jar:glib-sharp.jar:atk-sharp.jar \
  GtkDemo.java
$ mono $IKVMDIR/ikvm.exe -classpath \
  .:mscorlib.jar:gtk-sharp.jar:glib-sharp.jar:atk-sharp.jar \
  GtkDemo
```

Where to learn more

IKVM is under aggressive development, as both Mono and Java itself are evolving to incorporate features such as generics. The best place to go to learn more about IKVM's operation is the *http://www.ikvm.net/* web site.

For information about the Java class libraries that IKVM supports, visit the home page of the GNU Classpath project, at *http://www.gnu.org/software/classpath/*.

Run a Development Version of Mono

The beauty of open source is that you can contribute and make changes yourself. Furthermore, when development happens in the open you can very often get bugfixes and feature requests met on a daily basis. There may well come a time when you hit on a bug or need a feature from Mono that's only available from the unreleased source code the Mono developers are using themselves. This lab demonstrates how to get the latest in everything.

Keep abreast of the latest changes to Mono, and prepare yourself to get involved in its development.

The place to start is, as ever, the Mono web site at *http://www.go-mono.com/*. Although we make our best efforts to ensure that the URLs we give here are accurate, the Mono team has the right to change them as they want. If you get stuck, the best advice is to go to the Mono site and use the navigation they provide.

To get the most from this lab, you must be familiar with conventional Mono installation as outlined in Chapter 1. The procedure for Linux is described here: for Mac OS and Windows you will need to make the necessary adaptations. You need to be happy with compiling and installing programs from source and have a C development environment set up.

How do I do that?

There are two options for getting the latest Mono. First, the Mono team makes daily packages of source code available. These can be downloaded and installed as this lab describes shortly. The second way is to check the sources out from Mono's anonymous CVS source repository. If it's a one-off test you're after, use the packages. If you want to start tracking the project daily and get involved with its development, use CVS.

To get a daily snapshot, visit *http://go-mono.com/daily/* and download the most recent package named *mono-*. We're going to be building from the source. If you don't want the hassle of compiling Mono yourself, download the *monocharge-* packages. These are prebuilt.

Unpack the source. Configure, compile, and install:

```
$ wget http://go-mono.com/daily/mono-latest.tar.gz
$ tar xfz mono-latest.tar.gz
$ cd mono-0.31.99.20040326
$ ./configure --prefix=/opt/mono
$ make
$ sudo make install
```

Set up your environment to use the development installation, and take a look at the version of Mono you're running:

```
$ export PATH=/opt/mono/bin:$PATH
$ export LD_LIBRARY_PATH=/opt/mono/lib:$LD_LIBRARY_PATH
Mac OS X users should set DYLD_LIBRARY_PATH instead
$ export PKG_CONFIG_PATH=/opt/mono/lib/pkgconfig
$ export MONO_PATH=/opt/mono/lib
$ mono --version
Mono JIT compiler version 0.31.99.20040326, (C) 2002-2004 Novell, Inc
and Contributors. www.go-mono.com
        TLS:           NPTL
        GC:            Included Boehm (with typed GC)
        SIGSEGV      : altstack
        Globalization: none
```

Advanced features of Mono can be enabled by using different parameters to the `configure` script. To enable to the integration with IKVM, the Java bytecode compiler for Mono, use `--with-ikvm-jni=yes` and specify the root of the Java JDK installation using `--with-jdk=/usr/lib/j2se/1.4`, adjusting the path as appropriate. The use of IKVM is described in "Run Java in Mono." To enable a preview of the C# 2.0, supporting generics, specify `--with-preview`. Generics are described in "Use Generics."

Now let's look at the CVS approach. The Mono anonymous CVS repository is mirrored from the developers' repository on an hourly basis. You can't commit changes to Mono, but you can get the very latest from the core developers. You'll need *autoconf*, *automake*, and *libtool* installed.

Compiling from CVS involves *bootstrapping* the compiler, *mcs*. The compiler is itself a C# application, so you need a working Mono installation to compile it. Furthermore, you need as recent an installation as possible. This means you must install from the snapshot packages before trying the CVS compile.

```
$ export CVSROOT=:pserver:anonymous@anoncvs.go-mono.com:/mono
$ cvs login
Use a blank password to log in when prompted
$ cvs -z3 co mcs mono
$ cd mono
```

Be careful not to blow away your working version of Mono when you're installing the development version. Install it into a different prefix from your normal installation, such as /opt/ mono.

```
$ ./autogen.sh --prefix=/opt/monocvs
$ make bootstrap
$ make install
```

Once you have the development version of the compiler and class libraries, you may want to install the live development version of the Gtk#
libraries too. Gtk# doesn't have snapshot packages, so you must use CVS:

```
$ export CVSROOT=:pserver:anonymous@anoncvs.go-mono.com:/mono
$ cvs login
Use a blank password to log in when prompted
$ cvs -z3 co gtk-sharp
$ cd gtk-sharp
$ ./autogen.sh --prefix=/opt/mono
$ make
$ make install
```

*Compiling Gtk#
needs the
development files
for the GTK+ 2.0
libraries installed.
More information
can be found on
from the FAQ at
http://gtk-sharp.
sourceforge.net/.*

To keep up to date with CVS sources, simply run cvs -z3 update -APd
for each of the source modules you wish to update. You may need to
autogen.sh again if the source code has changed substantially. The make
fullbuild command ensures that the build starts from clean.

Where to learn more

The main reason to use the development version of Mono or Gtk# is to
take advantage of bugfixes that haven't yet made it into a release. Alternatively, you may want to participate in the development of Mono or a
related project.

To be aware of current problems or changes in the project, it is a good
idea to read the Mono mailing list, and the Mono development mailing
list. The denizens of the Mono IRC channel can also be a helpful source
of information.

Remember that before reporting bugs or asking questions you should
make sure that you have checked your configuration. Always describe
exactly your environment including Mono version and your operating
system version.

If you want to start contributing to Mono or its satellite projects, be sure
to study carefully the *README* and *HACKING* files in the source distributions. Follow the mailing lists and establish the etiquette and procedure
for participation.

The Mono web site, *http://www.go-mono.com/*, should be the first port of
call for up to date information about Mono development. In particular the
sections entitled "Beginning," "Debugging," and "Contributing HOWTO"
are essential reading. Additionally, the Mono mailing lists are linked from
the home page. You can follow the archives online or join the list.

Many of the Mono contributors write about their Mono activities in a weblog. These are collected and published on one site, "Monologue." This can be found at *http://www.go-mono.com/monologue/*. If you use an RSS aggregator, you can add Monologue's RSS feed. These contributors can often be found on the Mono IRC chat channel. This is available on *irc.gnome.org*, channel *#mono*.

When tracking down or reporting problems, the most useful resource is the *Bugzilla* bug tracker at *http://bugzilla.ximian.com/*. Instructions for its use are available linked from the Mono web site, including directions on bug posting etiquette.

Use Generics

Generics are a feature of the C# 2.0 language specification, implemented as part of the Mono 1.2 feature-preview that comes with Mono 1.0. Familiar from other object-oriented languages such as C++ and Eiffel, generics are "template types." Essentially, generics allow similar sorts of polymorphism to those that can be implemented with object and type-casting, but with compile-time checking.

Generics are a feature from the future that can save you time today!

This lab implements a simple collection class, Crowd, to illustrate the use of generics in Mono. As generics are not a released feature of Mono 1.0, this lab only provides an overview of their functionality.

How do I do that?

To use generics in Mono, you must use the *gmcs* compiler as opposed to the usual *mcs*. The generics compiler is available from the *mono-preview* RPM packages or can be built by specifying --with-preview=yes when compiling Mono from source.

Consider a program designed to keep track of a number of people in a crowd. For convenience, each person will be represented by a string containing their name. This might reasonably and naively be implemented with an ArrayList as shown in Example 8-14.

Example 8-14. Crowd as list: 05-generics/CrowdList.cs

```
using System;
using System.Collections;

public class ArrayListDemo {
  public static void Main (string [ ] args)
  {
    ArrayList c = new ArrayList ();
```

Example 8-14. Crowd as list: 05-generics/CrowdList.cs (continued)

```
    c.Add ("Fred");
    c.Add (23);
    c.Add ("Wilma");

    foreach (string person in c) {
      Console.WriteLine (person);
    }
  }
}
```

A brief glance at the code in Example 8-14 will tell you that disaster looms, however, as can be seen when the program is run:

```
$ mcs CrowdList.cs
$ mono CrowdList.exe
Fred

Unhandled Exception: System.InvalidCastException: Cannot cast
from source type to destination type.
in <0x000de> GenericsDemo:Main (string[ ])
```

The problem is caused by the lack of type-safe collection classes in Mono. Without the power of generics to help, the tidy solution to making this situation safe is similar to that shown in the *DateTimeCollections.cs* listing from "Manage Collections of Data" in Chapter 3, where a specialized collection for a particular type is made, using OnInsert to check that the member to be added was of the required type.

Example 8-15 shows a generics-based solution to making the crowd collection type-safe.

Example 8-15. Generic Crowd: 05-generics/Crowd.cs

```
using System;
using System.Collections;

public class GenericsDemo {
  public static void Main (string [ ] args)
  {
    Crowd <string> c = new Crowd <string> ();
    c.Add ("Fred");
    c.Add ("Barney");
    c.Add ("Wilma");
    Console.WriteLine (c.Contains ("Fred"));
    c.Remove ("Fred");
    Console.WriteLine (c.Contains ("Fred"));
  }
}

public class Crowd <CrowdMember>
{
```

Example 8-15. Generic Crowd: 05-generics/Crowd.cs (continued)

```
  ArrayList list;

  public Crowd ()
  {
    list = new ArrayList ();
  }

  public void Add (CrowdMember member)
  {
    list.Add (member);
  }

  public bool Contains (CrowdMember member)
  {
    return list.Contains (member);
  }

  public void Remove (CrowdMember member)
  {
    list.Remove (member);
  }
}
```

You can compile and run Example 8-15 using the following commands:

```
$ gmcs Crowd.cs
$ mono Crowd.exe
True
False
```

Notice that Example 8-15 doesn't even attempt to add an integer into the Crowd. Doing so (try it!) would result in a compile-time error similar to this:

```
Crowd.cs(9) error CS1502: The best overloaded match for method
'void Crowd!1[System.String].Add (in string)' has some invalid
arguments
Crowd.cs(9) error CS1503: Argument 0: Cannot convert from 'int'
to 'in string'
```

Although generics are a feature from C# 2.0, they also require support in the underlying CIL and runtime, which Mono 1.0 already has, in preparation for the generics support in Mono 1.2.

How it works

Generic class declarations are parameterized by one or more types, enclosed in angle brackets (< >). When a generic class is instantiated, the target type or types are again specified in angle brackets. The name of the substituted type is used throughout the class implementation as if it were the actual type.

Writing all the angle-bracketed generic types can quickly become tiresome. The versatile using keyword can help out here:

```
using StringCrowd = Crowd <string>;

public class GenericsDemo {
  public static void Main (string [ ] args)
  {
    StringCrowd c = new StringCrowd ();
    ...
```

There is an interesting wrinkle here, in that a generic can be parameterized by either reference types or value types. A common idiom to indicate some sort of noncritical failure status is to have a method return null. Consider the implementation of this in a generic class. As soon as that generic is instantiated with a value type such as int, returning null becomes a nonsense. To get around this, instead of null, the special function default is used. So evaluating default (T) where T is a reference type gives null, but 0 where T is int, and so on. An example use might be in reading from some sort of queue:

```
public T ReadNext ()
{
  T ret;

  if (Queue.DataAvailable) {
    ret = new T (Queue.Head);
    Queue.MoveNext ();
  } else {
    ret = default (T);
  }
  return ret;
}
```

What about ...

...Constraining the types a generic can be instantiated with? After all, there are some operations that don't make sense on certain types. Consider this small program:

```
public class Comparer <T> {
  public bool LessThan (T a, T b)
  {
    return a < b;
  }
}
```

If you try to compile this, the compiler complains with the message Operator < cannot be applied to operands of type 'T' and 'T', and rightly so. The compiler has no way of determining if the less-than operator will ever make sense for any given type. Instead the way to ensure that the type T is comparable is to write:

```
public class Comparer <T> where T : IComparable {
  public bool LessThan (T a, T b)
  {
    return a.CompareTo (b) < 0;
  }
}
```

To test this out, try and compile Example 8-16 with *gmcs*. Because the class Wine has no implementation of IComparable, the example simply won't compile. Replace Wine with something like int, and all will be well.

Example 8-16. Incorrect attempt to use Comparer: 05-generics/Comparer.cs

```
// 08-advanced/05-generics
using System;

public class ComparerDemo {
  public static void Main (string [ ] args)
  {
    Comparer <Wine> c = new Comparer <Wine> ();
    Wine zinfandel = new Wine ();
    Wine chardonnay = new Wine ();
    bool result = c.LessThan (zinfandel, chardonnay);
  }
}

public class Wine {
}

public class Comparer <T> where T : IComparable {
  public bool LessThan (T a, T b)
  {
    return a.CompareTo (b) < 0;
  }
}
```

Where to learn more

By far the best reference to C# generics is on Microsoft's MSDN site, in an article by Juval Lowy called "An Introduction to C# Generics." Search for the title from the search box at *http://msdn.microsoft.com/*. An interesting interview with Anders Hejlsberg, the lead C# architect, about generics and how they compare to C++ and Java generics is available online at *http://www.artima.com/intv/generics.html*.

Until Mono 1.2 is released, working with generics in Mono is an extremely "bleeding edge" activity. If you intend to investigate them

If using a .NET
2.0 class like
System.Collec-
tions.Generic, set
your MONO_PATH
to /opt/mono/lib/
mono/2.0:
$MONO_PATH,
adjusting for the
root of your Mono
distribution.

further, ensure you are subscribed to the Mono mailing lists described in "Join the Mono Community" in Chapter 1. Also, you may well find you need to run a development version of Mono, instructions for doing which can be found in "Run a Development Version of Mono."

If you're feeling really brave, try improving the code in Example 8-16 to support some useful interfaces such as ICollection. You'll need to use the generic collections interfaces from the namespace System. Collections.Generic. For instance, the class declaration for Crowd will look something like this:

```
public class Crowd <CrowdMember> : ICollection <CrowdMember>
```

A solution to this problem can be found in *08-advanced/05-generics/ FullCrowd.cs*, available from the code listings on this book's web site.

Write Mono Programs in Basic

The Mono Basic compiler is one of Mono 1.0's preview features. It aims to be compatible with Microsoft Visual Basic .NET. Although Basic has found little popularity with Linux developers, it is in widespread use in the professional Windows programming world. For this reason its support within Mono is advantageous for those wishing to migrate either software written in Basic, or programmers trained in it.

Get back to the
1990s and program
some Basic!

This lab introduces a few of the fundamentals of the Mono Basic language and demonstrates use of the Basic compiler.

How do I do that?

First, you must have the preview features of Mono 1.0 installed. You can find out how to do that in "Use Generics." To find out if the Basic compiler is installed properly, run the command mbas. You should see the version and usage information for the Basic compiler printed to the console.

Although C# and Mono Basic compile down to the same CIL bytecode, the languages are significantly different in their syntax. What C# implies through syntax shortcuts, Basic tends to make (sometimes painfully) explicit. To get an instant impression of this look at Example 8-17, which shows that faithful retainer of language tutorials everywhere, "Hello World."

Example 8-17. 06-basic/HelloWorld.vb

```
' 08-advanced/06-basic
Module HelloWorld
```

Example 8-17. 06-basic/HelloWorld.vb (continued)

```
Sub Main ()
   System.Console.WriteLine ("Hello, World!")
End Sub

End Module
```

Compile and run Example 8-17 using these commands:

```
$ mbas HelloWorld.vb
$ mono HelloWorld.exe
Hello, World!
```

The brevity of Example 8-17 does not leave much to be explained, except for the Module keyword. A Module is a special kind of class in which all the methods are declared to be static. Except that Basic doesn't use the term "static," but *shared* instead.

As Mono Basic is fully built on the Mono runtime, it has access to all the normal assemblies, including those that are part of Gtk#. Example 8-18 shows a simple Gtk# based program, introducing a few new language features on the way.

Example 8-18. 06-basic/HelloGtkWorld.vb

```
' 08-advanced/06-basic
Imports System
Imports Gtk

Module HelloGtkWorld

   Sub Main ()
      Dim Win as Window
      Dim Btn as Button

      Application.Init ()
      Win = new Window ("Hello BASIC World!")
      Btn = new Button ("Click me!")
      Win.Add (Btn)
      Win.SetDefaultSize (150, 150)
      Win.ShowAll ()
      AddHandler Win.DeleteEvent, AddressOf WindowDelete
      AddHandler Btn.Clicked, AddressOf ButtonClicked
      Application.Run ()
   End Sub

   Sub WindowDelete (o As Object, args As DeleteEventArgs)
      Application.Quit ()
   End Sub

   Sub ButtonClicked (o As Object, args As EventArgs)
      Console.WriteLine ("I was clicked!")
```

As mbas is part of the Mono preview, it is not yet finished software. This shows in that only /r: rather than -r: can be used to reference an assembly.

Example 8-18. 06-basic/HelloGtkWorld.vb (continued)

```
  End Sub

End Module
```

Compile and run Example 8-18 like this, ensuring that MONODIR is set to the root of your Mono installation.

```
$ mbas /r:$MONODIR/lib/mono/gtk-sharp/gtk-sharp.dll \
    HelloGtkWorld.vb
$ mono HelloGtkWorld.exe
```

Example 8-18, following the pattern of the programs demonstrated in Chapter 4, attaches an event handler to the Gtk.Window.DeleteEvent event. This is a case where the Basic syntax of AddHandler is arguably more helpful than the use of the += operator in C#. Basic's AddressOf operator makes explicit the notion of delegates as function pointers. As in C#, any variable must be declared with a type. In Basic, this is done with the Dim keyword.

As with the Java examples in "Run Java in Mono," the most tangible way to demonstrate to the unbelieving mind that Mono languages work painlessly with each other is to write your own code and see it interoperating. While doing that, the opportunity is ripe to demonstrate writing library assemblies in Basic.

Example 8-19 shows a class, Adder. Adder is a somewhat contrived collection of functionality, for the purposes of demonstrating several features in a small amount of space. Adder has a property, Name, a method SayHello and a static method Add.

Example 8-19. 06-basic/Adder.vb

```
' 08-advanced/06-basic
Imports System

Namespace MonoDN

  Public Class Adder

    Private myname As String

    Public Sub New ()
      MyBase.New ()
      myname = "Fred"
    End Sub

    Public Property Name () As String
      Get
        Name = myname
```

Example 8-19. 06-basic/Adder.vb (continued)

```
      End Get
      Set (ByVal Value As String)
        myname = Value
      End Set
    End Property

    Public Sub SayHello ()
      Console.WriteLine ("Hello, I'm {0}", myname)
    End Sub

    Shared Function Add (A As Integer, B As Integer)
      Return A + B
    End Function

  End Class

End Namespace
```

Notice also in Example 8-19 that the Adder class is in the MonoDN namespace. Compile the code with:

```
$ mbas /target:library Adder.vb
```

Example 8-20 shows a small C# program to exercise the main features of the Adder class. Compile the AdderClient program, run it, and observe the output.

```
$ mcs -r:Adder.dll AdderClient.cs
$ mono AdderClient.exe
Hello, I'm Fred
1 + 2 = 3
Hello, I'm Margaret
```

Example 8-20. 06-basic/AdderClient.cs

```
// 08-advanced/06-basic
using System;
using MonoDN;

public class AdderClient {
  public static void Main (string [] args)
  {
    Adder a = new Adder ();
    a.SayHello ();
    Console.WriteLine ("1 + 2 = {0}",
        Adder.Add (1, 2));
    a.Name = "Margaret";
    a.SayHello ();
  }
}
```

Where to learn more

If you want to learn more about Mono Basic, any resource on Visual Basic .NET (the .NET bit is important!) will prove useful. For beginners, Jesse Liberty's *Learning Visual Basic .NET* (O'Reilly) is a good start. Further reference can be found in *VB.NET Core Classes in a Nutshell* and *VB.NET Language in a Nutshell* (O'Reilly).

As Mono Basic is a preview feature of Mono, if you intend to investigate it further it's wise to join one or more Mono community forum, described in "Join the Mono Community" in Chapter 1.

Index

<% %> (angle brackets), parameterizing
    generic class
    declarations, 255
<% %> block, XSP, 200
<%= %> block, XSP, 200
<%@ %> block, XSP, 202, 205
-> (arrow) operator, C#, 24
@ (at-sign)
  around variables in templates, 236
  prefixing strings, 54
\ (backslash), filename path
    separator, 242
. (dot files), GConf as alternative
    to, 130
. (dot) operator, C#, 24
:: (double colon) operator, C++, 24
+= operator, C#, 38
+ (plus sign), concatenation
    operator, 54
/ (slash), filename path separator, 242

A

accelerators, keyboard, 101, 103
AccelGroup class, 103
AC_SUBST directives, 235
action area, 93
Activated event, 104
AddAccelerator() method, MenuItem
    class, 104
AddAttribute() method,
    TreeViewColumn class, 111
AddButton() method, Dialog class, 94

AddNotify() method, GConf.Client
    class, 135
ADO.NET, 226, 231
ADO.NET Cookbook (Hamilton), 231
ADO.NET in a Nutshell (Hamilton;
    MacDonald), 231
Albahari, Ben (C# Essentials, 2nd
    Edition), 95
Alt keys (mnemonic keys), 101
Anakrino tool, 67
angle brackets (< >), parameterizing
    generic class
    declarations, 255
animation, timeout handler used
    for, 145
Ant build system (see NAnt build
    system)
Apache web server, 195–198
APIs (see assemblies)
App class, 122
AppBar class, 122
appbars, 120
AppDatadir property, Program
    class, 156
AppendFormat() method, StringBuilder
    class, 55
AppendItem() method,
    DruidPageStandard, 142
AppendPage() method, Druid
    class, 142
AppendValues() method, ListStore
    class, 110
AppendValues() method, TreeStore
    class, 110

We'd like to hear your suggestions for improving our indexes. Send email to *index@oreilly.com*.

Application class, 81, 120
applications
  cross-platform, 241–244
  distributing, 232–241
  Mono executable, location of, 237
  networked, remoting and, 210–215
  source packages for,
    building, 232–241
Applied Cryptography (Schneier), 225
array reference types, C#, 28
ArrayList class, 60
arrow (->) operator, C#, 24
ASMX files, 203–206
ASP.NET, serving with Mono and
  Apache web
  servers, 195–198
ASPX files (see XSP)
assemblies, 44–48
  attributes in, 45
  compatibility assemblies, xv, 4
  decompiling, 67
  for Mono application, 237–240
  in GAC, 7
  Mono assemblies, xv
  resources for, 48
  using in multiple applications, 47
  viewing IL for, 63–67
  (see also mcs command, -pkg
    options)
AssemblyInfo.cs file, 9, 45, 237, 239
Assert() method, Assertion class, 77
AssertEquals() method, Assertion
  class, 77
Assertion class, 77
AssertNotNull() method, Assertion
  class, 77
AssertNull() method, Assertion
  class, 77
AssertSame() method, Assertion
  class, 77
AsymmetricAlgorithm class, 224
AsyncCallback class, 149
asynchronous operations, 53,
  143–149
at-sign (@)
  around variables in templates, 236
  prefixing strings, 54
attributes
  C#, 39–41
  in assemblies, 45
  of files, 51

autoconf tool, xix, 232–241
Autoconnect() method, Glade.XML
  class, 129
automake tool, xix, 232–241
Autotools build system, xix

B

background computations, 146
backslash (\), cross-platform
  compatibility and, 242
Basic language, writing Mono
  programs in, 258–262
Beck, Kent (Test Driven Development:
  By Example), 78
BeginInvoke() method, Delegate
  class, 149
binary serialization, 212
BinaryReader class, 52
BinaryWriter class, 52
binfmt command, 8
BitArray class, 60
books (see resources)
BorderWidth property, boxes, 85
boxes, packing widgets in, 82–86
boxing value types, C#, 32
bugs in Mono, tracking or
  reporting, 20, 253
Bugzilla bug tracker, 20, 253
buttons, subclassing, 94

C

C# compiler (see mcs command)
C# Developers Center web site, 25
C# Essentials, 2nd Edition (Albahari;
  Drayton; Merril), 95
C# language, xviii, 22
  array reference types, 28
  assemblies and, 44–48
  attributes, 39–41
  boxing value types as reference
    types, 32
  class names compared to source file
    names, 23
  command-line arguments for, 23
  compiling (see mcs command)
  decompiling IL into, 67
  delegates, 36–39
  enumeration types, 30
  events, 36–39
  exception handling, 32–36

Druid class, 138
DruidPage class, 138
DruidPageEdge class, 138, 142
DruidPageStandard class, 138, 142, 143
druids, 137–143
DTD, validating XML using, 183
DYLD_LIBRARY_PATH environment variable, 4

E

Eclipse IDE, 16
Edited event, CellRendererText class, 112
editors, text, xx, 13
Emacs text editor, 13
encryption, 220–225
    of hash value in assembly, 47
    resources for, 225
Entry class, 89
enum keyword, C#, 30
enumeration types, C#, 30
environment variable settings for Mono installation, 4
Equals() method, System.Object class, 28
error handling (see exception handling)
escaping special characters in strings, 54
event handling
    C#, 36–39
    drag and drop functionality, 117
    druids, 142
    graphics, 99
    Gtk#, 79–82
    menu items, 104
    signals in Glade, 125
    subclassing and, 95
    TreeView class, 112
    XML validation, 183
    XSD validation, 186
events, xviii
Exception class, 35
exception handling, xvii, 32–36
.exe suffix, executing Mono programs without, 7
executable assembly for Mono application, 237–240
ExecuteNonQuery() method, 228
ExecuteReader() method, 228

ExecuteScalar() method, 228
executing Mono programs, 5, 6, 23
    passing command-line arguments to, 23
    without .exe suffix, 7
Exit() method, System Environment class, 23
ExpectedException attribute, 77
Expose event, Widget class, 99
Extensible Markup Language (see XML)
external libraries, C#, 41–44

F

Fail() method, Assertion class, 77
FCL (Framework Class Library)
    collections, 59–63
    file access classes, 49–53
    processes, 68
    regular expressions, 56–58
    strings, 53–55
    threads, 70–74
Fedora Core, 2
    (see also Linux)
File class, 49–53
file systems, cross-platform compatibility and, 241
FileAttributes enum, 51
filename path separator, cross-platform compatibility and, 242
files
    accessing, FCL classes for, 49–53
    asynchronous file I/O, 53
    attributes of, 51
    dropping into applications, 113
    permissions, 51
    reading binary data from, 52
    searching with regular expressions, 56–58
FileStream class, 52
FileSystemWatcher class, 38
Fill() method, MySqlDataAdapter class, 230
finally syntax, C#, 34
Flush() method, StreamWriter class, 208
Focused event, Widget class, 81
fonts used in this book, xx
Format() method, string class, 55
Framework Class Library (see FCL)
Freeman, Jay (Anakrino tool), 67

cross-platform compatibility
          and, 243
      designing, resources for, 86, 106
      (see also Gtk# toolkit; widgets)
using directive, C#, 24

V

ValidationEventHandler delegate, 183
ValidationEventHandler event, 183
ValidationType property,
          XmlValidatingReader
          class, 183
value types, C#, 29–32
VB.NET Core Classes in a Nutshell, 262
VB.NET Language in a Nutshell, 262
VBox class, 85
version of Mono, determining, 5
viewer.glade path, 127
Vim text editor, 13
virtual methods, 28

W

WaitForExit() method, Process
          class, 69
Walsh, Norman (DocBook: The
          Definitive Guide), 158
web applications, running, 198–202
web (see networking; web sites)
web server
      Apache web server, 195–198
      connecting to, without
          sockets, 206–208
web services, 203–206
web sites
      Anakrino tool, 67
      Apache web server
          documentation, 198
      Asynchronous File I/O, 53
      Bugzilla bug tracker, 20
      C# 2.0, changes in, 82
      C# Developer's Center, 25
      conglomerate XML editor, 154
      Consuming Unmanaged DLL
          Functions section, .NET
          Framework Developer's
          Guide, 44
      Dashboard, 21
      DocBook DTDs, 154
      for this book, xxi
      gettext tool, 159

Glade downloads, 123
GLib source packages, 4
GNOME CVS repository, 20
GNOME Documentation Project, 158
GNOME Human Interface
          Guidelines, 86, 106
GNU Classpath project, 250
GTK+ 2.0 Reference Manual, 95
GTK+ 2.0 Tutorial, 82
Gtk# source code, 4
IKVM, 250
IL, MSDN documentation, 67
Improve, Eclipse IDE, 16
JUnit, 78
make program documentation, 18
Metadata and Self-Describing
          Components, .NET Framework
          Developer's Guide, 48
Microsoft-focused forums, 17
Mono, 18, 252
Mono Contributor Howto, 78
Mono daily snapshots, 250
Mono downloads, 2
MonoDevelop, 8
Monologue, 19
MSDN (Microsoft Developer
          Network), 18
MySQL, 231
Novell Forge, 20
NUnit, 78
O'Reilly, xxi
O'Reilly Network online
          magazine, 19
Pango Reference Manual, 90
Reflector tool, 67
regular expressions, MSDN
          documentation, 58
RELAX NG, 192
SAX API, 172
scrollkeeper tool, 158
The Secrets of Strong Naming, 48
SharpDevelop, 13
System.Globalization, 159
X11, 3
XCode, 13
Ximian Red Carpet package
          manager, 2
XmlCsvReader class, 172
xmllint tool, 154
XML-RPC, 216, 220
XPath, 178

About the Authors

Edd Dumbill is Editor-at-Large for the O'Reilly Network. He also writes free software and packages Bluetooth-related software for the Debian GNU/Linux distribution. Edd is the creator of XMLhack and WriteTheWeb and has a weblog called Behind the Times.

Niel M. Bornstein, with over ten years of experience in software development, has worked in diverse areas such as corporate information systems, client-server application development, and web-hosted applications. A clear and engaging writer, Niel is a frequent contributor to XML.com, an affiliate site of the O'Reilly Network.

Colophon

Our look is the result of reader comments, our own experimentation, and feedback from distribution channels. Distinctive covers complement our distinctive approach to technical topics, breathing personality and life into potentially dry subjects.

The *Developer's Notebook* series is modeled on the tradition of laboratory notebooks. Laboratory notebooks are an invaluable tool for researchers and their successors.

The purpose of a laboratory notebook is to facilitate the recording of data and conclusions as the work is being conducted, creating a faithful and immediate history. The notebook begins with a title page that includes the owner's name and the subject of research. The pages of the notebook should be numbered and prefaced with a table of contents. Entries must be clear, easy to read, and accurately dated; they should use simple, direct language to indicate the name of the experiment and the steps taken. Calculations are written out carefully and relevant thoughts and ideas recorded. Each experiment is introduced and summarized as it is added to the notebook. The goal is to produce comprehensive, clearly organized notes that can be used as a reference. Careful documentation creates a valuable record and provides a practical guide for future developers.

Sarah Sherman was the production editor and the proofreader for *Mono: A Developer's Notebook*. Matt Hutchinson, Reg Aubry, and Claire Cloutier provided quality control. Angela Howard wrote the index.

Hanna Dyer designed the cover of this book. Emma Colby produced the cover layout with QuarkXPress 4.1 using the Officina Sans and JuniorHandwriting fonts.

David Futato designed the interior layout, with contributions from Edie Freedman. This book was converted by Joe Wizda to FrameMaker 5.5.6 with a format conversion tool created by Erik Ray, Jason McIntosh, Neil Walls, and Mike Sierra that uses Perl and XML technologies. The text font is Adobe Boton; the heading font is ITC Officina Sans; the code font is LucasFont's TheSans Mono Condensed, and the hand-writing font is a modified version of JuniorHandwriting made by Tepid Monkey Foundry, and modified by O'Reilly. The illustrations that appear in the book were produced by Robert Romano and Jessamyn Read using Macromedia FreeHand 9 and Adobe Photoshop 6. This colophon was written by Colleen Gorman.